AF556181

Theories and Principles of Librarianship

Theories and Principles of Librarianship

M. Ram

RANDOM PUBLICATIONS
NEW DELHI (INDIA)

Theories and Principles of Librarianship

ISBN 978-93-5111-341-6

Published in 2014 in India by

RANDOM PUBLICATIONS

4376-A/4B, Gali Murari Lal, Ansari Road
New Delhi-110 002
Phone : +91-11-43580356, +91-11-23289044
e-mail: randomexports@gmail.com, sales@randompublications.com,
info@randompublications.com

Reprinted 2019

Type Setting by : Keystoneprintads, Delhi-110051
Digitally Printed at: Replika Press Pvt. Ltd.

Preface

A librarian is a person who works professionally in a library, and may hold a degree in librarianship. Traditionally, a librarian is associated with collections of books, as demonstrated by the etymology of the word "librarian". The role of a librarian is continually evolving to meet social and technological needs: a modern librarian may deal with information in many formats, including books, magazines, newspapers, audio recordings, video recordings, maps, manuscripts, photographs and other graphic material, bibliographic databases, web searching, and digital resources. A librarian may provide other information services, including computer provision and training, coordination of public programs, basic literacy education, and assistive equipment for people with disabilities, and help with finding and using community resources. Appreciation for librarians is often included by authors and scholars in the Acknowledgment sections of books.

The present book ' Theories and Principles of Librarianship ' is written to explicit the various facets of special libraries and librarianships. It is believed this book will be useful for the students studying the special libraries and librarianship as a subject at graduation and post-graduation level.

I would like to thank my team for standing beside me throughout my career and writing this book. My special thanks go to "Random Publications" who have published the book.

— ***M. Ram***

Contents

1

Accountability in Library Management: Issues and Strategies for the 21st Century

If libraries were to be judged on their own merit, in isolation from their parent organisations, the majority in the ASEAN countries can be said to be excellent, even in comparison with libraries in more developed countries. However it is only when libraries are judged in the context of their parent organisations that their contribution is seen to be more peripheral rather than integral. For example, most university libraries are not fully integrated into the teaching–learning process which forms the core business of universities. This is partly due to pedagogical constraints, in that teaching-learning strategies at the university do not encourage resource-based learning, causing libraries to be side-lined.

It may also be due to the fact that librarians are not regarded as "academic" by the academia, "inferior" in status and ability. These are realities that exist at universities and in different other ways at other types of library environments. At the national level, it is librarians who have always assumed that libraries are critical to national development while not many outside the library community acknowledge the importance of the library's role.

There are sufficient indicators that reflect this lack of recognition:

- Changes in nomenclature from 'librarians' to 'information professionals/specialists,' 'librarianship' to 'information science' propagated by librarians themselves, beginning in the 1970's. It is as if prior to the 1970s, libraries had not been involved with information provision and dissemination.
- Librarians not awarded the same recognition as other professions and this is reflected in schemes of service and salary scales despite the fact that librarians have academic and professional qualifications at entry point.
- The proliferation of members of other professions taking the lead role in information provision and dissemination.

The issue therefore is, against this background, are librarians in the position to cope with the demands and challenges of the 21st century?

ARE LIBRARIES READY FOR THE 21ST CENTURY?

To fight, one has to recognise the enemy – so it is with libraries. Unless libraries understand what is demanded of them by the 21st Century, it would be difficult for them to face the onslaught of the changes that the century will bring. To prepare themselves for the onslaught, they would need to not only assess their current "strengths" and "weaknesses" but to also recognise the "opportunities" or "threats" presented by the 21st century.

A SWOT analysis of libraries is important because it provides libraries with a more 'clinical' approach to library development, minimising trial and error in the process.

The SWOT analysis is not based on research data but based on the perception and certain assumptions on the part of the authors, resulting from their reading of the relevant information literature as well as their experiences as Chief Librarians. The SWOT analysis is used merely to illustrate the need for librarians to be introspective and understand their capabilities as well as to be aware of developments taking place in their surrounding environment.

Internal Environment:

- *Strength*:
  - Collection
  - Reputation
  - User Education
- *Weakneses*:
  - Collection
  - Staff
  - Funds
  - Usage
  - Peripheral role
  - Non-integrated Strategic Plan

External Environment:

- Opportunity:
  - Lifelong education
  - Innovative technology
  - Knowledge management
  - Globalisation
  - National policies and Objectives
- *Threat*:
  - Proliferation of information providers
  - Globalisation

DEFINING THE LIBRARY'S ENVIRONMENT

INTERNAL ENVIRONMENT

Any assessment of the library's strengths and weaknesses must be based on user feedback in the form of complaints or user studies or benchmarking. In the absence of such feedback however and purely for the purpose of this chapter, the authors have drawn on their own experiences as Chief Librarian and Consultant Librarian to identify the strengths and weaknesses of the library.

Strengths

Three areas can be identified as the library's strength, notably:

- Collections
- Reputation
- User Education

Collections

Collections are the library's greatest strength because without collections, there can be no library. The strength of the collections however depends on its size and uniqueness. In the 1950s and 1960s, the size of the collection is the measure of the library's worth. As such weeding exercises were seldom undertaken for fear that large libraries will lose their competitive edge. Today, the issue of size is not the main criteria to assess the library's stature because with the advent of digital libraries, the world's collections are easily accessible. The uniqueness of collections however has became a more important criteria for assessing the library's strength because of their heritage value and their potential as a national asset.

In the case of Malaysia, the various Malaysiana collections at the National Library of Malaysia, at the 17 public university libraries, at government research agencies in the form of research collections, at the State Public Libraries in the form of the state collections, are examples of unique collections that are found in the country. Collectively, the collections found in all types of libraries in any country can be deemed to be the country's national asset. The fact that they are professionally organised for easy retrieval makes library collections indispensable for national development. However, while the monetary value of these collections may be easy to quantify by totalling the annual budgets of each library, their academic and cultural value are priceless. But the main issue in question is: Are the collections used? However priceless the collections, their value will come to naught unless used.

Reputation

Libraries exist today because people believe in the traditional concept of the libraries as being at the heart of learning. Since the education system provides the nation's manpower and serves as the catalyst for national development and advancement, libraries are accorded the same value. They believe that a literate population is the country's foremost asset and critical for national advancement. This belief has prevailed till today but it is a perception that has not been substantiated by library usage. It is obvious that while libraries are still regarded as an important tool for education and a mechanism for development of manpower for the country, reputation alone is not sufficient. The perception that libraries are important must be replaced by a more realistic view of the library's worth.

User Education

Teaching users how to retrieve materials via the library systems, whether manual or electronic, has long been undertaken by libraries. However, user education programmes have become more urgent in recent years when library systems became ICT-based. The underlying premise of all user education programmes is that however excellent the library's collections and systems are, if not used they serve no purpose.

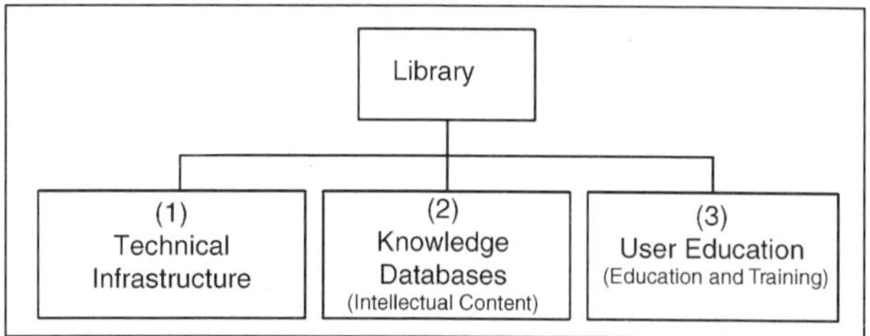

User education programmes are now offered by most libraries, both formally or informally. It is the best way to promote libraries and library use because not only do these programmes enable librarians to come into direct contact with the clients, demonstrate to the clients the proficiency of librarians in both the academic aspect of library work as well as the technical aspect, it also provides libraries with the opportunity to.

- Be integrated into the teaching and learning process in the case of university libraries or
- Develop literacy skills among members of society in the case of public libraries.

Weaknesses

Unfortunately, there are more weaknesses than strengths in our analysis of the internal environment:

Collections

Generally, notwithstanding the size of their collections, libraries have in their collections, materials that contain data more archival than current. They are excellent for scholars and researchers from the academia but users of the 21st century are weaned on ICT and expect information at a press of the button.

Library collections are mainly passive collections, sitting on library shelves for years, unused. Consisting mainly of printed secondary and tertiary sources, they stand the risk of being replaced by e-books, e-journals and internet. It has become very common for libraries to have e-books, e-journals and internet services provided by commercial vendors at a very high cost. It would not be a surprise however that later in the 21st century, access to Internet and electronic databases will themselves become passé and by the end of the 21st century, materials would be more readily available in palmtops and accessible while showering in the bathroom or driving in cars. Will libraries have the funds to update and upgrade their collections will be the main issue facing libraries in the 21st century.

Unless libraries have collections that are relevant and can meet the demands of the 21st century, library collections comprising of secondary and tertiary data, will be rendered obsolete. The main weakness of library collections however lies in the fact that they are not used to the optimum, giving rise to management debates on whether or not it is cost-beneficial to maintain libraries when alternatives are available on-line.

Staff

In order for libraries to be dynamic, library staff must have the right qualifications and competencies for the job in hand, as well as the right attitude towards service. In the current situation, the majority of library staff can be said to be generally passive and not proactive. This is where library education plays a part. Librarians of the 21st century must be multi-skilled, have sound subject knowledge and good leadership. Library schools would have to be more responsive to these needs and take into account that librarians of the future will not be sitting at a desk in a library but will work in a virtual environment with PC(s) as colleagues. Multi-skilled, she will need to communicate well, preferably in several languages, be knowledgeable in specialised subject areas, innovative in the use of ICT, personable and independent.

Funds

Lack of funds is a perennial problem faced by all libraries. Notwithstanding the fact there are libraries that are well-endowed funds are never adequate to fulfil all objectives. This has resulted in libraries undertaking resource-sharing of collections and services to reduce expenditure and optimise usage. In some countries, libraries have embraced the concept of 'corporatisation' through which libraries have imposed membership fees and service charges. Other libraries depend on sponsors and donors for funds. The issue is: will libraries in the 21st century have to be self-funding?

Usage

The most important issue in library usage is the need to provide evidence of usage. Much of the professional literature has alluded to the fact that despite their importance, libraries are not used to the optimum. Also, with the establishment of digital libraries, which makes remote access easy, library visits will soon be more for pleasure than for information gathering. In a recent survey of undergraduates at the University of Malaya Library only a small percentage visit the library every day (17.2%), with the majority (54%) visiting a few times a week. The survey also shows that the majority of students do not use the electronic databases preferring the printed books instead. There is a need to market library services to increase usage, whether on-site or remote.

At the OUM Library, statistics obtained from log-ins of e-books and e-journals show that:

- Remote access is greater than on-site access and
- Usage of e-books higher than e-journals.

Peripheral Role of Libraries

Is the role of library passive or proactive? There is no real evidence to show that libraries are integrated into the core business of their institutions, especially academic libraries and special libraries.

In the case of University libraries, while there is no evidence of a correlation between usage of library resources and academic achievement evidence of Faculty-library integration can be discerned by asking the following questions:.

- *Teaching*: Is there resourcebased teaching? Are library resources integrated into teaching activities?
- *Learning*: Is there resource based learning? Are library resources integrated into learning activities?
- *Research*: Is there evidence that the more specialised the research, the less need there is for library resources?

With regard to the library's role in learning, in a survey undertaken at the University of Malaya, to determine whether the user education programme is useful for their learning, the majority of students surveyed replied in the affirmative.

EXTERNAL ENVIRONMENT

To be prepared for the 21st century, libraries would have to be aware not only of developments taking place in the world outside library walls but to interpret these developments into "opportunities" or "threats" for libraries. Those that can be considered as "opportunities" must be taken advantage of while taking steps to be prepared for those that are considered as "threats". These "opportunities" and "threats" found beyond library walls must however be seen in the right perspective, against the background of the library's capabilities or its "strengths" and "weaknesses".

Weaknesses

What can be interpreted as 'opportunities' can be subjective, depending on how the librarians perceive them to be.

For the purpose of this chapter, the authors have identified five areas:

- Innovative Technology.
- Globalisation.
- Lifelong Learning.
- Knowledge Management.
- National Policies and Objectives.

Innovative Technology

The phrase "innovative technology" is deliberately used here to denote the innovative aspects of technology because not since the wheel has there been a development so global that it has not touched every aspect of life and every level of society – *e.g.* e-learning, e-government, e-business. From the Parliament to shopping, technology has become part of life. Reaching the moon, artificial intelligence, cloning of genes have become mundane news – innovative technology has made them possible.

The advantages provided by innovative technology can be summarised as:

- More efficient work processes, with less mistakes and greater output
- Provides global access to information
- Encourages independent learning

But the issue that confronts libraries in the 21st century is: To what level should librarians be trained in technology?

In the case of libraries, innovative technology has been identified to facilitate:

- Day-to-day tasks such as acquisitions, cataloguing, loans etc.
- Interaction with users via the use of portals. The development of information gateways or portals has made it possible for library and information professionals to upgrade their services. Information portal can offer users one stop work stations where they can search across a multitude of resources and retrieve electronic and book resources in one station. Information portals can provide integration of sources for searching and for location and delivery of materials – in whatever format they exist. Portal brings the opportunity to develop elibrary services – to meet the growing expectations of the student population.
- Enables user education programmes to be conducted in large groups with hands-on sessions. Undertaking user education programmes provides libraries with the opportunity to optimise usage because users are taught lifelong learning skills such as information–retrieval skill and ICT skills. Implementing a portal can change the environment in which users discover information and get better access to the wealth of contents.

Globalisation

The term "globalisation" is associated mainly with business – giving rise to concepts such as 'global economy', 'global markets', 'global competition' or hyper competition', etc. A global economy is one in which goods, services, people, skills and ideas move freely across geographic borders.

Relatively unfettered by artificial constraints, such as tariffs, the global economy significantly expands and complicates a firm's competitive environment". Is globalisation relevant for libraries? The authors are of the opinion that since 'information delivery' is a business and globalisation is basically a business concept than globalisation will have an impact on libraries. Innovative technology has made it possible for business to be conducted in a global environment but how does globalisation affect librarians?

Self-Efficiency vs. Outsourcing

Concept of self-sufficiency has given way to global outsourcing by cutting out the role of the middle man, including the librarian. This has implications for the library in matters relating to human resource and organisation structure.

Examples:

- *Acquisitions*: Librarians do not need to go though local agents. There are many more companies on Internet who can acquire anything for libraries, ranging from equipment to books.
- *Cataloguing*: OCLC is a case in point although it does not contain records for non-English items.
- *Information Services*: It is a matter of time before information services are conducted on a global basis replacing libraries and librarians except for the provision of local information which however may be taken over by local companies with enough entrepreneurial acumen to take over the information market.

Demand for Wide-ranging Information

Imagine providing information services for the whole world, when most libraries cannot even satisfy the information needs of their own clientele. Theoretically, however, this is what globalisation could generate.

Do librarians have the potential for it? In reality, no. Working on the premise that no one person can provide all information on everything, it will be a massive task but if libraries do not do it other more enterprising professionals would.

It is worth a thought. For example, libraries in Malaysia need not confine themselves to providing information merely about Malaysia but through databases subscribed and information networks established via the universities and ministries, librarians can play a role. This will have implications for the library in terms of collections, human resource and job expertise and skills.

The question that begs to be asked at this juncture is: Do we still need libraries and librarians in the face of globalisation?

Lifelong Learning

The move towards a more democratic form of education in the 1960s and 1970s resulted in a shift in the concept of education from one that was authoritarian and elitist to one that advocated 'equal opportunity in education'. 'Equal opportunity in education' was seen as the democratic right of all individuals–irrespective of race, status, age or ability but at the same time 'equal opportunity' does not mean the same treatment for everyone. For equal opportunity to be meaningful, however, education must be extended on a continuous lifelong basis with opportunities for success provided at every stage of the continuum.

Any attempt at early elimination would render the democratisation process ineffective and make a mockery of the principle of 'equal opportunity' Conceptualising education as a lifelong process was an effort at translating democratic principles into educational practice. Democratising education on the principles of equal opportunity meant a re-appraisal of traditional aims and methods.

Unlike the traditional concept, the modern concept of education believes that education should produce a learning society, not a learning minority. In simple language, higher education should be catering to the masses. The change in emphasis in educational aims and objectives has made it necessary for teaching and learning methods to be reviewed, giving rise to a productive learning environment with the focus on learning and the learner rather than teaching and the teachers, in greater emphasis given to differentiation in needs, abilities and personalities in the development of independent and active learning the democratisation of higher education has given the concept 'equal opportunity' a new meaning, encompassing a wider scope of educational aims and objectives. It has given modern education certain characteristics.

Greater and More Flexible Access to Higher Education

Greater access does not mean mainly increasing the number of people enrolled in mainstream university programmes but also to provide opportunities for those previously "excluded" for various reasons. Propagating lifelong education would ensure that any one who wishes to acquire qualifications at any stage of his life would be able to do so because there are alternative means by which the opportunity is provided

Learner-centred Approach to Learning

The importance given to the learner in the modern approach to education ensures that learner needs are given priority. In lifelong learning, the focus is on teaching the learner how to learn, not what to learn. In modern terms, it would mean "empowering" the learner such that he can be independent and resourceful throughout his lifetime of learning experiences. This also means that the learner is given the opportunity to learn at his own pace and according to his own style. He can undertake his learning anywhere, anytime, anyhow. Learning therefore becomes flexible, at a pace dictated by the learner and in accordance with negotiated objectives.

Variety of Teaching Strategies

With the learner's interest at the heart of the teaching-learning process, the method and strategy of instruction need to adapt. Instruction has now to be skills-based, not subject-based, consistent with the need to prepare learners for lifelong learning, so as to teach them how to learn rather than what to learn. Instruction is individualised to cater to individual differences of the learners making it necessary for small-group teaching rather than the whole-class approach which assumes that learners learn at the same pace.

A greater variety of teaching strategies have been devised in recent years to cope with the learner-centric pedagogy such as interdisciplinary team-teaching, project work, problem-based teaching and with greater ICT capability, web-based teaching, e-teaching, etc. What implications does lifelong learning have for libraries?. Bearing in mind that lifelong 'students' are now not confined to the 5-14 age cohort but more likely 5-65 years age cohort as the learning population moves from primary schools to universities, libraries will have to reassess its collections, services and delivery systems to accommodate this learning continuum.

There will be traditional as well as non-traditional universities. In the case of the non-traditional universities offering open and distance learning programmes, libraries will need to focus more on digital collections, services to be more flexible providing for remote access and delivery systems need to be efficient. The issue is: When libraries move from providing library-centred to usercentred services, the library can no longer be a building but a system.

Knowledge Management

The concept of Knowledge Management (KM) is basically one that advocates sharing of knowledge within a company or agency such that with the sharing of knowledge it will help the company or agency to combat competition and provide it with the competitive edge.

It is a process that involves:

- *Knowledge creation*: Recording information from top management downwards and vice versa. It includes documenting unwritten knowledge or in other words, documenting experiences of people relevant to the company operations. This is not an easy task because the information may not be current and people are not forthcoming, preferring to be secretive.
- *Knowledge organisation*: Documenting and using retrieval systems to store and make accessible the necessary information. What to document, how detailed and for whom are issues related to KM. In

certain agencies, there will be a committee or jury of specialists to decide which information to document and store.

- *Knowledge dissemination/sharing*: KM was introduced to reduce barriers in information/knowledge sharing in companies to facilitate decision-making and prevent unnecessary duplication of effort. Knowing what others are doing in other department will help departmental heads to make more informed decisions. Knowledge sharing is more effective if it involves all levels of staff – from top management downwards and vice versa. The logic of sharing strategic and operational knowledge is to make processes more efficient and intradepartmental communication more effective. As for its role in ensuring the company's monetary gains it has been reported in the professional literature to be 'successful'. KM has also been described as "organisational learning" because in sharing the information or knowledge the whole organisation goes through a learning process. The success of KM is difficult to quantify because it is difficult to measure the success of knowledge-sharing or to ascertain to what extent organisational learning takes place.

But what does KM mean to libraries?

- The library can become the Centre for Knowledge Management in the institution by being involved in documenting, organising and disseminating the information or knowledge gathered from within the organisation This is particularly viable for all libraries e.g. in the case of university libraries information about teaching, learning and research activities can not only be documented via published reports but also by interviewing the VC, Deputy VC's, Deans, lecturers, students, Ministry of Education officials, etc. In special libraries at government agencies or private companies, there may be problems with access to confidential information like pricing of commodities, marketing policies, marketing research results, etc. In Malaysia, these are a few successful agencies undertaking KM. From their experience, it can be said that the success of KM depends on the support of the management of the organization while the main problem is that colleagues are not cooperative and not forthcoming with information, especially tacit information.
- The library can create primary "live" information, instead of dealing with "passive information" which is often second-hand, outdated, irrelevant and insignificant.
- Staff must be trained or retrained in certain areas in order to function effectively. The ability to interview effectively, the ability to relate to people without either intimidating them or being intimidated by them, knowledgeable in relevant subject areas, proficient at handling ICT information delivery systems, etc.

- Allows library to be creative because there is neither universal approach to KM, nor one or best way of implementing it.
- Recognition that information is an important commodity but like any other product needs good marketing strategies. If the library wants to function as an information centre it has to convince its own market and society at large of the importance of its role as information provider.

National Policies and Objectives

All countries have long-term strategic plans. In Malaysia, it is a 25-year plan which forms the basis for national development till 2020. Briefly, the V2020s aim is to make Malaysia an industrialised nation by the year 2020.

In order to achieve this aim, nine thrust areas were identified to drive the V2020. One of the thrust areas is to make the Malaysian society a knowledge-based society. In this case of Malaysia, not only is the public sector committed to achieving the strategic objectives of V2020 but the private sector as well.

Knowing where the nation is heading towards and the role played by each sector of society is important to the library and although the role of libraries is more indirect than direct, libraries do have in their custody the nation's intellectual wealth which should be optimized in the development of the knowledge society. Considering the wealth of information resources located at libraries throughout Malaysia, if they had been read and used, Malaysia does not need to wait till the year 2020 to have an information-rich society.

Threats

Proliferation of Information Providers

A potential threat is the proliferation of non-library information providing companies and agencies that provide information via Internet. They may impose charges for the information but the information is usually current. How can libraries compete when the collections available at libraries are mainly secondary information found in print and electronic media?

There are three areas that the new breed of information providers has found foothold:

- Delivery systems
- Content development
- Content management

At the International Conferences of Asian Digital Libraries, held in Kuala Lumpur in December 2003, it was remarkable to listen to ICT specialists who have devised systems for information delivery. The focus was systems rather than content but it gave a good indication of what is imminent in the near future. Much as librarians were awed by the current developments, it also gave the impression that unless libraries take on a more pro-active approach, libraries will be by-passed as information centres. So the issue is: Can libraries compete?

Globalisation

There are two aspects in globalisation – the positive and the negative, depending on how one views it.

There are two potentials:

- Ability to outsource certain aspects of library functions such as acquisitions, cataloguing and information sources.
- Provide information services beyond home shores. It will be a daunting task as there will be a need to upgrade staff expertise but notwithstanding this, we need to explore the possibility.

From the negative point of view, it will spell the end of library services as we know it now, specifically with regard to information delivery. The library will remain the centre for loans and reference, using print and electronic resources. These materials can be accessed on-site or from the home or office. But the critical issue is currency and variety of information that cannot be supplied by libraries. Globalisation will then take away from the library its information delivery function because in speed and variety libraries will not be able to compete with information centres worldwide despite the cost.

ACCOUNTABILITY IN LIBRARY MANAGEMENT

Having defined the environment it is obvious that while in the internal environment there are more weaknesses than strengths, in the external environment there are more opportunities than threats. How then can libraries take advantage of the opportunities that the 21st century has to offer when library resources are inadequate and their role more peripheral than integral? The answer is to strategise – through well-designed strategic plans, efficient organisation, capable leadership and effective control measures. It is only when these management tools and strategies are in place can libraries ensure the achievement of their goals and objectives. The onus therefore lies with the libraries to maximise their opportunities and be accountable for the success of their performance. Seen in this light, accountability therefore is the key factor to whether or not they can meet the demands and challenges of the 21st century

STRATEGIC PLAN

A well-designed plan would provide direction, minimise uncertainty and impact of changes, reduce waste and establish standards for goal achievements.

The planning process incorporates the following steps:

- Setting of goals and objectives

- Formulating strategies
- Developing action plans
- Coordinating activities
- Monitoring accomplishment of goals
- Review/ revise plan

For the libraries, it is crucial that they understand what their core business is, which is SERVICES. Their core business must be integrated into the core business of their organisations

In designing the strategies, the library has to first determine a strategic focus which will be incorporated in its:

- Vision,
- Mission and
- Objectives statements.

Where does the issue of accountability arise in the formulation of the strategic plan? It is in the quantitative methods used to measure the accomplishment of goals and objectives, in the time frames given to accomplish each activity and in the quality measures used in the performance such as monitoring, setting standards (ISO) and benchmarking. But however brilliant the plan, unless implemented, it is useless.

ORGANISING

The organisation structure should facilitate the achievement of goals so it is important that the organisation structure is designed to facilitate work flow (whether via function, specialisation or process), define the chain of command (whether hierarchical, flat, etc.), define the span of control (the wider the less effective) and clarify issue such as centralisation vs. decentralisation.

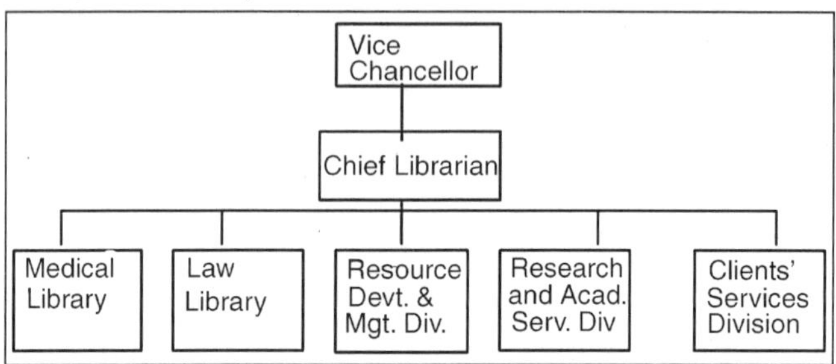

Fig. Example of a Simple One-site Organisation Structure

The library management would have to structure the organization in such a way as to ensure that the organisation structure facilitates rather than hinder the achievement of goals. The library management is therefore accountable in this aspect.

LEADING

Leading is influencing others to carry out tasks towards the achievements of goals.

There are different types of leaderships but there are certain traits or characteristics that reflect good leadership:

- Develop corporate of excellent staff
  - Staff development plan
  - Motivation
  - Competency training
  - Leadership training
  - Performance measurement
- Monitor activities
- Monitor achievement of goals
- Flexible and adaptable leadership
- Establish value culture – leadership by example

Leadership is not confined to being the Chief Librarian or the Library Director but leadership is found at all levels. Leaders may be managers but not all managers are leaders. The quality of human resource in any organisation depends on the quality of leadership. In this way, the library manager should be held accountable if staff cannot perform and goals cannot be achieved.

CONTROL

Control measures must be in place to monitor activities and ensure that goals are achieved. The effectiveness of any control system depends on how effectively it can facilitate the achievement of goals. Why is a control system important?

- It is a means of measuring whether goals are met and if not why. You can have well-formulated strategic plans, well-designed organisation structure, highly motivated staff but without control there is no measure of goals achievement.
- It is a management tool that can be used to monitor and measure activities with greater objectivity.

There are basically three types of control measures that libraries can use:

- Monitoring
- ISO
- Benchmarking

2

Total Quality Management: A Perspective Approach for Librarians

INTRODUCTION

The increasing expectations of users have challenged libraries to improve their quality of services. Limited by increasingly tighter budgetary restrictions, library managers feel more pressure to fully exploit available resources. Therefore, several libraries and information services have adopted quality management practices in recent years.

Among the various initiatives implemented include:

- ISO 9000 standards,
- 5S movement, and
- benchmarking.

By adopting quality management, the library's image and service quality can be improved, and librarians can increase productivity while focusing on the customer's needs. Quality management has been extensively applied within the manufacturing industry for over a decade.

More recently, the service industry has increasingly emphasised this area. The public sector has also put forward major initiatives to improve quality. Closely examining available quality management techniques in service industries and the public sector reveals their effectiveness and positive impact on the customers. Quality management is increasingly integrated into library services, following their perceived success in manufacturing industries, with particular emphasis on improving service quality.

Libraries have developed numerous programmes to fulfil user requirements. In general, libraries concentrate mainly on maintaining administrative activities, building the collection, and serving the users.

Therefore, the functions of a library can be broadly categorised as administrative management, technical services and public services. Administrative management defines the objectives of the library, allocates the resources to achieving such objectives, co-ordinates related activities, and assesses the performance of related services. Technical services largely focus on building the collection and making the collection more accessible for users. The activities of technical services include acquisition, information organisation, and preservation. While all library activities strive to, public services serve the customers most directly. Related activities consist of circulation, reference and access service. Library services can be viewed as an open system with materials, resources and information needs of customers as input. In other words, the activities involved in providing and using library services are more interrelated than isolated.

While the library only exists for serving customers, the service delivery system should be user-oriented. Although all functions and activities focus on customers, the direct interaction between library and customers occurs in public services. That is, librarians working in circulation, reference and access service respond and translate the customer's expectations to the technical service department and administrative management.

Depending on the ability of public services to accurately interpret customer requirements, all functions of the library can be directed to satisfying the quality requirements and information needs of customers. Quality management in libraries and information services has received considerable attention, with a majority of those investigations describing quality concepts, quality management principles, related processes, and limitations. From the perspective of library services, adopting quality programmes increases the effectiveness of the library and satisfies increasingly higher customer expectations. Most quality management- related literature is based on experience drawn from industrial organisations, particularly on the manufacturing of tangible products delivered to the end-user at a later stage.

Past years have witnessed the increasing acceptance of quality management into services-related and non-profit organisations, such as education. Despite the significant level of adaptation within service organisations and the public sector, there exists missing link between quality management principles/tools and the implementation of quality management in libraries and information services.

Johannsen foresaw the risk:

- . . . As the general principles of quality control have originally been developed in private sector and industrial environments, you may expect problems, when you wish to use those principles to manage quality of an intangible resource, information, in organizations, where structures, culture, management style, business strategies and customers are often very unlike industrial organizations.

Effectively→ implementing quality management in libraries and information services requires an understanding of the following:

- The unique characteristics of library operations
- The nature of interaction between librarians and customers
- The making of recommendations on the application of appropriate quality management concepts and techniques.

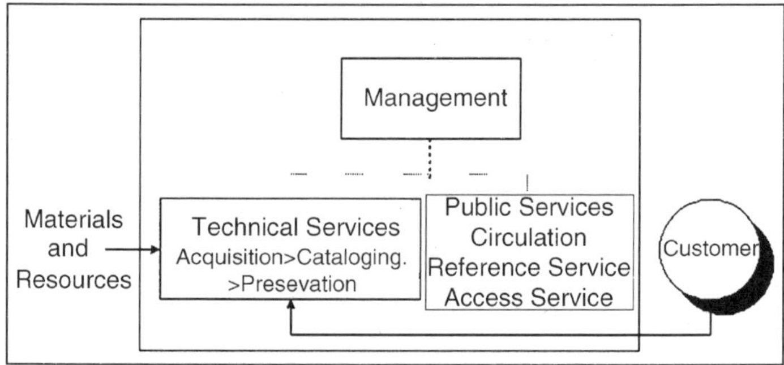

Fig. A Systemic View of Library Services.

QUALITY MANAGEMENT APPROACHES

Quality management approaches can be categorised broadly into three stages according to the evolution of management control. Management can implement control before an activity commences, while the activity occurs, or after the activity has been completed. Consequently, three types of control are feedforward, concurrent and feedback. The most desirable type of management control is feedforward control that is future-directed and takes place in advance of the actual activity.

Feedforward control is advantageous because it allows management to prevent anticipated problems rather than having to cure them later and to avoid wasting resources. Concurrent control, as its name implies, takes place while an activity is in progress. When control is enacted while the activity is being performed, management can correct problems before they become too costly. The most conventional means of control relies on feedback. The feedback control takes place after the activity.

However, a disadvantage of this approach is that the damage will have already occurred by the time that the manager has the information to take corrective actions. Consequently, feedforward control is the most economic approach and can meet the requirement of customers, followed by concurrent control and feedback control, respectively. Interestingly, quality management approaches developed and applied to assess and improve product quality can be related to types of management control from the perspective of an open system. Quality management approaches were originally developed as being product-oriented. Feedback control, an inspection-based quality control approach, was introduced to detect inferior products at the after-production stage. Realising that quality could not be improved by merely inspecting the finished product, subsequent efforts switched the emphasis of quality management from inspection to process control: from feedback control stage to concurrent control stage.

The underlying premise regarding quality in the concurrent control stage is that quality is equivalent to meeting or exceeding customer expectations.

Manufacturing products that reflect the diverse needs of customers, is more of a function of good design than of good control of a process. Therefore, quality management has gradually shifted to emphasis on the design phase: from concurrent control stage to feedforward control stage.

Quality by Inspection

The inspection-based system was perhaps the first scientifically designed quality control system to evaluate quality. The system is applied to incoming raw materials and parts for use as inputs for production and/or finished products. Under this system, some quality characteristics are examined, measured and compared with required specifications to assess conformity.

Therefore, the inspection-based system is a screening process that merely isolates conforming from non-conforming products without having any direct mechanism to reduce defects. Reducing the damage to final products, sampling plans were developed to control product quality. Although an effective technique, a quality control system based on sampling inspection does not directly achieve customer satisfaction and continuous improvement. Producing fewer defects through process improvement is the only means of reducing defects.

QUALITY BY PROCESS CONTROL

Defects inevitably add to the production cost and waste resources. Therefore, a business strives for zero defects. The quality management system based on sampling inspections has been replaced by the approach of continuously improving the process. This concept, as pioneered by Deming, moves from detecting defects to preventing them and continuing with process improvement to meeting and exceeding customer requirements on a continuous basis. The continuous cycle of process improvement is based on the scientific method for addressing problems, commonly referred to as the Deming cycle.

Deming's approach consists of four basic stages:

- A plan of what to do;
- Do or carry out the plan;
- Study what has done; and
- Act to prevent errors or improve the process.

The planning stage consists of studying the current situation, gathering data, and planning for improvement.

Related activities include:

- Defining the process, its inputs, outputs, customers, and suppliers;
- Understanding customer expectations;
- Identifying problems;
- Testing theories of causes; and
- Developing solutions.

In the do stage, the plan is implemented on a trial basis to evaluate a proposed solution and provide objective data. The study stage determines whether or not the trial plan is working correctly and if any further problems or opportunities are identified. In the final stage, act, the final plan is implemented and the improvements become standardised and implemented continuously.

This process then returns to the plan stage for further diagnosis and improvement. The Deming Cycle can enhance communication between the staff involved and help employees to use the wheel to improve processes. Some of the specific tools used to improve processes are control charts, process capability studies, seven tools, seven new tools, and seven creativity tools. However, the appropriate tools must be applied for the specified purpose.

For example, cause-and-effect diagrams and process flow charts could be more appropriate during the planning stage of the Deming wheel, whereas control charts may be most appropriate during the stage of checking.

QUALITY BY DESIGN

The Deming approach shifted the focus of quality management a step back from inspection to process control. The approach of quality by design makes a further step back from process to design. By definition, Quality by design implies that quality must be built in early in the development and design stage. By doing so, the final product can satisfy the customers.

Two important techniques for designing quality products are:

- Quality function deployment (QFD) and
- Failure Mode and Effect Analysis (FMEA).

Quality function deployment is a structured approach that:

- Identifies and ranks the relative importance of customer requirements;
- Identifies design parameters that contribute to the customer requirements;
- Estimates the relationship between design parameters and customer requirements and among different design parameters; and
- Sets target values for the design parameters to best satisfy customer requirements.

A QFD matrix is frequently used to translate prioritised customer requirements into identifiable and measurable product specifications and engineering requirements to reduce functional variation and costs, thereby facilitating the decision-makers in making designrelated decisions. Many investigators have successfully applied QFD in product and service design. Failure Mode and Effect Analysis is a methodical approach to examine a proposed design for possible ways in which failure can occur.

FMEA consists of:

- Identifying and listing modes of failure and the subsequent faults;
- Assessing the probability of these faults;
- Assessing the probability that the faults are detected;

- Assessing the severity of the consequences of the faults;
- Calculating a measure of the risk;
- Ranking the faults on the basis of the risk;
- Attempting to resolve the high-risk problems; and
- Verifying the effectiveness of the action by using a revised measure of risk.

In addition to providing preliminary information on reliability prediction, product and process design, FMEA helps engineers identify potential problems in the product earlier, thereby avoiding costly changes or reworks at later stages. Closely scrutinising quality management reveals that many techniques are based on experience derived from manufacturing tangible products. Whether or not quality management practices can be transferred to a service industry delivering intangible services has received considerable attention.

Many investigators confer that:

- The service and manufacturing industries differ in terms of the characteristics of quality,
- Different criteria must be used for measuring these industries, and
- The focus of quality management is rather different than similar.

The final manufacturing products can be measured objectively, while the quality can be managed by output control. Meanwhile, the deliverables of services are frequently intangible, which is difficult to measure objectively. In addition to the simultaneously delivery and consumption of services, the quality certainly cannot be managed by either output control or process control. Brophy and Coulling indicated that with the broad applications in the service sector, the sector has come to the recognition that some aspects of quality management must be approached somewhat differently in the service industry.

The most distinguishing characteristic between service and manufacturing industries is that in the former, there is usually a direct interaction between the customer and the service. Libraries and information services have intensive direct interaction and also indirect contact with the customers. Because of the immediacy of the interface, libraries must develop their own framework when integrating quality management approaches into libraries.

FRAMEWORK OF QUALITY MANAGEMENT APPROACHES IN LIBRARIES

Having different characteristics, library services require special approaches of quality management that go beyond the simple adoption of manufacturing techniques for a product. Quality management related to library functions can be viewed in three phases: before service, during service, and after service. Library services ultimately focus on satisfying the information needs of customers. Before services are provided, the technical service departments should have required books and information resources collected and value-added to enhance their value to the customers. Therefore, the customer-oriented library should regard technical services as resource development system to ensure that every customer has resources properly acquired, organised, displayed or accessed. Having direct contact with customers, the public services should be regarded as information service delivejry system and focus on providing information to customers accurately, promptly, and responsively to help customers solve problems, and build up customers' knowledge and ultimately enhance their productivity.

Administrative management should be regarded as the service support system to coordinate and allocate resources as well as provide support for technical services and public services to satisfy customers' needs, and to evaluate service performance periodically and to continuously improve service quality. Figure shows the quality management approaches and techniques associated with the stages of service delivery in libraries.

Resource Development System

Largely concerning itself with backstage activities, a resource development system is the off-line preparation for public services and has no direct contact with customers. For services in which the customer need not be present, the service transaction can be de-coupled and standardised. For example, acquisition is considered to be a customised service. Convenient access to Web-accessible public access catalogue, however, has weaned customers from present interaction with live librarians to interaction via online purchase request and, consequently, only routine order preparation and communication is required.

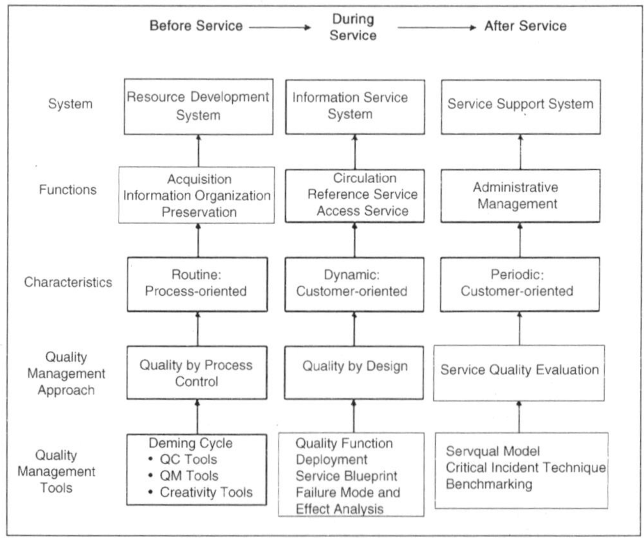

Fig. Framework of Quality Management Approaches in Libraries.

Most activities related to technical services have technical and procedural standards to follow, accounting for why each function is characterised by a high routine and process-orientation.

International or domestic rules govern the cataloguing, classification, and information organisation. In addition, standardised practices also exist for acquisition and preservation, *e.g.* how order requests are to be formulated and transmitted.

In fact, many practices in technical services are standardised by actual work routines and formalised based on a detailed and systematic study during library automation. Therefore, the quality management of a resource development system should emphasise the concurrent control of process to ensure that all books and resources have been accurately collected, accessed and valueadded appropriately. Quality by process control is the best quality management strategy for a resource development system.

Deming's PDSA cycle, together with the seven quality control tools, the seven quality management tools, and the seven creativity tools can be applied in technical services to improve service quality. The PDSA Cycle is focused on satisfying customer needs. This requires an attitude of putting the customer first and a belief that this principle is the object of one's work. Implicit in the Deming PDSA approach is that improvement in quality results from continuous, incremental turns of the wheel.

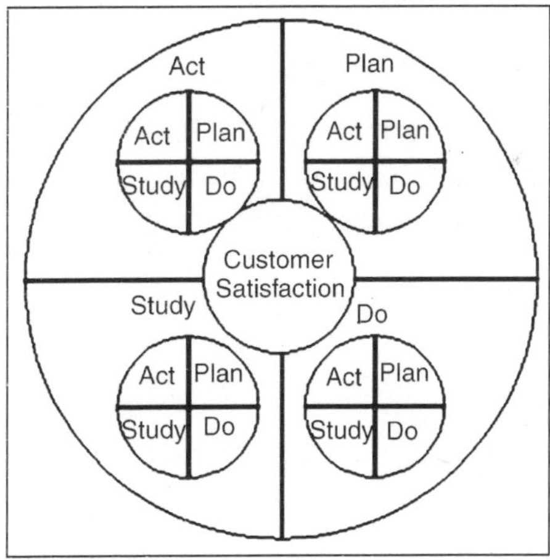

Fig. The Deming Circle

Seven simple tools — cause-and-effect diagrams, run charts, scatter diagrams, flowcharts, Pareto diagrams, histograms and control charts — have been termed the Seven Quality Control. In the early 1970s, as Total Quality Control (TQC) expanded to service and administrative areas, it became clear that the 7QC tools were not always appropriate. So, the seven new QC tools or the seven management tools – affinity diagrams, interrelationship digraphs, tree diagrams, matrix diagrams, prioritisation matrixes, process decision programme charts, and activity network diagrams–were developed under the leadership of Nyatanni. Among these the affinity diagram is a tool for organising language data. After ideas are brainstormed and written on cards, they are grouped together with similar ideas. A header card is created which captures the meaning of each group of ideas. This is a creative, right brain, activity.

The Seven Creativity Tools are problem definition, brainstorming, brainwriting, creative brainstorming, word and picture association, advanced analogies, and the morphological chart. While the original seven QC tools are oriented towards the analysis of quantitative data, the seven management tools and seven creativity tools are designed to handle unstructured, verbal information in group-base problem-solving or decision- making processes. All these tools can be used separately or complementarily. For example, the acquisition department can use control chart to evaluate the performance of dealers, and build partnership with the best dealer.

The serial department can use the cause-and-effect diagram not only to analyse the causes of missing issues but also use relation diagrams to control the order status of critical serials to ensure the completeness and promptness of serials collection. In addition, the Pareto diagram can be used in the cataloguing department to collect the data on bibliographic verification and copy cataloguing for further analysing the feasibility of enhancing productivity and shortening the processing time.

INFORMATION SERVICE SYSTEM

The information service system is a service delivery system that has direct contact with customers. In circulation, access and reference services, the customer often serves as the co-producer and works with the librarians and the library system to produce a final product which enhances knowledge, skills, or promotes the enjoyment of leisure activities. The service encounter is always initiated by the customer. Therefore, the major function of an information service system is dynamic and customer-oriented. Because of direct interaction with public service librarians, customers require the service to be done right the first time and to be consistent every time.

Consequently, quality by design is the best quality management strategy for information service system. Quality management tools that can be applied are quality function deployment, failure mode and effect analysis, and service blueprinting which is specially designed for effectively managing the service encounter. Reference service has direct encounters with customers, and the service quality depends highly on the performance of the reference librarians and their interactions with customers. Therefore, the design of reference service can adopt the techniques of quality function deployment.

Library activists proposed a modified framework of quality function deployment for reference service. There are four phases to facilitate communicating service requirements from the customer to the activities related to quality management of reference service delivery. The first phase is to identify the customer's needs and requirements. The second phase is to define the service requirements and design the co-service system so that the right quality is built in from the very beginning of service design.

The third phase consists of process planning which is a matter of selecting the co-service process "best" producing what the customer needs. Phase four involves the planning of the quality management activities. It emphasizes translating reference processes into quality management activities in order to ensure quality both before and during the reference encounter. The first task of applying QFD to reference services is to identify customer needs, which are descriptions in the customer's own words of the benefits they want the reference services to provide. The opinions posted on the library web site or BBS, customer complaints, records of reference interviews, previous user studies, and so on, will all contribute to the list of customer needs.

In reference services, the primary customer needs might be categorised as "good employees", "right answers" and "nice environment". In order to manage the customer needs, the primary needs need to be structured into a hierarchy. For example, the primary need for "good employee" might be elaborated as "good attitude" and "good skills" in serving customers. And the "good attitude" is subdivided into "kind and polite", "does not have to wait", "assists users in looking up information" and "properly dressed".

Each customer need is, then, to be met in terms of professional terminology – that is, service requirements. For example, the words "kind and polite" express the customer's concept, but librarians need these words translated into their vocabulary in order to actually build a service delivering standards and quality management activities. In delivering reference service, "kind and polite" may be described in terms of the responsiveness, approachability, attentiveness, and courtesy. The service requirements of reference services translated from customer needs might be grouped into answer, process, and environment, using an Affinity Diagram.

For example, the quality of answer might be evaluated according to two perspectives – results and sources. And the quality of source might be evaluated according to the indicators of credibility, acceptability, accessibility and availability. After the service requirements have been identified and prioritised, the most important requirements must be linked to reference process to design the co-service system to satisfy the customer needs.

Circulation and access service is the major contact between the customer and the library, and is usually the starting point for customers to use all other library services. With information networks, most customers can remotely access the webpac or search networked databases. After identifying the availability of certain books or documents, the customer is physically present in the library to check out those books or photocopy the required documents.

If the collection or documents needed by the customers are unavailable, the customers can also apply for an interlibrary loan or document delivery service. Encounters between the customer and library are integral and continuous, with each customer possibly encountering many points of services and interacting with varying service facilities and librarians.

Therefore, the circulation and access service should be designed by integrating all of the service points to provide seamless services to customers. The service blueprint is a customer-focused service process analysis tool. Figure gives an example of a typical service blueprint for access service. A service blueprint is a detailed map or a flow chart of the service process. However, creating a flow chart can only depict the workflow of internal operations from the perspective of the librarian.

Such a flow chart neither provides understanding of the interaction between the librarian and the customer; nor can it integrate these encounter points with related activities that support these encounters. Therefore, the concepts of "line of interaction" and "line of visibility" are used in a service blueprint to improve service encounters. Consequently, the service delivery process can be simultaneously viewed from the perspectives of the librarian and the customer. The line of interaction differentiates actions performed by the customer from actions performed by the librarians. Customer actions are placed above the line.

Actions performed by the librarians are located below the line. These actions are charted on the service path proceeding from left to right. Along the line of interaction, the encounter points, *i.e.* the points in the service process where the customer receives the access services, can be easily specified. The line of visibility in a service blueprint distinguishes those processes that are visible to the customer from those that are behind the scenes.

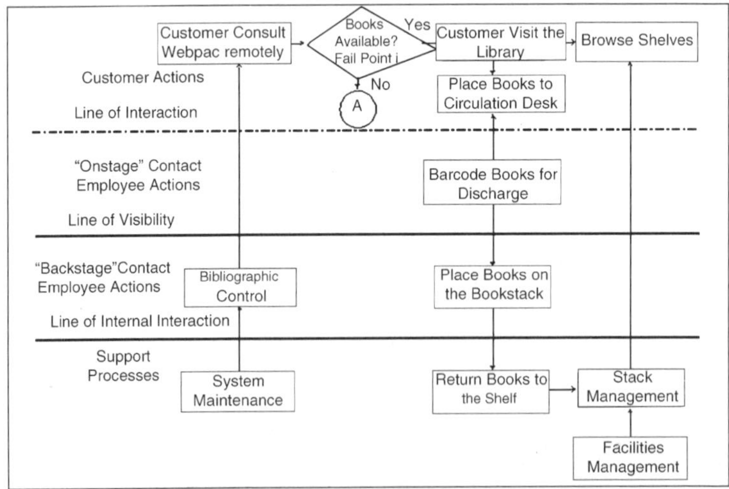

Fig. Framework of Service Blueprint - A Case of Access Service.

This concept facilitates the understanding of the interconnection between "below-the-line" and "above-the- line" service processes and the recognition that the latter processes where the customers' experiences directly depend on the former processes that customers do not experience. The blueprinting exercise also provides librarians with opportunities to identify potential fail points and, then, use the failure mode and effect analysis to design "foolproof" procedures to avoid such an occurrence, thereby ensuring the delivery of high-quality services. The purpose of failure mode and effects analysis is to identify all the ways in which a failure can occur, to estimate the effect and seriousness of the failure, and to recommend corrective design actions. An FMEA usually consists of specifying the following information for each critical component: failure mode, cause of failure, effect on the product or system within which it operates, corrective action, and comments.

SERVICE SUPPORT SYSTEM

The performance of a customer-oriented library should be evaluated on the basis of quality and quantity. Quantitative evaluation in terms of output measure is the basic element of a statistical report, which is mainly prepared for accountability not for improving service. Meanwhile, customer satisfaction significantly contributes to improving service quality. Based on the evaluation results, the service support system should allocate resources to those services that customers deem as having low satisfaction. In practice, the SERVQUAL model, critical incident techniques and benchmarking can be used to evaluate and improve service quality in library services. Parasuraman, Zeithaml, and Berry developed a multiple-item scale called SERVQUAL for measuring the five dimensions of service quality. A score for the quality of service is calculated by computing the differences between the ratings that customers assign to paired expectation and perception of each of twenty-two statements. This instrument has been designed and validated for use in a variety of service encounters.

In addition, many investigators have adapted the SERVQUAL measures to evaluate the service quality of libraries. Critical incident techniques can be used to analyse the service encounters between the customer and librarians. Customers and employees are interviewed separately to describe their experiences of the service experience. By doing so, the cause of success or failure of the service encounter can be analysed; the critical factors of service encounters can be identified as well. Correspondingly, staff training and development courses can be designed to enhance the capacity of librarians and library instruction. Moreover, information literacy programmes can be designed to equip the capacity of customers. For every quality dimension, some organisations have earned the reputation of being "best in class" and, thus, a benchmark for comparison. Benchmarking, however, involves more than comparing statistics. It also includes visiting the leading organisation to learn firsthand how such outstanding performance has been achieved.

3

New Librarian`s Skills and Qualification

INTRODUCTION

The appearance of the internet and the WorldwideWeb, as a final stage of an evolution started many decades ago with the introduction of computers and network technologies, has created a new information and social environment, radically different from the functional environment of the traditional library. This fact has led to a considerable research and discussion concerning the form, the role, the position and the functions of the social institutions known as "libraries" within this new context.

At the same time, and as it might be expected, another discussion is under way, concerning what may be considered as the human parallel of the institution, that is the librarian or the information professional that runs the library. This discussion concerns many aspects and problems of the information professional in the new environment and especially the types, the education needed, the skills and qualifications required, the extent to which the profession should or will change etc. In an attempt to determine and understand these changes and, mainly, to analyse the data that will lead the profession to the new century, several works with various types of predictions, analyses and proposals regarding the future of the profession have been published. A brief overview of the relevant literature follows so that the findings of our research are considered in the suitable context. According to these works, thus, the modern librarian should be a professional that possesses standards and values that function effectively and smoothly in a technological environment.

He fully understands and knows sufficiently the conventional library practices. He constantly wishes to change, to develop and to learn. He adapts easily in a permanently altered environment of information, he has experience in education and possess a considerable amount of communication skills. His survival will be ensured by the fundamentals of his science and the skills and roles that emerge from them. The role of intermediate and instructor will still be essentials and librarian will focus into helping the user identify the information he needs and providing tools for evaluation and use.

Audunson believes that the modern academic courses in LIS should aim to create the "complete librarian", while Researchers points out that the education should not only focus on the technical matters of Library Science, such as the creation of a digital library, but should also be orientated towards the development of survival and affective skills. In the modern environment procedures and practices in education should convergence with those found in an actual working environment.

Librarians must emphasize in the learning environment they create themselves and not solely to technology. He also demonstrates ten tendencies of the contemporary environment of information that influence librarian's function and role such as: virtual is a place not a format, communities of interest are no longer bounded by geography and every profession's relevance is in question. According to him, one of the most important future roles is that of information councelor. Identification of the most important issues that affect – within the modern environment – the behaviour and attitudes of every librarian is also accomplished by Melchionda. Technostress and techno-phobia, lack of standardisation and quality, competition with search engines and commercial tools are few of the factors that influence the role of librarian in the modern environment.

An important issue should be the examination of the real cause of changes in the librarian's profession, regardless of time frame, and through a more realistic point-of-view. In fact, the goals of our profession are still the same and they are affected from the expectations of the market, the working environment and ethics. Specialization or hybridization should not pose a dilemma, since the profession must be considered as a whole set that is constantly changing and revised. Regarding the "hybridization" of our profession, Biddiscombe believes that the hybrid library poses the need for "hybrid" information professionals.

Although it is difficult for one person to acquire a large number of skills, he states that every modern librarian must be able to recognize informational needs, manage users and encourage people with different skills to work in the same team. Such "hybrid" teams will play an important role as far as management of future information systems is concerned. Librarians should also focus on evolving their internet skills and four basic points regarding that evolution should be mediation and assistance, teaching and training, partnerships, design and production.

Also, according to Pace every online library experience should be consisted of quality, expertise, integrity and longevity. Concerning the skills needed by a modern librarian, Fisher analyses a set of skills and points out that at the same time with the traditional roles, the librarian will create organizational information management systems, will use the techniques of Information Architect, will manage access in digital documents and will support every possible learning procedure. A profile of skills and qualification is also demonstrated by Partridge and Hallam, according to which qualifications are divided into technical and generic ones.

Ashcroft identifies six basic skill categories:

- Professional.
- Marketing and promotion.
- Evaluation.
- Communication – negotiation – collaboration.
- Censorship.
- Personal transferable skills.

In addition, Marion conducted a research on job advertisements and she concluded that a new category of "digital librarian" is not yet necessary and library is still a part of an evolving automated environment, rather than of a digital one. She also found communication skills to be the most wanted qualification. Kwasik's analysis on job ads regarding skills for serials librarians found communication skills to be the second most desired qualification. In general, she found traditional skills to be more desired than then ones originating from the digital world. The importance of ICT skills is underlined by Biddiscombe as he believes are necessary for any learning, educational or research procedure in a learning environment, but at the same time, information specialists should maintain some of their traditional skills and qualifications.

Steele and Mechthild also believe that ICT skills, along with communication and administration ones will be essential for every modern librarian. They also state that the use of many terms in order to describe the new librarian is the result of the uncertainty of what the role of a librarian should be.

Concerning the roles served by a modern librarian, Fourie's literature survey identified several roles:

- Publishing;
- Negotiating;
- Teaching;
- Advising;
- Retrieving – researching; and
- Archival management.

In addition, she suggested three more:

- Environmental scanning;
- Active identification of new niche markets; and
- Action research.

Moreover, England states that the librarian will function as researcher, organizer and publisher, member of the digital library design team, teacher and consultant, while Garrod analyses seven roles for a modern librarian, such as metadata specialist, marketing – public relations and learning facilitator. Finally, Nageswara and Babu's research reflects some of the most current trends in LIS as impressed through the roles they identify; search intermediary, facilitator, trainer – educator, web site builder – publisher, researcher, interface designer, knowledge manager, shifter of information resources.

RESEARCH

A total of 200 job advertisements were studied from UK, Canada, Australia and the USA in 2006 and 2007. The aim of the research is to have the qualifications and the skills of librarian's profession investigated, as they are impressed through the job ads.

The elements of this research – substantially the qualifications and skills that the libraries ask for – were used so that a basic profile for a modern librarian would be created, which presents the skills through classes and subclasses. The job ads concern positions in various types of libraries and their departments.

Table. Skills and Qualifications Identified through Job Advertisements

Skills/qualifications	%
Degree in LIS	82
Working experience	68
Communication skills	65
Collection development – management	53
Service orientation	38
Working in a team	38
Administration – organizational skills	36
Knowledge of current developments in LIS	32
User education	30
Digital collection development – management	27
Use of software applications	27
Library automated systems	25
Creation – management of web pages	25
Personal traits	22
Knowledge of library's subject content	21
Working alone	20
Markup languages	16
Databases	13
Programming languages	12
Use of p/c	12
Sets priorities	11
Networks	11
Programme management	10
Problem solving	10
Foreign languages	10

Development of personal career	9
Attention to detail	8
Metadata	7
Serial collections management	6
Knowledge of current developments in ICT	6
Marketing	5
Critical thinking	5
Multimedia	5
Alliances – consortia	4
Administration experience	3
Digitalization	2
Typing	1

FINDINGS

The findings of this research are:

- A total of 38 skills and qualifications were identified through the job ads. Their percentage of appearance was recorded and it's the basic element for the final findings of this research.
- Degree in LIS and working experience skills were expected to be the ones with the highest percentage, and should be considered "de facto" for all librarians, without any further value into this research's findings.
- Communication skill appears in over 60 per cent of the ads and should be considered a desirable skill for every modern librarian. We can assume that this need for communication skills, no matter if the librarian works in technical or public services, comes from the rapid development of the web and the increase of possible ways and means of communication among LIS professionals and the librarian and the user.
- Development of digital collections skill appears in the 10th place. The "equivalent" originating from the traditional environment appears in twice as many advertisements. This finding is an important one regarding the need for development of a completely new set of skills that will originate from the digital world. Instead, it is concluded that the skills that the librarian has developed for decades and regard the knowledge and use of traditional library systems are still important.
- Interpersonal skills, in general, have a high percentage of appearance in the job ads.
- The need for administrative-organizational skills underlines that a modern librarian should have the ability to manage and organize weather it is about the library and its departments or research groups and projects.

- ICT skills often have a higher percentage than the "digital skills". Although ICT skills have a relatively low percentage, we can expect that this will change in the future. General use of software and the knowledge of creating and maintaining web pages are two of the most desirable skills in this category.
- Skills related with the management and use of digital content have a small demand and that was an interesting finding. Especially when compared with the "traditional" skills we can conclude that, at the time being, professional practice dismisses the need for a new category, the "digital librarian".
- Probably the most important aspect of professional development and advancement for the modern librarian is adaptation of current skills in new practices and motivation in acquiring new skills when needed.
- The qualifications and the personal skills a librarian must possess does not change according to the developments in technology, but goes along with the change in organisational and administrative structure of information services.
- Qualifications for a modern librarian are a mix of old and new ones and that synthesis derives from the need in organising documents and information in a hybrid environment.
- Social skills are important not only for professionals working in public services, but should be considered a distinct category of skills, along with professional skills, important for every modern LIS professional.

PROFILE

There has been an analysis in two major categories: professional and general skills. As professional are comprehended the skills that are directly interwoven with the working practices, the use of professional standards and the daily activity of the librarian regarding various technical services.

In this category are included the practices of traditional librarianship, new tendencies that prevail in the management of digital content, the general ICT skills and, finally, various subclasses of general administrative and educational type.

In the category of general skills in which it would, rather, be more appropriate the term social skills, are included all those abilities that the librarian develops daily through his working environment without, however, being related directly with his daily occupation with activities such as cataloguing. The belief that was expressed in various cases, often by persons that did not originate from the traditional librarianship, for the necessity of developing a new set of qualifications and skills, directly and uniquely originating from the digital world, is erroneous.

Table. Profile of skills and Qualifications

Professional skills	Generic (Social) Skills
Process: Management of conventional materials	Personal traits
Automated library systems	Individual talents
Collection development	Critical thinking
Collection management	Attention to detail
Experience in selecting, acquiring and processing	Problem solving conventional material
Self-marketing	
Serials collection management	Ethics
Process – management of digital materials	Business skills
Metadata tools	*Interpersonal skills*
Design and management of databases	Working in a team
Evaluation of internet informational materials,	Communications skills
sources and services	Ability to work alone
Collection development	Understanding user demands and informational
Multimedia	needs
Digitalization	Leadership
Electronic publishing	Service orientation
ICT skills	Participation – development of library consortia
Markup languages	*Experience*
Design, creation and maintenance of web pages	Reference experience
Technical knowledge in computers	Knowledge of library's subject content
Use of software applications (O/S, Office, etc.)	Ability to accept change
Distance education software	Administration experience
Programming languages	Prioritize work
Networks	Insight in transferring traditional operations in an Ability to compare software, hardware online environment and technologies
Lifelong learning – continuing education	
Administrative – organizational skills	Planning personal career
Library facilities management	Ability to learn constantly
Financial resources management	Knowledge of current developments in LIS
Human resources management and	Knowledge of current evaluation
developments in ICT	Evaluation of library services
Interviewing skills	

Marketing
Projects management
Understanding organizational structure
Education
LIS degree
Participation in conferences – seminars
Participation in library associations – organizations
User education – online education
Typing
Foreign languages

Even though the librarians are facing challenges for new and emerging skills, the most important aspect of this change is to be able to adapt the existing skills – many of which are traditional librarianship skills – and the ability to remain flexible in a working environment that is constantly changing. Thus, we can talk not only about a new set of skills and qualifications, but, rather, about the suitable mentalities that should be developed and be adapted in the working culture.

The librarians need to maintain those skills that gave them respect in the traditional environment and they should, simultaneously, continue being open in new ideas, being interested to approach user needs and develop all those new skills they need, in order to ensure access to information. And we must keep in mind that the state of the evolving librarian is not a new condition, but rather a continuation of what librarians have always done.

4

Flattering a Library Manager: Library Skills and Managerial Challenges

Chances are that at some point–while in library school, while working as a paraprofessional, while working as a front-line librarian, or even while utilizing your favourite library–you had visions of how you could arrange things better if you "ran the zoo". Chances are that at some point after becoming a library manager, you realised that now that you *do* run the zoo–or at least the monkey house—it can be harder than you envisioned to implement those changes you have always wanted to make.

Merely sitting in the zookeeper's seat, further, may transform both your perspective and your priorities. Many of us are accidental managers; that is a given. What is not a given is the way you approach and grow into your management position. Parenting expert Dr. Spock once reassured parents everywhere with the classic line: "Trust yourself, you know more than you think you do."

The same can be said for most accidental library managers. Everything you have learned–as a library worker, from previous supervisors, on the job, from mentors, from volunteer work, from committee involvement, in nonlibrary managerial positions, from classes, from workshops, from the professional literature, as a parent, or from coworkers–will be useful as you settle in. Start from the assumption that you know more than you think you do and that you can trust in your own common sense.

You know how to treat people the way you would yourself like to be treated. You know how you would like the library, or your own small part of it, to work. You know how you respond to stress, to challenges, and to other people. Now, move forward from here. Library management comprises more than just making the changes you have always wanted. You must make those changes in the optimal fashion for your institution, in the context of its larger goals, other departments' activities, and your patrons' needs. You must learn to prioritize your own and your staff's tasks and goals, and to carry out these tasks in a logical order that allows each of your moves to build on your previous actions.

Your interactions with and management of the various members of your staff always need to work towards allowing the institution to carry out its mission and to serve its customers. Management as a whole involves achieving institutional goals through the people and resources available to you. Adult Services, Mount Prospect Public Library, Illinois, explains: "My biggest challenge was learning what it means to be a manager. It's not just writing reports and keeping an eye on the budget, but it's also a lot of interaction with others".

LIBRARY SKILLS AND MANAGERIAL CHALLENGES

Our skills and background as librarians can both help and hinder our managerial exfforts. If we think consciously about these linkages, we can learn to become more effective in any managerial position.

Positive connections include:

- *The ability to collect and analyse information:* Throughout your managerial career, you will need to utilize these skills in activities ranging from creating a budget, to strategic planning, to writing a marketing plan.
- *The urge to share information:* Any organization benefits from the free flow of information; close-mouthed managers foster inefficiency, rumors, and resentment.
- *The ability to organize knowledge:* Again, this will be useful in activities as large as strategic planning and as seemingly small as keeping updated and organized personnel files.
- *The tendency to build networks:* No manager can "go it alone," and librarians' propensity to share information, stories, experiences, and acquired knowledge with one another will stand you in good stead here.
- *The belief in the principle of equity of access and treatment:* As useful when it comes to staff as when dealing with library customers.

On the other hand, tendencies you need to be careful of as a library manager include:

- *The notion that "the patron is always right:"* When you extend your wish to make life comfortable for your patrons to bending over backward to make life easy for your staff, you run the risk of not pushing your people to their fullest.
- *The wish to avoid conflict:* Studies and personality tests consistently show that librarians tend to tip the introverted and conflict-avoiding side of the scale. This is a generalisation, but watch for these tendencies in yourself and be willing and able to step in to manage conflicts among your employees and with your patrons.
- *Emphasis of the philosophical over the practical:* Library school tends to foster a black-and-white worldview of philosophical idealism; managers eventually need to learn to compromise.

Additional linkages will be emphasized in the appropriate chapters, but always be open to understanding the ways in which your background as a librarian affects your work as a manager. Make a conscious effort to manage as a librarian. Overall, remember that you are a *library* manager, and that the ways in which you manage your people and institution need to be true to the principles and practices of librarianship. Ultimately, working effectively as a library manager demands developing a new way of thinking and behaving, while remembering your roots as a librarian or building a background in librarianship.

MAKING THAT TRANSITION

As you adjust to your management role, the first transition from managed to manager can be the hardest. As a nonmanagement employee, you may have been provided with an orientation, directions, and fairly explicit instructions on your day-to-day duties when settling into a new position. As a manager, you may be thrown into a new job with little direction or instruction on how to proceed; management positions are often largely what you make of them. Although you will have a broad outline of your administrator's, board's, or institution's expectations, part of your job will actually be to define your own specific responsibilities and role within your department, library, or section.

Even after the first transition or two gives you an idea of what to expect, the transition into any managerial position can be tricky throughout your career. Transitional periods are inevitably stressful for both you and your new staff, as everyone involved is dealing with a fairly major change and needs to renegotiate relationships and work patterns. But while your staff members' daily work will most likely remain relatively constant, providing them with an underlying stability to draw upon while weathering the changes your arrival brings, you will face the additional task of redefining yourself as a supervisor, a department head, or an administrator. The first few months in a managerial position can be critical in establishing your credibility, settling comfortably into your new role, and setting out your management style and strategies.

This transitional period, while difficult, also presents the opportunity to begin as you mean to continue, to build relationships and alliances with your staff, supervisors, and colleagues, and to lay out your vision for your department, section, or organization. It is always harder to switch gears later than to chart your course from the outset.

Take time, however, to get to know your staff, their personalities, their strengths, and their weaknesses before launching into a major change initiative. In some ways it can be especially difficult to take over a position from a previous manager who seems to have run the zoo in a less than optimal manner. Library staff will have developed an understandable mistrust of those in a management role. Much of your time at the outset may be spent undoing the damage your predecessor left behind, rather than in moving forward with your own initiatives and ideas. As one manager survey respondent notes: "Be aware that your staff may not trust you or your motives at first." This can be frustrating, so work on maintaining your own energy and enthusiasm. New library managers often come in brimming with ideas, but need to have the willingness first to learn the library's organizational culture and to lay the groundwork of trust needed for their initiatives' success. Also think about the ways in which succeeding an ineffective manager can actually work in your favour.

Any moves you make may lead to improvements—and there will be a general predisposition towards change. If you were promoted from within, having suffered with the rest, you will also have insight into what not to do when you move into a management role. Another manager survey respondent even explains her theory of management as: "Having seen library management done badly, I try to think: what would my old boss have done–and do the opposite."

One staff survey respondent suggests: "Never forget what it's like to have a bad boss, and don't turn into one yourself." If you have experienced a history of incompetent or ineffective managers, though, it may take you some time to overcome your own distrust of management and realise that you are now one of "them". Librarians who are promoted into a managerial position from within will find that their former coworkers will have particular preconceptions and expectations for their behaviour as a manager, based on past conversations and behaviour as an employee. Your former colleagues may no longer be quite sure how to interact with you. Oregon State University Librarian for Systems Applications says that: "the biggest surprise for me was that people I had worked with for more than five years viewed me as a different person simply because I had become a manager."

They would sometimes agree to concepts that I presented, even though in reality they had very different views on the issue. I found this disconcerting because I wanted and expected them to express their honest opinions. As any manager, your relationships and interactions with nonmanagerial staff members will inevitably change. Katharine Salzmann, Archivist/Curator of Manuscripts, Southern Illinois University at Carbondale, explains:

"I don't know if it was exactly a surprise, but the biggest adjustment I had to make was simply realizing that I was a 'boss.' I wasn't fully prepared for the role and how people's expectations of me would change, or how my working relationships with individuals would change."

This is not to say that you cannot have good, friendly working relationships with your staff members, but your relationships as manager and managed will tend to take on a different flavour than that of your relationships with your professional peers. You need to consider how important it is to you to be liked, as opposed to being respected as a manager. If you have tended to find most of your friends through work, you may need now to extend that circle outside your institution's walls. If, on the other hand, you come from the outside to assume a management position in a given library, your first step before defining any new goals will be to familiarize yourself with the institution's existing mission and organizational culture, as well as with the people who will be working for you. You will need to settle into your new environment and to give people a chance to settle into the inherent change your arrival brings.

You will of course have your own theories, ideas, and priorities–as well as responsibility for those imposed from above and outside. If you appear to be swooping in with a completely new agenda, however, you will undoubtedly meet with fierce resistance from existing staff. People need a compelling reason to move out of their comfortable routines, and need to feel as if they are a part of any change. Make it a point to learn from and work with your staff from the very beginning.

Realise also that the fact that your administration made the decision to hire from the outside rather than promote from within may mean that it is consciously looking for new perspectives and fresh ideas. Capitalize on this desire for change by enlisting administrative, institutional, and/or board support for your initiatives from the outset. Your goals have a greater chance of success if they receive consistent support throughout the management hierarchy of your organization. Successful management is undoubtedly more complicated than just "doing the opposite" of what your previous less-than-competent boss used to do.

A good first step, though, as you begin defining your role as a manager, is to think back to all of your experiences as someone who has been managed, inside or outside of a library environment. Identify both the role models you do, and those you do not, wish to emulate. Debbie Hackleman notes that "in some cases I learned by observing others–both what worked well and what I would choose to do differently. Observing negative examples is often quite useful." Of course, it is always easier to identify negative experiences and to dwell on what not to do. This is a useful beginning, and you should always keep your previous managers'–and your own– missteps firmly in mind. Dwelling on the negative, however, fails to provide us with a solid foundation for deciding what *to* do, for making the decisions that help propel both our careers and institutions forward, and for establishing our own management style. The next task, therefore, involves deciding where to go and how to begin. Before implementing any changes, you will need to identify the goals for your institution, section, or department, within the larger goals of the organization, larger institution, or system.

You need to provide yourself and your staff with a larger context for your work, in order to successfully define both what you do and why you do it. Lastly, realise that, in any management situation, you will also be compared to your predecessors. Whether comments tend to run along the lines of: "That's not how Ms. X used to do it," or: "We're so glad not to have to waste our time pleasing Mr. Y anymore," it will take staff some time to settle in and become accustomed to your way of managing things. Remember, you are not the first person to ever face this transition— and, if you should ever leave your position, your staff will be equally as glad to explain to your successor just what she is doing differently. Do not get hung up on people's tendencies to bring up the past; libraries are long-lived institutions, and each library's history includes a long line of managers and management styles. Focus on carving out your own place and creating your own part of your institution's history.

WHAT A LIBRARY MANAGER DOES

The ways in which library managers spend their time of course vary among institutions and different levels of management—and in a sense, this is what this entire book is about! But there are some similarities among the roles and responsibilities of most managers. The basic job of any manager is to direct her resources and people towards accomplishing the defined goals of the institution. Higher-up managers may be responsible for defining these larger goals; section or department managers may set goals for their part of the whole in terms of the larger mission of the library; and libraries, as service institutions, need overall to define and to prioritize these goals in terms of the needs of their patrons or customers. As a library division manager at the Josephine County Library System, Oregon, explains: "Fight for the patrons, and every decision that is made should be made because it will make it easier for the patron." Any traditional managerial activity fits into this broad definition. You supervise and evaluate library staff in order to ensure that they work effectively to provide the services your patrons need and expect.

You keep the technology and facilities in your institution humming along so that customers have a comfortable, safe, and useful place to work, as well as the tools to meet their informational needs. You help create a culture of customer service, realizing that your approach and that of your employees goes a long way towards creating an atmosphere in which you can effectively serve your community.

The way in which you manage people largely defines their attitudes towards their work, which in turn defines how smoothly the organization runs. You hold the authority to make decisions within your institution, and are responsible for making those decisions in the way that will best accomplish institutional goals. You are responsible for ranking the importance of various activities in terms of these goals, for prioritizing goals themselves, and for allocating resources to best accomplish library goals.

WOMEN IN MANAGEMENT

Although librarianship is still a female-dominated profession, many observers have noted that men hold a disproportionate number of administrative positions, that they tend to receive higher compensation than women in the field, and that subfields of the profession with a higher concentration of male workers tend to be higher-paid. These discrepancies are beginning to change in some subsets of the profession; female *Association of Research Libraries* (ARL) directors, for example, now make slightly more than their male counterparts, although there are fewer of them overall. This change in the salary structure of the top positions at large research institutions, however, fails to extend to other management positions and library environments. Female library managers can network with others to work to conquer these and other challenges. ALA's Library Administration and Management Association, for example, has a women administrator's discussion group.

ALA also has a *Committee on the Status of Women in Librarianship* (COSWL), which has among its goals that of helping women advance into managerial positions, and maintains a Feminist Task Force. Although still under-represented, especially in "top" jobs, relative to their presence in the profession, women make up an ever-increasing proportion of those in library management positions. This in turn results in an ever-increasing number of other female managers with whom you can network. You can also network with female managers in other professions; there are a number of organizations for professional women that will help you. Women are also more likely to face interruption of their careers for family reasons.

The lower pay in librarianship relative to that in many other professions means that female librarians may be more likely to take time for child care, elder care, and other personal responsibilities than will their more highly paid nonlibrary partners. Work to create the same flexibility and opportunity for your staff as you would appreciate from your institution. Be open to job sharing, flexible schedules, and telecommuting options, when the type of position and an individual's personality and work ethic make these ideas a reasonable possibility. A number of library responsibilities can be effectively carried out off-site, including functions such as collection development and Web design.

Libraries that fail to support flexible work options risk losing some of their best employees. Further, be supportive of pay equity efforts; do not dismiss them now that your own salary has increased with the assumption of your managerial duties. Some argue that women have a distinct managerial style, that their ways of interacting with people inevitably differ from the "male" style of management and communi-cation. Depending on who you read, you will find arguments that female styles of management are either a better or a less effective way of managing. Remember that you will need to develop your own style—as appropriate to your organizational culture, your staff, your own personality, and your library's goals.

NON–LIBRARIANS AS LIBRARY MANAGERS

Non-MLS holders face particular challenges as library managers. Those new to the library environment may find that, although their existing managerial skills are transferable, it still takes time to understand and fit into the library world. Paraprofessional mid-level managers may encounter a prejudice for the MLS among degreed administrators and other department heads. Non-MLS library managers must develop a deep understanding of the functions of their institution, especially of the particular section or project for which they are responsible.

As one manager survey respondent stresses:

"I think it is essential for a library manager to know the basics of the functions he or she is managing. For example, I wasn't familiar with the specific tool my cataloger used at my last job, but at least I knew cataloging, so I could help her when needed and know when she was or wasn't doing her job."

You need to understand the work your staff is doing in order to properly evaluate whether they are doing this work well and efficiently. The process of developing this insight may be as simple as taking the time to observe and ask questions, or it may take some reading or coursework, depending on your situation and background. While MLS librarians value the degree, they also generally value experience and expertise. The best way to impart that value and to elicit their respect is by example.

PARAPROFESSIONAL MANAGERS

Paraprofessional managers occupy a unique place in a library's hierarchy. Although you may fill a managerial position that appears in an equivalent level on an organization chart as your MLS peers, you may have a more difficult time promoting your ideas to those administrators that have an unconscious preference for the degree—and you may receive a lower salary. This observation is not intended to rekindle the ongoing debate over the value of the MLS, but rather to make you aware of some of the issues you might face as a paraprofessional manager in many library environments.

If your organization will help cover the costs of a degree and you can see a clear career path for yourself, you can consider going back to school and earning your MLS. The fantastic combination of a library degree and your previous library and management experience should equate to higher salaries and more options in your future, if you intend to stay in the library field. Many librarian managers got their start in paraprofessional positions and then earned the degree after working in the field for a number of years, enabling them to move up and to advance their careers in library management.

In any case, realise that library school, while it may prepare people to be librarians, rarely prepares them for a career in management. Your MLS counterparts have no particular advantage *as managers.* The library skills and outlook that help create a good library manager, further, are by no means unique to degree holders.

VOLUNTEER MANAGERS

You may be entering a library management position in a small and/or remote library as a volunteer manager, on a full- or parttime basis, without specific library experience—and without compensation! Much of the information in this book will also be applicable in a volunteer situation, but you will need to adapt any advice, as appropriate, to smaller libraries and to your unique circumstances. As a volunteer manager, you also may be responsible for all library activities, from organizing a collection, to checking out materials, to managing others.

Non-MLS library managers thrown into or assuming one of these library management positions should investigate Dave Sutton's *So You're Going to Run a Library: A Library Management Primer*, which is a useful guide for any manager new to libraries, especially in small institutions. If you are a volunteer manager, congratulations on feeling so strongly about the value of libraries that you are willing to donate your time and effort to keeping one going in your community or in your institution. One of your first steps should be to try to find a more experienced library manager to serve as your mentor and to help answer your inevitable questions about both librarianship and management. Again, here, a willingness to learn and to grow in your position will serve you well. Part of being a good volunteer manager may also include inspiring others to volunteer, as well as constructively directing and praising their energies.

NON–LIBRARIANS (NEW TO LIBRARIES)

If you enter library management from another profession, you may be taken aback by the amount of controversy the appointment of a nonlibrarian to a library administrative–especially a director–position in a larger institution can cause. This can be especially difficult if you begin calling yourself or are hired as a "librarian." As a non-MLS administrator, realise that you have walked into an ongoing argument about the importance of the MLS degree.

Some of the professionals who have spent the time, money, and effort to earn a master's in library and information science feel strongly about the value of the degree, pointing out that non-M.D.s who work in doctor's offices are never called doctors; public school employees without degrees and certification are not considered qualified to work as teachers. Institutions that call nondegree holders "librarians" and award them with administrative posts, in this view, merely contribute to an erosion of the value of the MLS degree.

This feeling is exacerbated by a general public perception that all library workers are "librarians" and questions such as: "You have to have a master's degree for this?!" as well as an ongoing internecine argument about the value of the degree and about the quality and rigor of some graduate programmes. Your assumption of an administrative position can stir up all of these feelings and arguments, but realizing that the tension stems from a number of factors can help you take criticism less personally and prepare yourself to field people's concerns. If there seems to be an argument or an undercurrent of feeling among staff that you are less entitled to your position due to your lack of an MLS, you may begin to feel defensive about your ability to do the job.

This is a situation in which you will do best by expressing your willingness to learn from your staff. As Mary Pergander, Head Librarian, Lake Bluff Public Library, Illinois, notes of her pre-MLS management experiences: "I did not know as much about libraries as my staff did. I trusted them to teach me, they trusted me to lead them. It worked out fine." Although you may understand the basic similarities among the duties involved in administrative positions in different environments, only time will demonstrate your ability to serve effectively as a *library* administrator. Acknowledging the strengths and knowledge base of your employees, while also demonstrating the unique perspective and skills you bring to your position, is the best combination to begin winning over your staff.

Any good manager learns from her staff in any environment; you will need to do so more overtly, and will need to rely on your professional staff in areas where your knowledge is lacking. Make a point of learning about the issues that affect today's libraries. Keep up to date, for example, by reading Weblogs and library news sites each morning. Start with major resources such as *American Libraries* and *Library Journal*, each of which posts breaking library-related news stories online.

Then, branch out further to include a couple of resources in your library's area of specialty. Librarians value information and the informed. Your interest in issues important to the field will help you assimilate into the library culture. As one respondent to the staff survey states: "My current manager does not have an MLS, nor does he have much knowledge of libraries. While I do appreciate his dedication to his work and his willingness to take action, I wish he would take more opportunities to understand and observe our work." Also be sure to join relevant local and national associations and to network with other managers, library workers, and librarians.

MANAGING YOURSELF

Beyond this commitment to learning, there are also a number of personal qualities that will help you become a better manager—as well as those you should try to curb.

Habits and patterns to overcome include:

- Procrastination. Many libraries are able to hum along for quite a while even when some managerial tasks are put off, masking the fact that their internal foundations are crumbling. Do not let a façade of well being allow you to put off potentially unpleasant tasks such as managing conflicts or making needed budget cuts.

- Impatience. Although in certain situations impatience can be quite useful in getting tasks done on a timely fashion, it has little value when dealing with library staff. As Amanda E. Standerfer, Library Director, Helen Matthes Library, Effingham, Illinois, suggests: "I would tell a new library manager to be patient. Not everything is going to work out in the first few months or years. I wanted to fix everything right away, and it just wasn't possible."
- Defensiveness. New managers sometimes develop an unfortunate tendency to take comments personally, or to jump to lay blame on others. While defensi-veness may grow out of uneasiness in your new position, your staff will be more concerned about your behaviour than the reasons behind your actions. Accept that you will make mistakes; be willing to take blame as well as credit and to learn from your errors.
- Miscommunication. Effective communication goes beyond communicating clearly and providing staff with pertinent information, and includes watching your own behaviour and communication style. There is no room for sarcasm towards your staff, for example.

Habits to cultivate include:

- *Listening*. You need to pay attention to, and learn from, your staff, peers, customers, and administration. As Kari Baumann, Branch Manager, Centennial Park Branch Library, Greeley, Colorado, says: "I think the most important thing any new manager can do is to listen—to her staff, and to library staff that she doesn't supervise—to understand the organization as a whole."
- *Assertiveness and self-confidence*. Many new library managers have difficulty transitioning, not only into dealing with staff as a manager rather than as a peer, but into dealing with their own bosses and colleagues in a self-confident and effective manner. Take charge from the beginning. Start out as you mean to continue. Understand the power that you have in the organization, and do not be reluctant to use it to influence people and influence change in your library. Librarians with a tendency to be less extroverted can find this more difficult, but a certain level of assertiveness is necessary in order to maintain your influence in the organization.
- *A willingness to be proactive*. Why wait for problems to pile up or for complaints to find you? Look for ways to improve library service, working conditions for staff, workflow, or funding, and then act on achieving your goals in these areas.

- *Communication.* The importance of maintaining open and frequent communication with anyone you supervise—or report to.
- *Lifelong learning.* Library manager can afford to stagnate in her position.

People skills are essential to any effective manager—especially in libraries!—and much of the discussion here and throughout the book reflects that fact. Of course people skills are also important in most subfields of librarianship, but they are especially necessary for managers in any library setting, type, or department.

CHARTING A MANAGEMENT PATH

The earlier you start consciously charting your career path as a library manager, the more successful you will be in your career as a whole. Some schools are proactively meeting the concerns of students seeking additional education in the management aspects of library science.

If you are just joining the profession and you have a clear vision of a library career path that includes management, you can investigate graduate library and information science programmes that offer a heavier emphasis on the administrative side of the field. Several schools now have joint programmes that offer a heavier exposure to the management aspects of librarianship; Kent State and UCLA, for example, each offer a joint MLIS/MBA degree programme, which can be especially useful to those whose career goals include management of a very large institution.

Mentors and Role Models

Earlier, the discussion focused on deciding whom *not* to emulate during your career as a library manager. Equally, if not more important, are the qualities of those you do choose to emulate. If you have lacked good managerial role models in your career so far, you can consider enrolling in a formal mentoring programme–either within your own institution, or one sponsored by a library-related or other organization. Alternatively, seek out more informal mentors – online, through networking at local events, through contacting people writing on issues that interest you.

Seek out expertise wherever it lies, and be willing to ask your mentors for their support and help. Realise also that it can be useful to find multiple mentors to help you with the various facets of and different decisions involved in your position.

Everyone has his or her own area of expertise, and a mentor can be anyone with experience or knowledge that you lack. Author and Webmaster Priscilla Shontz advises: "Find yourself some good mentors, either at your organization or elsewhere. This is important in any position, but in a management position you can sometimes feel very alone–especially if you manage a small library where you are the only manager. It can be incredibly helpful to have friends, mentors, and colleagues to whom you can turn when you have a question or when you just need to vent! For example, if you manage a branch library, you may want to develop relationships with other branch managers, so you can ask for advice when facing a decision or problem. Library activist suggests that new managers "find a mentor to help show you the ropes in your organization and give you pointers on management skills."

A one- or two-year graduate programme, of course, can be hard pressed to fit in all the coursework needed to prepare someone to become a librarian, let alone to teach management skills as well. However, the lack of practical information presented in even the most basic library management courses was overwhelmingly cited as a problem by manager survey respondents—and, given the predicted upcoming wave of library retirements, this should be a concern for schools charged with preparing future library managers to fill these anticipated upper-level vacancies.

Many respondents to the manager survey suggested that more hands-on courses would have been useful, especially those incorporating role-playing, jobshadowing, and/or presentations and advice from actual working managers in different library settings. Others suggested internships or other real-world activities. A number of library managers do take advantage of continuing education opportunities to fill in the gaps left by their alma maters, or to build up their skills in specific areas. As a manager, you will likely need to take responsibility for your own ongoing learning and professional development. There may be no one above you that will suggest you take a class, attend a conference, or otherwise push yourself professionally, whereas as a nonmanagement librarian you may have been used to your supervisor suggesting that you engage in these activities.

Never fall into the trap of assuming that, because you have progressed to a certain point in your career, you need no further professional development. Realise also that more official professional development activities such as workshops and meetings serve as excellent networking as well as professional development opportunities, and can keep you energized and focused on your career and your profession. Cessa Vichi, a library division manager at the Josephine County Library System, says: Attending any training is always beneficial for ideas, new ways of looking at old problems, inspiration and growth as a leader.

As a leader, the responsibility for organizational/division growth falls on you. New ideas, fresh input, and different approaches are vital to learning and growing as a leader." You can locate official professional development and management training opportunities in a variety of ways, from reading your local library system's newsletter to attending ALA conferences. Also, be open to learning through your professional reading. Professional development includes all of your lifelong learning, from reading to on-the-job experience. Lifelong learning means precisely that: learning through all of your experiences, whether planned or not. Always try to think beyond your current job, and about how you can learn, grow, and move forward in your library career.

Take advantage of professional development and networking opportunities. Look at these not as an imposition on your time, but as an opportunity to reenergize, learn, and open to new possibilities. Libraries, especially today, do not remain stagnant–you need to stretch yourself to keep up! Warren Bennis and Robert Thomas note: "The ability to learn is a defining characteristic of being human; the ability to continue learning is an essential skill of leadership.

When leaders lose that ability, they inevitably falter. When any of us lose that ability, we no longer grow."2 As a librarian, you possess an inherent advantage over managers in other types of organizations. A major task of any manager is to identify and assimilate the information that will help her do her job. Who better to take on that task than information professionals? The only difference here is that, instead of compiling this information on behalf of your patrons, you are doing so for yourself and as is relevant in your own context. Most managers are made, not born, and you can use your library skills to help make your own way.

5

Identifying the Key Positions of Librarians

There are a variety of ways to identify key positions, and they differ from library to library. Generally, a key position exerts critical influence on library-wide activities operationally, strategically, or both. Traditionally key positions were limited to those at the top of the library's hierarchy, since, that is where most important problem solving and decision making took place. That is no longer the case. Problem solving and decision making have become diffused throughout libraries; they may reside at many points on the organisational chart, where, as often as not, employees are leading from all positions.

Criteria to be considered to assist in the identification of key positions include the following:

- *Critical task:* Do you have any positions that would stop a critical task from occurring if the incumbent were to leave, such that the library would suffer in the absence of this function?
- *Leadership positions*: Depending on the size of the library, consider taking the analysis of leadership positions further. For each leadership/management position, ask what function it uniquely contributes to the library's current mission and to the accomplishment of the strategic plan. If the position were vacant, would the function still operate effectively and efficiently? If the answer is no, then you are looking at a key position.
- *Future projects:* These positions are based on where your library is heading in the future from a strategic stand-point. They may include a director of outreach where one does not exist or a coordinator of innovation or strategic initiatives when such a focus is desired.
- *Consequences of a vacancy:* Are there any other positions which, if vacated, would raise an uproar and bring severe consequences (decisions not made, customer complaints not satisfied, branches not open, computers not started, materials not ordered)?
- *Other:* What other mission-critical positions exist in your library? One could be the archivist, especially if, as in Yolo County Library, there is only one and she serves as both county archivist and records manager for the county. Who oversees government documents,

between services, or your state historical room? Who runs your branch that provides services to the blind and physically handicapped? to Russian immigrants? How difficult would it be to fill these positions? These are possible key positions.

Libraries should follow a consistent format in tracking key positions by answering the following questions for each position:

- What are the requirements (knowledge, skills, abilities, competencies) for this position?
- Who holds this position now?
- Is anyone ready to replace the incumbent if needed? Are there specific positions that could provide needed developmental experience for these key positions?
- What are the career or retirement plans of the incumbent(s)?
- Is this work critical?
- Can the work be split up and accomplished by one or more others? Can it be outsourced? Redistributed?

Sno-Isle (Wash.) Libraries did an excellent job conducting such a review. Pat Olafson, the libraries' HR director, clearly depicted many of these steps in an easy-to-capture spreadsheet.

Other Ways of Replacing Key Positions

Before a vacancy occurs and certainly before filling a position or planning for successors, a library should consider other options to filling the position, including not filling it at all. Look at the work to see if the position and its responsibilities still add value to the library. Does it still fit into the overall strategy and goals of the library? If not, do not fill the job. If it does fit in, ask if the work can be done differently and more effectively through process improvement or other methods. Assess whether the work is the right work.

For example, does the public library need two MLS catalogers? Is ongoing authority work critical to your mission and strategy, or can you let that go? Moving to other options, assess whether the work can be reallocated to others. Without overloading the others, can another department handle it, or can two departments merge and take over the work?

Can the work be contracted out at less cost or completed by a temporary employee, part-time employee, or substitute? Being even more creative, how about accomplishing the work via job rotation (developmental assignment) or library school interns? What about reengineering the work or calling in retirees? For example, Queens Borough Public Library offers incentives to retirees who want to stay on in some capacity and assist with the transfer of their knowledge and experience.

There are many possibilities for filling a position when a vacancy occurs. Keeping open about what needs to be done, what the right work is at this point in the library's history, and who needs to do it leads to a more effective workforce with resources assigned where they best meet the needs of your community. After you identify key positions, it is important to keep job descriptions up to date. Job descriptions and competencies are the source documents for work requirements needed to prepare possible replacements for key positions. The job description should lay out the essential functions of the job along with its duties and responsibilities.

Most libraries require job descriptions. Typically a job description describes the nature of the work to be done as well as its level of complexity, the supervision received or provided, the education and experience required, and the physical requirements of the job. People who work with job descriptions call these requirements "KSAs," short for knowledge, skills, and abilities.

A *competency* is "a cluster of related knowledge, skills and attitudes that affects a major part of one's job that correlates with performance on the job, that can be measured against well-accepted standards, and that can be improved via training and development." In other words, they are the skills, knowledge, and personal attributes that contribute to an individual's success in a particular position.

Two examples are "Uses teamwork and project management skills to benefit the library and its users" and "Models self management." Competencies and KSAs are related, but competencies go beyond the KSAs required for any individual job. They add, sometimes implicitly, the attitudes and values that are the foundation for behaviour and performance. Whether or not it is intentional, many job descriptions contain a mix of KSAs and competencies.

Consider these brief examples of statements related to intellectual freedom:

- *Competency:* Models the library's approach to intellectual freedom to ensure the community benefits.
- *Knowledge:* Knows the principles of intellectual freedom as set forth by ALA position papers and library board policy.
- *Skill:* Develops clear and timely written responses to complaints from customers about the library's collection. Consistently applies library board policy in making collection development decisions. Trains staff to respond appropriately and effectively to customer complaints.
- *Ability:* Ability to communicate effectively with a broad range of customers and staff about controversial issues.

Your strategic plan spells out what services the library wants to provide during the next several years. These services were defined by assessing the needs of your community—be it a city, county, or district, your students, the hospital staff, or the corporation you serve. The library's challenge is to respond to these needs with the staff it has now, can develop, or can acquire.

COMPETENCIES: JUST A BUZZWORD, OR IS

Competencies describe specifically what kinds of skills, behaviours, and personal characteristics all employees are expected to demonstrate. The goal in selecting and defining competencies is to ensure that they are consistent throughout the library regardless of job, level, department, or location. Once you have competencies in place, the job of selecting high-level performers as part of your succession planning and leadership development process becomes more concrete and less subjective. By engaging in this exercise, you reap huge rewards. Indeed, you will have outlined the criteria that define individual as well as organisational success in your library. We show you how to take a customised, culture-specific approach as well as some shortcuts to developing competencies.

The beneficial effects of competencies on the library can be seen in many ways:

- Competencies are tied to the values of your library and therefore serve to foster these values.
- Competencies provide clear and specific definitions that support the purpose of the library.
- Competencies provide clear guidelines as to what it takes for your library to be successful.
- Competencies provide practical tools and guidelines for performance management.
- Competencies target training needs required for the development of staff. This process results in the development of a library that has a continuous and dynamic learning environment— a necessity for survival in the twenty-first century.

As Josephine Bryant and Kay Poustie write in the Bertelsmann Foundation's 2001 report Competencies Needed by Public Library Staff:

- The [competency] system is behaviourally anchored so that both managers and employees can see what is expected of them. The system can also be used to integrate several human resources functions:
  - The model can be used as the basis for executive development, recruitment, selection, compensation, performance appraisal, career development, job design, and organisation design. In its crudest form, it is a yardstick for measuring how someone is performing, comparing current performance to an ideal, and suggesting actions that can be taken to improve that performance. What makes the competency model concept work is its simplicity, the prevailing conditions in the company that provide a fertile bed in which it can grow, managers believing in it, and employees accepting it.5

The outcome of the work of developing competencies is that you will have a list and description of what your library values and needs to achieve success at the organisational level and what employees and teams need to achieve success. This model does more than support succession planning and development; competencies can be at the center of many of your human resource policies and programmes as they specify performance management criteria, help plan careers, and highlight training and development needs, to name a few. A common approach to developing competencies is to focus on the people doing the job, that is, the knowledge, skills, and attitudes required to do their job successfully rather than the work itself. This means that cognitive (knowing), behavioural, and affective (feeling) factors are all at work in a competency.

Thus a competency includes:

- *Knowledge,* that is, what is known and understood about a subject in order to ensure successful performance on the job. An example might be knowledge and understanding of the social and intellectual needs of a library's customer group such as seniors or preschool children.
- *Skills* necessary to process this knowledge. An example might be effective communication skills.
- Appropriate *attitudes* and *values,* which are exhibited in behavioural characteristics that impact the way knowledge and skills are brought to bear on the job. These are usually internal evaluations of what might be considered good or important, such as the insistence on giving the best service possible at all times.

If you are a supervisor, you know that attitudes and values are important, but they are not the same as behaviours. We evaluate performance on the basis of observable behaviours, not on attitudes and values, which are often the invisible building blocks of behaviour. We know when someone values customer service in the same way we do, because we observe her using negotiation and listening skills to make appropriate exceptions to the rules for customers. But we coach and evaluate on observable behaviours—not on the competencies that build the foundation. Competencies define what success looks like within the context of a job such as manager, librarian, or supervisor.

Each competency developed by a library should consist of:

- A *definition* that contains all the critical elements of the competency, and
- *Levels* of proficiency, which are described as scales for assessment purposes.

Again, assessment here does directly translate to performance evaluation. In this context, assessment is most often used to identify and develop needed training across categories of staff. You will probably not find levels of proficiency in published competency sets, since, they are usually added as needed by the users.

You might consider a scale as simple as 1-2-3:

- Does not demonstrate.
- Often demonstrates.
- Consistently demonstrates.

Competencies fall into one of three main categories: core, behavioural, and technical:

1. *Core* (or basic) competencies usually reflect the competencies that are essential to the library's success. These competencies reflect what an organisation does best and are based on the values of the library. They are considered necessary for *all jobs in the library,* and all employees are expected to demonstrate these competencies. An example of such a competency is customer service.

2. *Behavioural* competencies apply to those performance characteristics that influence and drive performance. They are usually relevant to several jobs, job levels, or job families, across the library. Leadership competencies and teamwork could be placed in this category.
3. *Technical* or professional competencies relate to technical knowledge or skills that are critical for a specific job/role to be successful. Competencies in negotiating a reference interview, research skills, or learning new databases are prime examples for librarian positions.

In many ways, technical competencies are the least important set of competencies. Most of our staff members have the technical skills to do their jobs, or they pick them up in day-to-day observation and certainly as their performance is managed. In our work and client issues we see that it is the behavioural and interpersonal competencies, as well as those around problem solving and personal mastery, that really make a difference. As work changes, other key competencies staff members need are comfort with ambiguity and change, flexibility, and creativity.

Table. Building a Competency Model: Four Methods.

Method	Cost	Probability of Accuracy	Probability of Usage
1. Use outside consultant to interview a sample of top performers for each target population group and compare with interview of average performers. Capture what the top performers do more frequently.	High	High	Low
2. Use outside consultants to train insiders to do the tasks in method 1.	Medium	High	Medium
3. Begin with a model from another respected company (with permission); interview a handful of top performers to determine if the borrowed model accurately describes what the top performers do.	Low	High	Low
4. Assemble a group of managers and, using a facilitator, brainstorm about the attributes of top performers today and in the future.	Low	Medium	High

There are a variety of ways to build a competency model. Bryant and Poustie examine four methods in terms of cost, probability of accuracy, and probability of usage. Although you can look at and even adopt some of the competencies of other libraries, they really need to reflect *your* library's culture, needs, and values. An excellent place to start is the Competency Index for the

Library Field published online in 2009 by WebJunction. WebJunction has also linked to competencies published by library organisations around the country to make your research even easier. Competencies should hold true for several years to ensure stability and that development of staff can be focused, and yet they need to be fluid as they are affected by the changing work environment.

DEVELOPING A COMPETENCY MODEL THROUGH FOCUS GROUPS

To increase the probability of usage, ownership, and success, we have seen Bryant and Poustie's third model used successfully with some variation. The variation consists of two additional steps. The first step is to work with a committee that includes a cross section (diagonal slice) of library staff and management to select and validate the model or competencies selected. The second step is to hold focus groups to test the competencies and levels of proficiency. The cost and time factors increase slightly, but the probability of usage increases from low to high.

For good results, follow these ten tips as you use focus groups:

- Aim for a group of six to eight people.
- Invite staff to get the representation you need, whether that be geographic representation, different levels and kinds of jobs represented, length of service, or something else. Make sure you invite people who will speak up.
- Depending on how many questions you have, allow one to two hours for the session. It often takes a little more time than you expect, and it is better to dismiss people early than to shut down a conversation too soon.
- Establish a few ground rules at the beginning of the session, such as
  - Everyone is expected to contribute to the discussion.
  - Responses will be aggregated before they are reported, not attributed to specific individuals. (This is standard practice, even if you do not expect to discuss anything sensitive. It does affect people's willingness to be frank.)
- Determine whether you will take notes directly on a laptop or use chart paper and transcribe the notes later. In either case, consider inviting someone to help you take notes. Be sure to introduce the person (and her role) to the group.
- Use open-ended questions: What do you like about these competencies? What's missing? What would you change? How would you go about helping someone to develop these competencies? What else should we think about?
- If no one responds to a question immediately, allow a minute of "soak time" for people to process the question and prepare a response.
- Spend your time recording what people say, not explaining or defending. You are there to ask and listen, not to lecture. Ask clarifying questions if needed to be sure you record their responses accurately.

- Decide in advance whether you are willing and able to send the participants your draft notes and allow them to add comments. This is not a standard procedure, and it adds time to your process—so if you want to do it, allows plenty of extra time.
- Thank people for participating and tell them what your next steps will be.

DEVELOPING A COMPETENCY MODEL BY INTERVIEWING TOP PERFORMERS

An alternative to using focus groups is to identify exemplary performers—individuals who are particularly good at demonstrating a competency. Then interview them.

This process takes more time than conducting focus groups, but it has the advantage of being more flexible to schedule. In addition, it gives top performers a bit more recognition for being exemplary. And by taking some time one-on-one, the conversation may go deeper than that of a focus group. If you can interview only a few individuals and want broader input, you can also choose to compile interview results and ask a focus group or committee to provide their reactions. Record results in a form such as:

Use this interview guide to collect information about how to build competencies in the context of your library's unique culture. Select several exemplary performers who have been identified as especially good at demonstrating a given competency. Indicate that competency next to the label "competency" below. Then spend about 15 minutes to interview each exemplary performer using the questions appearing below. When you are finished, analyze the results by identifying common themes and patterns across all the interview results.

Competency: ____________________
Name: ____________________ **Title:** ____________________
Years of Experience in Job: ____________ **Date:** ____________________
Interviewed by: ____________________

1. Think of a time when you were asked to demonstrate this competency.
   a. What was the situation?
   b. When did this situation occur?
   c. What did you do?
   d. How do you believe the experience helped you demonstrate this competency?
   e. If you had a mentee or trainee, and she participated in an experience like this, would it help to build the competency?
2. Who are some people in this library who are exceptionally good at demonstrating this competency to whom you could refer your mentee or trainee?
3. What are some work experiences in the library that you believe your mentee/trainee should be given to build or demonstrate the competency?
4. How might the pressure to produce by specific deadlines help to build or demonstrate the competency?
5. Where would you send people—to what branch or department—to build and/or demonstrate this competency? (Where are the centers of excellence for this competency in the organization, and why do you think so?)
6. List special and specific work assignments that would be particularly useful in building or demonstrating this competency.
7. If someone asked you for advice on how to build this competency in this library, what advice would you give them?
8. Could you think of some upcoming or pending library projects that might be especially useful to build this competency? What are they, and why do you think they could help to build the competency?

The next step in identifying the competencies is to feed back the results to the exemplary performers to make sure that you heard what was said, to achieve consensus, and to verify that the assignments recommended would actually build the competencies. The competencies could then be linked to training and development needs as well as informing the succession planning and development process.

Fig. Interview Guide to Collect Competency Development Strategies.

CASE STUDY, PUBLIC LIBRARY: CITY OF TORONTO CORE COMPETENCIES

These core competencies for the City of Toronto were developed on the basis of the kind of organisation and culture desired and the city's values and aspirations. They apply to all municipal employees, including those at the Toronto Public Library.

The behavioural characteristics of the core competencies are as follows:

- Customer service orientation:
  - Clarifies expectations
  - Takes personal responsibility
  - Takes action for the customer
  - Addresses underlying customer needs
  - Uses a long-term approach
- Fiscal responsibility:
  - Understands key resource issues affecting one's responsibilities and business priorities using resources to increase customer value
  - Demonstrates fiscal prudence
  - Models effective utilisation
  - Advocates benefits for the organisation
- Innovation:
  - Seeks new solutions
  - Takes action new to the job or function
  - Introduces new ideas to the organisation
  - Introduces new ideas to the public sector
  - Encourages innovation in others
- Results orientation:
  - Wants to do job well
  - Works to achieve goals
  - Sets own standards to improve performance
  - Sets and strives to meet higher standards of performance
  - Conducts cost-benefit analyses
  - Takes calculated entrepreneurial risks
- Teamwork:
  - Cooperates and contributes
  - Promotes team cooperation
  - Builds a high-performing team

CASE STUDY, ACADEMIC LIBRARY: QUEENSLAND UNIVERSITY OF TECHNOLOGY

The competencies selected by the Queensland (Australia) University of Technology (QUT) were borrowed from the British Chartered Institute of Library and Information Professionals' research for the summary shown in table of the professional and information and generic skills library professionals need for the twenty-first century in order to best align library services with the university's strategic plan.

Table. Summary of Library Skills (Academic) for the Twenty-first Century.

Professional Information Skills	Generic Skills
Knowledge Management architecture Information and communication Technology skills Technical (traditional) professional skills	Project Management Information Planning and evaluation People management Research skills Bids and proposals
Subject Expertise	**Critical Skills**
Collection management Collection description Technical (traditional) professional skills	Thinking Planning and evaluation Analysis Problem solving Research
Information Technology	**Leadership**
Design Application User support (problem solving)	General management Communication skills Systems Strategic management People skills Financial skills
Service Development	**Promotion and market**
User information Surveys Service impact analysis appreciation Promotion and Marketing	Design appreciation Presentation skills Multiprofessional Planning and evaluation

They were adopted to align with the university's change in approach to learning and teaching, particularly with respect to providing students with more flexible learning. In addition, the university's strategic plan announced its intention to double the number of higher-degree research students and expand significantly its overall research capacity and performance.

The implication for the library in providing the range and level of services to support this growth was significant and indicated a changing role for the academic library as well as the need for librarians to work collaboratively with academics, researchers, learning designers, and IT professionals. QUT, along with its cohort the Librarians of the Australian Technology Network (LATN), commissioned a consultant to "identify overall issues and concerns related to succession and workforce planning among the libraries and their universities and to make recommendations for the LATN group as a whole and its individual members to address these issues."

The recommendations for the QUT library included the following: development of a workforce and succession plan; conduct of an inventory of skills and attitudes needed by the library for both the short and long term; revision of selection criteria (for positions) to focus on learning agility, personal attributes, and leadership qualities; consideration of all vacancies to see if requirements have changed or new priorities need to be addressed; encouragement of staff to take a proactive stance in their own career development; and identification of staff with leadership and management potential and allow them to take on greater challenges. As an outcome of these recommendations, their first task was to investigate the role of the faculty/ liaison librarian, which is the position at the development and delivery end of many of the new trends and services, especially in learning and teaching support and the identification and management of access to electronic information sources.

Through focused development of key competencies, not only will employees be better prepared to compete for vacancies, they will also be exhibiting the key attributes needed to drive the library's strategic plan.

Leadership development has been the focus of a great deal of study and work. It is of particular interest to us as we look to grow the next generation of library leaders. Building the leadership capacity of staff at all levels suggests that developing leadership competencies deserves focused attention. Libraries, of course, are not the only organisations interested in developing leaders. In fact, we can learn a great deal from the work of other organisations—particularly those in the public sector. This group of organisations has a lot in common with both public and academic libraries. Libraries are often publicly funded (in whole or in part), making them a part of the public sector. More than that, they are usually part of a local, state, or national political environment and must function well in this milieu in order to survive.

PUBLIC SECTOR LEADER COMPETENCIES

In her research of public sector succession planning practices, Mary Young found several themes related to the competencies that are most important to help leaders acquire.

The three primary development needs are:

1. *Knowledge and understanding outside the employee's own department or functional area:* In many cases, employees' previous career experiences have not exposed them to other areas of government. As a result, they need to understand what other departments or functions do and how that work is connected to their own. Translating to libraries, this would be about helping the employee learn more about what

happens in the branch if they have not worked in one for years, how books get selected and processed, or even how the marketing department's work brings customers of all ages in.

2. *Knowledge and understanding at the enterprise level:* In part, this content area is an aggregation of learning about other departments and functions; it is about how all the pieces fit together. In addition, it is about work at the executive level—the tasks, functions, and challenges that are important at these levels above departments or agencies, including knowledge and understanding of the organisation's relationship to its broader environment. Again in the library world, how does your library determine strategy? Who makes that decision? On what knowledge and with what input
3. *A broad network of relationships:* Knowledge and understanding are important, but they do not assure a leader's effectiveness. The third critical area libraries need to help leaders develop is building a broad network of relationships—across departments and functions, at many levels, and in the library's wider environment. Do employees in your library realise that they are a department in a college or local jurisdiction?

Why are these particular items so important in developing leaders? Not because they are the most critical skills or hardest to develop, but because *these are the competencies that individual employees are least able to develop on their own.* These three competencies are "boundary-spanning: they are about stretching employees' knowledge, understanding, and working relationships and exposing them to people and aspects of the organisation outside their current sphere. These objectives have important implications for how libraries go about developing leaders." Another way of looking at these three development needs is that they help people develop competencies around political awareness and operate effectively in a broader political environment.

We have seen some libraries identify these competencies as critical and begin to help staff develop them. For example, the California Library Association's Competencies for California Librarians in the 21st Century includes political awareness as a core competency for librarians. California libraries such as those in Fresno and Santa Clara counties encourage involvement in local business and community organisations and with local government and non-profit agencies to help staff identify and enlist the help of strategic partners. Structuring learning opportunities for staff around internal (library) and external (government and community) decision making, as the libraries in Fresno and Santa Clara counties have done, is a way of helping them grasp the bigger picture. As can be seen with recent budget cuts and changes to the political climate, acquiring these skills, and being comfortable using them, might be one of the competencies that separates senior leaders from others.

In addition to these three competencies, Young found the following specific skills that managers and leaders typically need to develop:

- Getting things done in this government or in this organisation/ jurisdiction.
- Managing change.
- Managing conflict.
- Managing the public.
- Managing the media.

To a more limited extent, some respondents reported several more basic supervisory skills that even experienced managers need to develop:

1. Managing employees, including influencing, motivating, developing, and retaining
2. Dealing with civil service and personnel policies
3. Professional skills such as making presentations, managing projects, facilitating meetings, evaluating performance, and leading teams

Sad to say, we have seen that too many managers in library systems are underdeveloped in these areas. The solution is not to penalise them for not having these competencies but to realise that they were not given (or did not take) earlier opportunities to develop them. Fortunately, we are seeing many libraries begin to address these issues by providing supervisory training opportunities for their managers. Some libraries open this training to staff who may want to move into supervisory positions as a way to help them decide whether that is something they really want to do and, if so, to prepare.

LEADERSHIP COMPETENCIES AND EMOTIONAL INTELLIGENCE

Leadership competencies run through your entire library, regardless of department, function, or position/ classification. Right Management studied emerging leaders, which it defined as those who (usually) manage others, contribute significantly to business results, are perceived as having potential for promotion or additional leadership responsibilities, and would cause pain if they left the organisation.

The highest rated competencies for these leaders were:

- *Focus on results:* Concentrates on the achievement of business results by effectively structuring and carrying out work.
- *Taking initiative:* Takes urgent action to accomplish objectives and achieve business results; is proactive; takes action to achieve goals beyond what is required.
- *Leadership:* Establishes and communicates a vision for the organisation. Inspires and empowers others. Leads by example.
- *Trust/integrity:* Trusted by others. Maintains reputation for truthfulness, credibility, confidentiality, and authenticity.
- *Self-awareness:* Understands personal strengths, limita-tions, needs, and values.

- *Building bonds/collaboration:* Builds positive working relationships with others. Demonstrates the willingness and capacity to collaborate and build partnerships with others.
- *Creativity/managing innovation:* Effectively manages and encourages the creativity of others.
- *Learning/self-development:* Demonstrates commitment to ongoing learning and professional self-improvement. Willing to be coached.
- *Self-management:* Demonstrates self-control. Maintains optimism, energy, and stamina. Manages stress well and models work/life balance.
- *Decision making:* Effectively collects and analyses data/input from others, considers alternatives, makes sound and timely decisions, collaborates in group decisions, and understands the impact of decisions on others.
- *Political savvy:* Accepts and understands the political dimension of organisational life, anticipates political consequences, and maneuvers effectively through complex situations.
- *Delegating:* Effectively transfers responsibility and authority to others and holds them accountable for achieving results

The biggest gaps found in the study came under self-awareness, political savvy, delegating, self management, leadership, and decision making. Our experience affirms these gaps. We are sure they do not surprise you, and you may even find the same in your own library. You may note that some of these competencies relate to the concept of emotional intelligence (EI) as developed by Daniel Goleman. Emotional intelligence "defines how we manage behaviour, navigate social complexities, and make personal decisions that achieve positive results."

Although it is beyond the scope of this book for us to discuss emotional intelligence and its importance in the workforce, we list the EI components of the Bar-On Emotional Intelligence Inventory as examples:

- Intrapersonal scale:
  - Self-regard
  - Emotional self-awareness
  - Assertiveness
  - Independence
  - Self-actualisation
- Interpersonal scale:
  - Empathy
  - Social responsibility
  - Interpersonal relationship
- Adaptability scale:
  - Reality testing
  - Flexibility
  - Problem solving

- Stress management scale:
  - Stress tolerance
  - Impulse control
- General mood scale:
  - Optimism
  - Happiness

We believe emotional intelligence to be critical to the success of leaders in any organisation and at any level. It has been shown that it is the key to 27–46 per cent of workplace success (per Dr. Reuven Bar-On) and that it accounts for 85–95 per cent of the difference between a "good leader" and an "excellent leader" (per Goleman).

It has also been shown that one can use emotional intelligence to boost job performance. It is so critical to success, write Bradberry and Greaves, that it "accounts for 60 per cent of performance in all types of jobs. It's the single biggest predictor of performance in the workplace and the strongest drive of leadership and personal excellence."

Although we mention it in this section on leader competencies, we hope you consider helping employees at all levels in your library to develop and strengthen their emotional intelligence. As we said earlier, these competencies rather than technical competencies are now most likely to be the drivers of potential, performance, or success at any level.

CONNECTION, CONTRIBUTION, AND COLLABORATION

Today's organisation is usually characterised by its networked, flat structure. Change is the expected, not the unusual. Flexibility and adaptability are inherent and required of everyone.

The values in such a library system are relationships; sharing information; localised solutions that fit the culture of the branch, department, and *your* library; and a culture that values openness and effectiveness as opposed to (only) efficiency.

In Winning with Library Leadership, Christi Olson and Paula Singer note that leaders in such complex systems as academic and public libraries find themselves needing to focus around three key competencies: connection, contribution, and collaboration:

- *Connection:* Making the right connections between people and organisations, linking people together for a common goal; uses the approach of power "with" rather than power "over."
- *Contribution:* Making explicit to each employee how her work or job ties to fulfilling the library's strategic goals; team or group members setting, clarifying, and sharing expectations, leading to commitment and ownership.
- *Collaboration:* Creating a shared understanding and interdependency among staff and others who come together to solve a problem; applied in complex, new, unfamiliar, and challenging situations.

TECHNICAL, LEADERSHIP, AND IMPLEMENTATION SKILLS

Another way to view competencies is in terms of three major categories: library and information system– related skills and knowledge, leadership skills, and implementation skills. Leadership competencies are often personal attributes, and implementation competencies are how one gets things done.

Paul Cantor, in "Succession Planning: Often Requested, Rarely Delivered," tells a wonderful and clear story from the Bible that really illustrates the difference:

- In the Bible, Noah demonstrated the differences among these three types of competencies. God told Noah that it was going to rain and that he wanted Noah to build an ark and put all kinds of animals on it. Therefore, Noah knew what the industry risks were (it's going to rain) and what should be done about it (build an ark and put the animals on it). However, *knowledge* of what the risks are, and what should be done about them, doesn't get the job done.
- But Noah, starting with the limited instruction on ark building provided by God, did get the ark built on time—and today we would say on budget—demonstrating that he had the *implementation skills* needed to take action and manage risk.
- Noah's implementation skills can be distinguished from his leadership skills. He demonstrated *leadership skills* by convincing all those animals to board the ark and not eat each other up during the voyage.

To select for future leadership, identify the competencies that best reflect your strategic direction. There are many competency directories that include competency definitions and assessment options. Library leaders can rely on their HR staff or a consultant to facilitate model development or appoint an individual or team to research and develop a model. A generic model is available through the U.S., Department of Labour as part of an initiative to assess future workforce needs. Johnson County (Kans.) Library, for example, used this model to select four competencies it wanted its current and potential leaders to acquire: leads change, influences people, achieves results, and fosters communication.

Johnson County's detailed definitions of these competencies, along with the competencies developed by the City of Toronto, the New Jersey Library Association, and the Ohio Library Council, follow. If the prospect of developing competencies is daunting, remember that you do not need to start from scratch, nor do you need an exhaustive set of competencies that covers everything staff need to demonstrate. Start with a few competencies that are most critical to your success. Remember the Johnson County Library example of looking at other models and picking four competencies to focus on.

Spend your energy on competencies that will bring your library the greatest return. Whether you are creating your own competencies or adapting ones used by others, you must involve staff and managers and get feedback, buy-in, and ownership. These are the competencies that will drive your succession planning and development process forward. You will be recruiting on the basis of these competencies, measuring performance against them, training and developing to them, and selecting high-potential performers who meet and exceed them in your succession planning process.

3NEW JERSEY LIBRARY ASSOCIATION CORE COMPETENCIES FOR LIBRARIANS

Preamble

These competencies pertain to the delivery of services to all ages, to all constituencies, and for all types of libraries. Competencies are the skills, technical knowledge and personal attributes that enable individuals to contribute positively to their organisations and the library profession. These Core Competencies apply to all librarians. Companion documents have been created to focus on the specific skills needed for specialised areas of librarianship. Throughout this document the terms patron, user, and customer are used interchangeably.

This document is intended for several purposes:

- To educate communities, governing bodies and funding agencies about the importance of the knowledge and skills of professional librarians.
- To develop job descriptions and evaluation tools for professional positions.
- To design policies, particularly as these policies relate to the organisation and staffing of libraries.
- To guide students attending graduate library school.
- To apprise library school faculty who are involved in the development of curricula of the continuously changing needs of the profession.
- To assist in planning staff development programmes.
- To motivate professionals to take responsibility for managing the development of one's own career.

Core Competencies

- Demonstrates a strong commitment to excellent customer service.
- Recognises and addresses the diverse nature of the library's patrons and community.
- Understands and supports the culture and context of the library and, if applicable, its parent institution.
- Demonstrates knowledge of the library system and the library profession.
- Understands the social, political, and economic context in which the library exists.

- Demonstrates knowledge of library and information science theory, information creation, organisation, and delivery.
- Adheres to the Code of Ethics of the American Library Association.
- Exhibits leadership skills including critical thinking, risk taking, and creativity, regardless of position within the management structure.
- Demonstrates commitment to working with others to achieve common goals.
- Acts within the organisation to implement the principles of knowledge management.
- Exhibits an understanding of the importance of a multidisciplinary and cross-functional approach to programmes and projects within the organisation.
- Monitors and implements changes in technology and information systems.
- Shares knowledge and expertise with users and colleagues.
- Displays excellent communication skills and is able to promote the library and advocate for its needs.
- Communicates effectively with publishers and other information providers to advance the interests of the library.
- Recognises the value of professional networking and actively participates in professional associations.
- Actively pursues personal and professional growth through continuing education.

JOHNSON COUNTY LIBRARY TIER II LEADERSHIP COMPETENCIES

Leads Change

- Learns Continually.
- Creativity/Innovation.
- External Awareness.
- Flexibility.
- Resilience.
- Service Motivation.
- Thinks Strategically.
- Vision.

Promotes the library's vision, goals, priorities, and values. Balances change and continuity; continually strives to improve customer service and programme performance; creates a work environment that encourages creative thinking; and maintains focus, intensity, and persistence, even under adversity.

Key Characteristics:

- Exercises leadership and motivates team members to incorporate JCL's mission, vision, and values into strategic planning as well as into the full range of the organisation's activities; encourages creative thinking and innovation; influences others towards a spirit of service; designs and implements new or cutting-edge programmes/processes.

- Identifies and integrates key issues affecting the organisation, including political, economic, social, technological, and administrative factors.
- Is open to change and new information; tolerates ambiguity; adapts behaviour and work methods in response to new information, changing conditions, or unexpected obstacles; adjusts rapidly to new situations warranting attention and resolution.
- Displays a high level of initiative, effort, and commitment to public service; proactive and achievement-oriented; self-motivated; pursues self-development; seeks feedback from others and opportunities to master new knowledge.
- Deals effectively with pressure; maintains focus and intensity and remains persistent, even under adversity; recovers quickly with setbacks.

Influences People

- Conflict Management.
- Leverages Diversity.
- Integrity/Honesty.
- Builds Teams.

Designs and implements strategies that maximize employee potential and fosters high ethical standards in meeting the organisation's vision, mission, and goals.

Key Characteristics:

- Provides leadership by inspiring, motivating, and guiding others towards goal accomplishment; empowers people by sharing power and authority.
- Effectively uses of the organisation's performance management system (*e.g.*, accurate performance plans and appraisals, and takes action to reward, counsel, and remove employees, as appropriate).
- Values cultural diversity and other differences; fosters an environment in which people who are culturally diverse can work together cooperatively and effectively in achieving organisational goals.
- Assesses employees' unique developmental needs and provides developmental opportunities that maximize employees' capabilities and contributes to the achievement of organisational goals; develops leadership in others through coaching and mentoring.
- Fosters commitment, team spirit, pride, trust, and group identity.
- Resolves conflicts in a positive and constructive manner.
- Recognises, encourages, and participates in the dynamic nature of leadership and follower-ship.

Achieves Results

- Accountability.
- Customer Service.
- Decisiveness.
- Entrepreneurship.
- Solves Problems.
- Technical Creativity.
- Political Savvy.

Stresses accountability and continuous improvement. Makes timely and effective decisions based on the library's mission, vision, and values. Identifies the internal and external politics that impact the work of the organisation.

Key Characteristics:

- Understands and appropriately applies procedures and policies; keeps current on issues, practices, and procedures.
- Exercises good judgement in structuring and organising work and sets priorities; balances the interests of patrons and readily readjusts priorities to respond to customer demands.
- Anticipates and identifies, diagnoses, and consults on potential or actual problem areas.
- Holds self and others accountable for decisions and work performance.
- Identifies opportunities to develop and/or promote new materials, programmes, and services within or outside of the organisation.
- Maintains appropriate skill level regarding current and new technologies.

Fosters Communication

- Influences/Negotiates.
- Interpersonal Skills.
- Oral Communication.
- Partners.
- Written Communication.

Creates an environment conducive to an open exchange of ideas. Explains, advocates, and expresses facts and ideas about the library when communicating with individuals and groups internally and externally.

Key Characteristics:

- Represents and speaks for the organisation and its work to those within and outside the library; elicits feedback, listens effectively, and clarifies information; facilitates an open exchange of ideas.
- Establishes and maintains working relationships within the library and throughout the community; approaches each problem situation with a clear perception of organisational goals; gets understanding and support from higher-level management.

- Collaborates with others; cooperates with others to obtain information and accomplish goals; facilitates win-win situations.
- Considers and responds appropriately to the needs, feelings, and capabilities of different people in different situations; is tactful and treats others with respect.
- Communicates effectively in written and oral reports, memoranda, and other documents in a clear, organised, and timely manner.

6

Changing Management Techniques as Libraries Automation and Organisational Change

IDENTIFICATION OF THE ISSUE

The example is only one instance of the large-scale changes that affect people's work lives. These types of changes raise many important issues for managers, from the level of director to unit supervisor. Some issues are primarily technological. What equipment will be needed? Is the technological infrastructure in place? Will the system crash when the date changes to January 1, 2000? Other issues are more social. How will the employees react? Will they accept the change or resist it? Can the change process be made easier? Unfortunately, this second group of issues can be easily overlooked. Managers often do not address human issues adequately, even though they are aware of them, and even though they consider their employees, clients, and other people to be important.

CHANGE ISSUES IN THE PUBLIC AND PRIVATE SECTORS

While the specific issue of library automation is located principally in the public sector, the processes and challenges of change are common to both areas.

HUMAN FACTORS IN LIBRARY AUTOMATION

Librarians, staff and patrons must make a number of adjustments as a result of any library automation project, whether it is an original implementation or a migration. One key area is the relationship between people and technology. People have to change the way they behave and think to work effectively in an automated environment. They skim through cards to find a catalogue record in a manual system. To find a catalogue record in an automated system they use computer commands.

In a migration scenario, this might be a change from typing keyboard commands to choosing buttons or menu items on a graphical interface. For long-term employees, this requires yet a third 'mental map.' These demands for change easily lead to stress reactions of fear or anger, especially when they are large-scale or frequent. Smith mentions several sources for these emotions, such as loss of control, worries about identity and security in the workplace, and breakdowns in interpersonal relationships. It is no wonder that people often resist change. However, Smith cautions against regarding human responses solely as a barrier to change. For leaders who pay attention to social issues, these responses provide valuable feedback and help to implement a more successful system.

HISTORICAL PERSPECTIVE

The early history of library automation can be divided into three phases, the Developmental Phase, the Operational Phase, and the Integrative Phase. The development phase was the period of early experimentation up to the early seventies. During this period a small number of institutions engaged in automation projects. While management hoped that systems could be transferred from one institution to another, this was not the case with these early efforts. Libraries did not have similar computer operating systems, they did not have standardised procedures, and they could not agree on outputs.

However, the development of the MARC record was a significant development that allowed libraries to communicate bibliographic records in a standard format.

The operational phase, in the mid-to-late seventies, saw the expansion of automation in a wider variety of libraries. Vendor-supplied systems, shared computer resources, and networking made this possible. Since, libraries were no longer forced to develop their own systems from scratch, it was an easier and less expensive task.

During this phase most library automation projects still focussed on discrete tasks, such as check-in or circulation. Operational areas were not integrated, and the overall workflow stayed basically the same, "it has been utterly possible to use the automated system as inefficiently and ineffectively and with as little knowledge of what is going on as with the manual system". Montague proposed that the next phase would be an integrative phase, in which the automation systems would cut across operational lines, actually change the way libraries do business, and improve service.

There were a number of obstacles during these stages of library automation:

- Lack of direction and oversight from library managers to systems staff;
- Lack of technical training for library managers;
- Failure to develop long-range plans;
- Lack of up and down communication between managers and staff;
- Lack of staff input;

- Lack of staff training;
- Lack of feedback mechanisms.

Overall, it appears that the several problems, training, oversight, input, feedback, all involved a general lack of communication.

MIGRATION—SECOND GENERATION SYSTEMS

Since, many libraries, including Notre Dame, have or plan to migrate to second generation library systems, it is important to consider whether the obstacles are the same. One view is that they are not the same. Migrations are said to be easier than initial implementations. Although there may be some staff apprehensions, staff morale is reported to improve. A significant advantage is that second-time buyers have a better understanding of what they want in a system, and focus more on quality and customer support, instead of low bids. There is one potential source of resistance, which is never present in an initial automation project, that is a hostile 'soon-to-be former vendor.' Another important distinction is whether the library is migrating after successful implementation of a system which simply no longer meets their needs, or whether the library is desperately seeking a new system after a failed effort.

The reaction of librarians to this viewpoint is to be mixed. Some libraries have reported a very similar degree of 'techno stress' during migration projects, with similar emotional responses. Staff are required to change procedures, and in many cases the new procedures are not clear-cut—of course, the procedures in the 'old' system were not clear-cut in the beginning either. On the other hand, the majority of directors in a survey of 33 libraries that had undergone system migrations felt that 'promoting' the system change to the staff was unnecessary. This seems to be primarily due to staff frustration with the old systems, providing a clear motivation for change.

The worse the original system, the less staff resistance there was to migration. However, there were still some symptoms of technostress. Many found the vendors training programmes to be inadequate, consisting of 'canned' presentations were did not apply to local needs. Due to 'rush jobs,' the staff at many libraries did not have adequate time to become familiar with the new system before it was made available to the public. In one particularly egregious case, the staff and patrons were given access to the system at the same time. The staff 'hated this.' A two-month lead-time between staff and public access gave optimum results.

PRIVATE SECTOR EXPERIENCES

While library automation, *per se*, is not a major issue in the for-profit world, automation in general definitely is. As such, experiences in the private sector provide helpful comparisons. One very familiar theme from corporate settings in the need to consult with users prior to any sort of migration or automation project. This is true even with systems that are not central to the users' jobs. Gaudin relates several stories of companies that tried to implement new systems without consulting users. One case involved replacing a mainframe e-mail system with a desktop system. After the company spent $3 million, the employees rejected it because it was not fast or stable enough.

In another case, FedEx introduced a scheduling system without consulting their own employees. This became one of the issues in a potential strike against the company. One manager pointed out the importance of remembering that 'users might like their old systems'. This is an important lesson for library managers to remember in a migration, especially when the original system was basically successful. Even a failed system may have features the employees liked. Another illustration is provided by Norman's study of a failed automation effort. An attempt to introduce the CASE system in a management information firm provides valuable lessons for both sectors. The goal of the CASE project was to establish a 2-1 ratio of CASE workstation usage among the MIS staff and achieve a 10 to 15 per cent increase in productivity. The project is considered to be a failure, because people are not using it. The company has lost business to competitors who do use the system. Norman identifies a number of factors in the CASE implementation, which contributed to its failure. From the beginning, the decision to implement CASE was made by a small high-level committee, without involving staff. There was a successful pilot project, following which the company attempted to expand the system.

Their main methodology was a staff-training programme. Management assumed that if they provided training, the programmers would use the system. While the training was described as 'adequate,' it was informational only, and there was no effort made to change attitudes. The most critical barrier identified in the study was the high learning curve for using CASE. Management did not make any effort to reduce this learning curve. Instead, each work group that attempted to use the system had to learn it on their own. There was no sharing of tricks or shortcuts, or any help given by those who had already started using the product to new users. Interdepartmental friction and a rigid chain-of-command that stifled communication between units prevented this type of cooperation.

A related factor was the lack of any visible benefits or rewards for using CASE. Instead rewards were based on completing projects under-time and under-budget. Since, CASE is intended to increase productivity, it might seem that this would reward its use. But "this means that the rewards are indirect and totally dependent upon the successful use of the tool". In conjunction with the high learning curve, this becomes a negative incentive – the system is likely to slow production in the short-term, until the learning curve is past. If the programmer fails to learn it quickly, rewards are lost rather than gained.

THEORIES AND STRATEGIES FOR CHANGE

In discussing theories of organisational change, many theorists divide changes into different types. Before delving too deeply into specific strategies for change, I would like to examine the relationship between library automation projects and descriptive theories.

CONTINUITY

In the Age of Unreason, Handy tells us that "Change is not what it used to be". He distinguishes continuous and discontinuous change. Continuous change is gradual and predictable, with one situation leading into the next. This is relatively comfortable for most people. But he asserts that the changes in the workplace now are discontinuous. That is, changes are abrupt and unpredictable, and hence, far less comfortable. Handy frequently links discontinuous change to technology. As such, it is easy to reach the conclusion that a library automation project is a discontinuous change. People who worked with paper switch to online systems, and their jobs are altered or even eliminated. But we should not be too quick to classify it this way. Particularly in the early automation projects, automated tasks were substituted for manual tasks on a one-to-one basis. Because of this, there was no drastic change in the overall workflow; even when specific tasks were drastically altered. It could be argued that automation has had a more significant impact since, that time, as library systems have become integrated.

CALM AND TURBULENT WATERS

Robbins focuses on the frequency of change. He uses two metaphors, 'calm waters' and 'whitewater rapids.' In the calm-waters scenario, change is the exception. Most of the time is spent in a state of equilibrium, until some crisis forces a change. After the change is past, the organisation regains a new state of equilibrium. In the white-water scenario, change is continuous, though in a different sense than Handy uses the word.

There is no state of equilibrium; instead one period of change is followed directly by another. It is very tempting to identify library automation projects with the 'calm water' metaphor. In fact, Saunders uses a very similar model in her article on library system migration. First various forces bring about a need for change, which requires unfreesing process. This is followed by a period of instability. When this is over, the library establishes a new state of equilibrium, as new patterns and procedures are frozen into place. Because automation efforts are not made frequently, this model appears to be a good match.

In an original automation project, the library has been using a manual system as long as it has been in existence. Once the project has been completed, the library will continue to use the new system indefinitely. Even in a migration project, the library may have been using its old system for many years, and certainly would hope the new system would be long-lived. One potential problem with this model is that it ignores the wider picture of overall changes. At the same time as a library is contemplating an integrated library system, the staff may be dealing with new online indexes, electronic journals, e-mail systems, computer operating systems, and even a building renovation. Taken in this larger context, the white water metaphor seems more appropriate to the library environment. It is often not just the project at hand that causes problems for staff and users, but the 'unrelenting demand' of changes in many areas. Another issue is the continuing change following the implementation of an automated system due to new releases and upgrades to the system.

Even after a new system is fully implemented, it may not be as 'calm' as the old manual system. One significant problem with the white-water model as a model for change is that it suggests a reactive style of management with unplanned changes. But most library automation and migration projects are planned, as are many of the other changes affecting the library staff. This model seems most apt for dealing with the external changes impacting an organisation.

THE FOUR MOTORS OF CHANGE

Van de Ven and Poole give a more fully fleshed taxonomy of change. They identify two crosscutting distinctions, the level and the mode of change. The level of change is whether the change involves single or multiple entities. The mode of change is either prescribed or emergent. A priori changes are planned, predictable or follow set rules or patterns. Emergent change is discontinuous and unpredictable.

This combination yields four 'motors of change:'

- Life-cycle (single entity, prescribed);
- Teleological (single entity, emergent);
- Dialectical (multiple entities, emergent); and
- Evolutionary (multiple entities, prescribed).

While these motors can be separated in theory, most real-life changes involve interaction between them. The four motors model provides a more complete description of organisational change, and avoids over simplification problems. If we examine library automation projects in this e-context of the four motors of change that Van de Ven describes, as suggested, find rather complex interactions. The teleological theory, which is characterised by planning and goal setting, provides the closest description of the first stage in an automation project. Libraries may have a variety of motivations for undertaking an automation or migration project.

In the case of migration, this might include negative factors, like dissatisfaction with the current vendor, as well as positive ones, like a desire to expand capabilities. These motivations provide the Aristotelian final cause for the project. Most libraries engage in goal setting activities, such as compiling lists of desired features. This stage may be described as teleological in Van de Ven's scheme because it primarily involves one entity and the process is emergent. At the beginning of this stage, it is not clear where it will finish. Although the process is planned the goals are identified during the process, and may provide a dramatic break with the existing manual or automated system.

The dialectical motor may be present to a lessor extant, as different stakeholders interact with each other, and occasionally present conflicting goals. This teleological description fits most, but not all migration projects. For 79 per cent of cases in a migration survey, the projects were planned. But in some cases, the libraries did not have time to develop plans due to legal or financial problems. In those cases, the teleological motor would only apply in a trivial sense, if at all.

Those cases are obviously not ideal scenarios. Towards the end of the selection process, the library must compare its goals and desires to the actual systems available. At this point, the process could be described as dialectical, involving the library and the vendors who would like to supply the system. Vendors and librarians both regard this process as different for migration projects compared to first-time automation efforts.

In a first-time automation, libraries tend to rely on numerical evaluation of vendors' proposals and claims. In migration projects, libraries find site visits to be the most effective way to evaluate quality and hands-on work issues. At some point either during the final selection process or shortly after a vendor is chosen, the process shifts to a life-cycle model. The life-cycle motor is also primarily concerned with the library as a single entity. At this point, the plan, which was developed in earlier stages, becomes the guide for the process.

The library engages is a series of steps that were laid out in the plan, possibly on a strict timeschedule. This includes all of the steps technically necessary to implement the system as well as steps to prepare the users. This process is imminent in, or prescribed by the plan, and is much more predictable than the earlier stages. The library may have even planned for contingencies. Once the actual conversion in done, and the new system is live, the process become somewhat less predictable. Procedures that worked on paper or in test may fail under the pressure of real-life use.

While none of the motors seem to be completely dominant at this point, the evolutionary theory is closest. Procedures that work 'survive' while others are discarded.

The changes may still be described as imminent, however, because they are constrained by the system. The others motors continue to play some role, as plans are made and carried out, and different stakeholders disagree on various issues. The dialectical motor may become dominant from time-to-time as the vendor announces new releases, or the library recommends enhancements for the system. At these times the possibilities for change are less constrained, and the results become more emergent.

STRATEGIES

The authors who describe actual automation projects also list key lessons and make recommendations. There are a number of general, and some very specific, suggestions along with a couple of common threads. One of the common threads is communication.

Whether it is between management and employees, between systems and users, or between the employees at large, it seems that more communication is always better. A related thread is the need to involve the users in the process as early as possible. Several of the authors suggested that users should be involved at the very beginning, during the selection process. Montage, Norman, Gaudin, Hallmark and Smith all cite lack of user involvement in the selection or planning stage as an obstacle to successful implementation. Since, these two threads stand out, we may conclude that if any overall strategy is too be effective, it must include a high level of communication and user participation.

STRATEGIES FROM THE CASE IMPLEMENTATION

Norman described three change strategies in his evaluation of the CASE implementation. These strategies could be used independently or in conjunction with each other.

Rational-empirical

This strategy focuses on training and information. It is presumed that teaching people to use the system and providing a rational explanation of why it is better will lead them to use it. This strategy could easily be applied to a library automation or migration project, as many of the authors indicated the importance of training programmes.

Normative-educational

This strategy focuses on group strategies for promoting acceptance of the new systems and providing motivation to use it. First, identify the attitudes that create resistance, and then develop programmes to change them. This is similar to developing training sessions in the rational-empirical strategy. The difference is that the sessions are intended to develop positive attitudes instead imparting information.

Power-coercive

In this strategy individuals are induced to use the new system by the threat of loosing their job or other benefits. This can be a fairly direct approach to implement change, but it also runs a high risk creating bad feelings, job dissatisfaction, and tension between management and employees. Threats, whether explicit or implicit, will also add to the fear and anxiety already identified as an obstacle to change. A variation of this strategy can be applied in a positive way by offering employees incentives for change. While this is can be regarded as a power-exercise it is less confrontational. In the CASE implementation, the main strategy that was applied was the rational-empirical strategy.

The normative-educational strategy was largely ignored, and the power-coercive strategy was inconsistently applied. Management made statements that employees were required to use the system, but did not follow-up when it was not used. Management also did not provide any direct positive incentives. This strategy may also be applied to library systems in the sense that when the old system is shut-off, employees will not be able to perform their duties without using the new system.

PHASED IMPLEMENTATION

Saunders recommends a strategy of phased implementation. The idea of this strategy is to minimize the impact of the new system has on staff by introducing modules in a gradual fashion. For example, a library might implement cataloguing or acquisitions functions first, and circulation latter. This strategy has some advantages. Successful implementation of one module should increase staff willingness to use another. Also, management can deal with the staff in smaller groups, concentrating on the area currently being automated, instead of dealing with all areas at once. The chief drawback of this strategy is found when the current system is already well integrated.

In this case, phased implementation may mean that user's are initially presented with a system that has fewer features than their previous system. There may also be technical difficulties that preclude phased implementation, as the two systems are not likely to communicate with each other well, if at all. Where it is usable, this strategy should also be combined with other strategies. Saunders specifically emphasises the importance of training and communication issues.

PARTICIPANT-ORIENTED CHANGE

Zeffane advocates the strategy of participant-oriented change, which is based on the premise that change works best when comes from the bottom up rather than from the top down. One reason for this premise is that if the employees introduce change, then they will not have an authority figure to rebel against. It is also based on the idea that collegial affiliation is a positive motivation for change. That is, employees will be more motivated to help with a changes initiated by someone at, or close to, their level. To use participant oriented change, management needs to shift the responsibility for change away from themselves and towards the employees.

This strategy goes beyond considering the users' needs, or soliciting input, to actually delegating authority to the participants. This strategy takes advantage of the fact that the employees who are closest to the hands-on work have the most detailed knowledge about it. This also frees the upper management from concentrating on this level of detail, and to concentrate on overall strategic planning. This strategy may not be effective in all types of organisations.

There are some essential elements for participative strategies to work. First, the employees given responsibilities for change must be well informed. Second, the employees must understand and agree with the mission of the organisation. Unless these requirements are met, management cannot expect that the decisions will be beneficial to the organisation. The third requirement is that this style of change must be supported by the organisation culture. The management must be comfortable with this type of delegation.

MANAGEMENT FUNCTIONS

The traditional roles of management are planning, organisation, coordination and control. These can be applied to these change strategies.

RATIONAL-EMPIRICAL

The rational-empirical strategy is primarily concerned with dispensing information, presuming that the plans for change have already been made. It involves the organising function of management, in the sense that the managers determine what information needs to be given to which employees in order to implement the changes. It also involves the control function, in that the management is seeking to influence behaviour through the information it dispenses.

NORMATIVE-EDUCATIONAL

The normative-education strategy is concerned with influencing attitudes and behaviour. As such, it involves the control function of management, but in an indirect manner. That is, rather than controlling behaviour directly, the management attempts to instill attitudes which are likely to result in the desired behaviour. Like the rational-empirical strategy, it also involves the coordinating function, as managers decide who should be involved in which programmes.

POWER-COERCIVE

The power-coercive strategy concerns the management role of control in a straight- forward fashion. It is mainly concerned with seeing to it that the change decisions are carried out as directed. To ensure this, it dispenses rewards or penalties to individuals or groups depending or whether they have implemented the changes. In the extreme, employees who fail to change are fired.

PHASED IMPLEMENTATION

Phased implementation involves both the planning and coordinating functions to a large degree. Planning includes determining the order in which to implement the modules and setting timetables for each phase. Coordination includes meshing together the efforts of different groups associated with each phase, and ensuring that each module is integrated with the previous ones when it is brought into production. As more modules are brought into the 'live' mode, coordination becomes essential in order to see that the different areas function smoothly.

PARTICIPANT-ORIENTED CHANGE

Participant oriented change involves the coordinating function of management. Since, much of the planning and decision making is delegated downward to the staff, management must integrate these plans and decisions. This is particularly important when implementing an integrated library system, as the activities of staff in one area will have more impact on other areas than they are accustomed to. The actual delegation of these responsibilities to employees involves the organising function. Determining how and to whom these responsibilities are delegated is in important part of the change process.

This may involve organising employees into self-managed teams, work groups, or interdepartmental task forces. How these groups are organised, the amount of authority they have, and how they will interact with each other are crucial decisions.

CONCLUSION

The participant oriented change strategy provides the best overall approach to managing library automation and migration projects. Of the strategies which have been outlined, it offers the highest degree of employee communication and participation. These are the same areas that caused the most problems if they were inadequate. One of the chief advantages of this strategy is that it involves the users of the system at the earliest possible stage of the project. That is during the teleological process of identifying reasons for the project and setting goals or criteria for a new system. Involving the employees at this stage reduces the need for normative attitude-adjusting sessions latter in the process.

This is not to say that managers who adopt this strategy can just ignore employee attitudes later on. Change will still be stressful, and people may still resist it at various points. But, management will not have to invest as much effort in convincing staff that the new system is better if the staff were involved in selecting it. The rational-empirical strategies of employee training programmes will still have a role to play, as the process moves on. As was demonstrated in the failed attempt at implementing the CASE system, this strategy is not sufficient by itself. But users must learn how a new system works if they are to use it at all. Within the overall context of participant oriented strategy, other employees provide much of that training. With their hands-on experience, employee led training can be more effective than vendor supplied 'canned presentations'.

This also promotes an atmosphere in which employees will be comfortable sharing their learning experiences, tricks and shortcuts following implementation. The other two strategies, phased implementation and power-coercive can not be recommended across the board. The power-coercive strategy is divisive, and is likely make the change harder instead of easier. This strategy aggravates fears about job security, which is one of the sources of change anxiety. While a degree of control needs to be maintained, a threatening approach is not desirable as a general strategy.

The strategy of phased implementation will be helpful for some situations, but not for all. For libraries currently using manual systems or automated systems that are not integrated, this method may help to ease the transition. For libraries that already have a well-integrated system, it could create even more chaos. Within the context of participant-oriented change, the choice of whether to include it rests with the employees who actually work with the system.

7

Strategic Planning for Librarians

A DEFINITION OF STRATEGIC PLANNING

Strategic planning is a tool for organising the present on the basis of the projections of the desired future. That is, a strategic plan is a road map to lead an organisation from where it is now to where it would like to be in five or ten years. It is necessary to have a strategic plan for your chapter or division. In order to develop a comprehensive plan for your chapter or division which would include both long- range and strategic elements, we suggest the methods and mechanisms outlined in this manual.

The plan must be:

- Simple
- Written
- Clear
- Based on the real current situation
- Have enough time allowed to give it a time to settle. It should not be rushed. Rushing the plan will cause problems.

BENEFITS AND PITFALLS IN STRATEGIC PLANNING

Since, the beginning of Special Libraries Association in 1909, it has experienced phenomenal growth in membership and influence. In the past ten years, growth has been particularly significant. Changes in the fields of special librarianship and information science have been dramatic and fundamental to the very way of doing business. The advent of on line systems and the computer age rapidly changed the way librarians/information managers operate.

The Association recognises that it can no longer merely react to issues as they emerge. If it is to continue as a leader in improving the profession, it must begin to anticipate future change rather than merely react to change. The Association as well as each chapter and division needs to consider this long-term future. Drawing on the resources it has, both human and financial, it needs to continue to grow. These resources are limited, and careful thought must be given to the allocation of these resources. To meet obligations to the profession, the public, and the membership, it is essential that the Association and its units use these resources in the most efficient manner by determining priority areas on which to concentrate. This means the identification of goals, pursuing those goals, and achieving them. Strategic planning will help build continuity in the Association's programmes, particularly in the areas of continuing education and publications. The Association has the gift of a great deal of diversity among the membership. The Association draws its strength from this diversity but at the same time, that diversity lessens the Association's impact in key areas because of a lack of cohesive focus by the organisation.

Therefore, it is necessary for each chapter and division to have a plan that is compatible with the overall strategic plan of SLA thus concentrating its efforts and greatly increasing its impact. There are several pitfalls associated with strategic planning. First, the plan may not turn out as well as expected because of changes in the environment in which the plan is supposed to operate. Also, strategic planning is worthless in getting an organisation out of a major crisis.

A crisis is a current problem not solved by a strategic plan. And, if the planning process itself is weak, the resulting plan may be weak and not satisfactory to the organisation. George Steiner in his Strategic Planning lists 50 major common pitfalls in starting, doing, and using strategic planning.

STRATEGIC PLANNING MODEL

In choosing the strategic planning model, two main things need to be considered. The first is whether you want the Association unit to plan as a not-for-profit, or as a profit organisation. Association planning is not the same as the planning for universities or businesses or government agencies. Associations need to be consistently receptive to the needs of the membership-at-large. The main purpose is to serve the members more than to make a profit or to increase the size of the organisation. The strategic plan needs to include a Mission Statement, Objectives, Goals, and an Action (or Implementation) Plan.

MISSION STATEMENT

This is the agreed-upon statement by the organisation and explains the reason for its existence. It is necessarily broad to encompass the diversity within the Association. The statement is not precise in its measurements nor does it need to be, but it does need to be periodically reviewed by the Association to see whether it still encompasses all of the relevant activities of the Association.

OBJECTIVES

The objectives are the areas of emphasis within the Association. Rather than specific statements with a specific goal, objectives state that the

Association plans to continue to do quality work in the following areas. These objectives or areas of emphasis need to be attained by discussion and review of the organisation's current activities as well as activities in which it would like to participate.

GOALS

These need to be both long-term and short-term goals; six months, one-year, threeyears, and ten-year goals need to be set so that the strategy for reaching these goals can be outlined in the plan. Most organisations recommend setting the long-term goals first and then setting short-term goals: those goals which can be reached as steps to attaining the long-term goal.

ACTION PLAN

The Action Plan should be designed after the main goals and objectives have been set in order to attain the mission in a straightforward and measurable way. With an Action Plan, the goals themselves can be obtained. Without the Action Plan, and the measures it entails, it would be impossible to implement the plan and measure its success. Being able to measure success would certainly be important both for maintaining our tax status as a not-for-profit organisation as well as to explain the use of it to the membership-at-large.

STRATEGIC PLANNING PROCESSES AND MECHANISMS

The publications 'A Guide to Nominal Group and Delphi Processes' by Andre L. Blebecq, et al, and "Guide for Leaders Using Nominal Group Technique" by James G. Cope and Carl Moore, describe the combination of nominal group and Delphi processes. Using these techniques, an organisation that is geographically separate can communicate and develop the working document in fairly rapid fashion.

GATHERING OF BACKGROUND INFORMATION

Background information is used by your Strategic Planning Committee for its review. By shifting through that information, the Committee would be able to develop a sound basis to continue their work. After existing information has been gathered, another information gathering activity should take place.

Develop a survey questionnaire to poll all members for their viewpoints on the directions your chapter or division should take. After the information has been synthesised from the questionnaires as well as from information already gathered, move to the second step.

A PLANNING WORKSHOP

The title of the article is 'Strategic Planning: Lead Your Association With a Plan for Tomorrow'.

Based on this article, your chapter or division needs to gather information on five basic questions:

- Where are we now? (The Situation);
- How did we get there? (Our Momentum);
- Where are we going? (The Direction);
- Where should we be going? (Desired Direction);
- How will we get there? (The Strategic Plan).

Bailey recommends that after gathering the background information, the planning workshop should take place. The first session would assess the current situation and how you arrived at that present situation. The second activity of this first workshop is to try to figure out where you are going and where you want to be. This is a very hard-hitting and difficult time for any association or business given the economic conditions and the change within our profession itself.

DESIGNING A PLANNING WORKBOOK

The planning Workbook will bring together all of the information gathered during the Planning Workshop, sift through the ideas put forward, and organise them into a meaningful body for review by the Planning Workshop attendees and other interested parties in the organisation.

SECOND PLANNING WORKSHOP

After the Planning Workshop information has been gathered into a workbook, another workshop should be planned. At this workshop (which should not be held too long after the first one), several things need to be accomplished. In the first half-day a Mission Statement should be adopted for the Association. The Mission Statement will include what the Association intends to stand for; what it hopes to contribute to the world-at-large. It should set goals for the Association and then, having set the goals, fulfill the Mission Statement by translating each goal into a specific objective. This means that the Mission Statement will be carried forth into a strategic plan.

THE COMMITTEE STRUCTURE

The Strategic Planning Committee should be composed of people who understand the organisation of Special Libraries Association, but also who have a constant feel for the Association and your chapter and division in general, and where it is moving. The Strategic Planning Committee should be made a permanent standing committee within the chapters and divisions with a rotating membership. This will encourage constant review and updating by the membership.

THOUGHTS REGARDING SHORT AND LONG RANGE PLANNING

In order to achieve a sound basis for the development of programmes and activities, systematic planning efforts must be undertaken. The following is a stream of ideas about planning which have been able to find their way to paper. They are presented merely for a point of departure and not meant for any other purpose--a 'Plan for Planning' so to speak.

PLANNING

Planning includes the ability to identify opportunities, analyse problems, establish priorities and needs, and allocate available resources. This also includes the establishment of priorities and needs, and allocate available resources.

This also includes the establishment of policies and procedures, objectives and standards of performance, forecasts and budgets, programmes and schedules:

- Planning is necessary:
  - Provides direction
  - Gives perspective
- Planning facilitates:
  - Involvement of concerned people and groups.
  - Communication
  - Coordination
- Steps in Planning:
  - Organising
    - *a.* Establish a structure
    - *b.* Group involvement
  - Setting objectives
    - *a.* Nature of objectives
    - *b.* Basis for objectives
  - Establishing priorities—based on needs, opportunities, interrelationships between elements.
  - Designing activities
  - Dividing action into feasible steps
    - *a.* Short range
    - *b.* Long range
  - Implementing action
  - Disseminating information
  - Evaluating—a continual process
  - Revising—at least annually

PROGRAMME

- Conceptual—why the programme should be undertaken:
  - Problem statement
  - Objectives
  - Hypothesis
  - Review of existing information

- Methodological—what has to be done and how it will be done:
  - Design Programme
  - Sampling
  - Analysis
    - *a.* Quantitative
    - *b.* Qualitative
  - Instrumentation selection or development.

CONTENTS OF PLANNING DOCUMENT

- Statement of philosophy:
  - General philosophy of the organisation
  - Philosophy of special libraries
- Needs assessment
- Goal of the Association
- Objectives of the Association
  - Something we want
  - Output—end product
  - Means—end product
- Establish programme alternatives
  - Fiscal—costs of conducting the programme:
    - *a.* Time
    - *b.* Resources
      - i. Human
      - ii. Non-human
    - c. Money
  - Programme—set of activities which are combined into some structure and are carried out to achieve some previously stated objective.
  - Limits and constraints:
    - *a.* An analysis of what we have to work with and work against
    - *b.* Specify time, money, programme requirements, people, and facilities within which the Association must operate
    - *c.* The statement of ground rules under which the Association must operate
  - Types of constraints:
    - *a.* Social
    - *b.* Technological
    - *c.* Administrative
    - *d.* Political
    - *e.* Legal
    - *f.* Economic
  - Forces affecting programme development:

a. Political
b. Outside interest groups
c. Administrative hierarchy
d. Users
e. Professional organisations

— Establish programme priorities
— Select best programme alternative
— Action plan
— Evaluation of programme

8

Implementation of Barcode Technology in Library Management

INTRODUCTION

The circulation work in an automated library involves keying in a large amount of data. Sometimes, the library staff at the counter has to retype the same information due to error in data entry. All this results in long queues at the circulation desk in our libraries. This voluminous work can be handled in a smooth manner in a much less time by the application of barcoding, one of the simplest coding technologies available in the market. The speed of data capture is three times faster than the speed at which a skilled data entry operator can input data' and also the error rate is negligibly small2. The barcode technology originated out of the need of retail stores and big industries to track down their inventory errors in a faster way. Due to the cheap human labour available in our country, the estimated barcoding market was a mere 12 crores in 1995-96', out of which libraries and miscellaneous services accounted for only 1 crore. Libraries need to adopt this technology as it helps retrieve and collect data quickly and efficiently.

BARCODE DATA TRANSFER

The information that can be encoded on the barcodes is rather limited and hence, it is up to the individual libraries to decide what information they need to barcode for efficient handling of collection and for better operation of services. Libraries can use accession numbers of books, the unique information that distinguish their collection, as the vital information entity to barcode their collection. Similarly, the identification number of a user stands distinct for each member, which can be used to barcode the user's cards. Accession number/borrower number exported from the library database/borrower database is converted to a series of black and white lines by the barcode software.

This can be printed by a dot-matrix/laser printer and pasted on all books and borrower cards. The light beam flashed from the barcode scanner on the barcode label undergoes reflection at the white lines and absorption on the dark bands. This reflected light is collected back and is converted into electric pulses by the photoelectric circuitry of the scanner. Further, these pulses are converted into binary information by the interface circuitry of the scanner before they are fed to the computer, for further processing. So, the information read from barcode acts as a substitute for the same information entered through keyboard, to handle circulation/other routines of the library database.

The barcode technology is essentially a data transfer device and hence, it works in perfect harmony with any of the computerised database systems. Any customisation needed at the user end can be done either by the in-house system personnel or by local solution providers. The barcoding setup includes the barcode scanner to read the barcoded information, its interfacing with the library computer, the software to convert the requisite information to barcodes, and the printer.

The barcode scanners may be classified into different groups like:

- As per design (handheld and fixed-mount).
- As per light source (infrared or visible).

Hand-held scanners contain no moving parts. They are compact, light and cheaper as compared to fixed-mount models. Hence, they are of interest to libraries desiring to optimise their budgetary resources. Infrared scanners can read mutilated labels; however, they need special printers. But recent times saw the dominant categorisation, as per technology, into CCD and laser scanners. In CCD scanners, light from the LEDs is used to read the barcode information, whereas laser light is used in the latter. Accordingly, laser scanners have increased scan width and range (distance from which the labels are scanned), but they are comparatively expensive. The vendors used to offer requisite software to generate barcodes from suggested fields of library database. Since, materials and readers are added only in prescribed number in a library, it will be better to avoid commercial printing of barcode labels.

All required lables can be printed either on normal paper or on purchased blank labels on a dot-matrixllaser printer, as per their availability in the library. While generating lables, provision may also be made to print some other fields like author/title/user riame in normal text to identify the labels easily, as one is more comfortable with text than numbers like accession/identification number. The user cards are normally laminated and to ensure long life of the labels on books (defective labels always lead to wrong/no reading of data), transparent cellotape can be pasted over these.

CODING FORMATS/ SYMBOLOGIES

The different code formats and how the information is encoded in bars is available in the litreature4. The same information can be encoded by different schemes; however, at the user and application level, it doesn't make much distinction and the user may use any of the schemes. The same information can be encoded to and satisfactorily decoded from more than one scheme without hampering efficiency or time. Limitations are imposed by the barcoding software one uses, and it is better to consult the individual operational manual for such information.

Some of the common formats are:

- *Universal Product Code (UPC)*: US standard to encode only digits, UPC-A to encode 12 digits or UPC-E to encode 6 digits.
- *European Article Number (EAN)*: European code to encode digits, available in two variations:. EAN-8 to encode 8 digits and EAN-13 to encode 13 digits.
- *Interleaved 2 of 5. (ITF)*: Supports only numeric characters but can be used for variable length.
- *Code-39*: Encodes capital alphabets, numerical and few special characters like $, +, per cent. Asterisk (*) must be used as the start and stop character. Lowercase alphabets cannot be encoded.
- *Code-1 28*: Encodes both the lower and the upper case letters, numeric and special characters found on the keyboard.
- *Codabar*: Encodes only numeric and few special characters and is the most widely used coding format. Generally, libraries use this symbology to encode books and borrower cards.

BARCODING AT THE IIT KHARAGPUR CENTRAL LIBRARY

The Central Library of the Indian Institute of Technology, Kharagpur, is one of the few libraries in the country to have a huge database of their entire collections. Initially, the computerised issue return of books6 was done by keying in the accession number of books and identification number of borrower, but this mechanism was prone to errors and. also resulted in long queues at the circulation grant desk.

Out of the project of ₹ 10 lakh received from AlCTE in 1994 for the conversion of the conventional central library into the electronic library, the Library procured 5 CCD barcode scanners and one HP-5Si Mx Laser Printer. It was decided to barcode books and hence, the details of books brought for issue/return were exported from the library database for generating barcode labels with accession number as the key field and the labels were printed on the laser printer using 'Softbar vl' software supplied by the vendor.

The Library also received a consignment of 'Nashua Laser Labels' in 30 labels per page format as gift from one of its alumni settled in US. The system generates three labels for each book to be pasted on the back of title page, secret page and last page. To fasten the process, personnel were given honorarium and encouraged to work overtime/on holidays to barcode the entire book collection. Side by side, new books processed by the technical processing section were also barcoded before release. Out of a special operating fund of ₹ 1 lakh received from the Institute in 1998, all the pending old books were also barcoded.

Now, the entire collection of over 2 lakh books is barcoded. From the academic year 1998-99, all B.Tech and M.Tech students were given a laminated barcoded library identity card and the practice of issuing separate borrower cards as per the entitlement was discontinued.

This facility will be further extended to faculty, researchers, and other staff in near future. This practice not only resulted in saving a large amount of stationery for printing numerous borrower cards but also a total saving of staff time which would have otherwise been spent for filing those cards. The user can have a book in one third of the pre-barcode issue time. The faculty, students and the personnel manning the circulation desk find the barcode technology user-friendly, efficient and fast.

ADOPTION IN OTHER LIBRARIES IN INDIA

Few of the computerised libraries in the country like American Centre, British Council, other ITs, some R&D libraries have already started barcoded circulation. With an investment of less than a lakh, the computerised libraries can procure barcode related hardware and software. A CCD scanner can be purchased for ₹ 15,000 and a laser scanner for ₹ 25,000 with comparable costs for relevant software. It is always better to have a feedback from the nearby libraries who use this technology before procuring one. Also, the potential vendors may be called to give a demonstration of this technology.

The procurement may be carried out in one go or in stages, so that those required for barcoding active collection may be purchased first and on completion of that work, more scanners may be bought. The accrued savings for the first few years will be more than what has been invested. Further, it will also improve the status of the library which will move one step closer to realise the fourth law of library science.

APPLICATIONS OF BARCODING

Barcoding offers a lot of comfort and ease to handle bulk routine tasks efficiently. The application of this technology for issue/return of books is widely identified and practiced in the developed countries of the world. A few of the computerised libraries in our country have also started experiencing the fruits of this technology. It is important to emphasise that this technology is not limited to circulation work. Newnham describes the barcoding of DNA samples in Britain. It is not out of place to ponder over future barcoding applications in a library. With the help of a data gathering device, the barcodes can be used to verify stock, as libraries have to resort to stock verification, at intervals.

If the provision for multiple barcodes or multidimensional barcoding is incorporated to handle call number information also, wrong shelving of books can be autodetected which would help the staff to rectify the same. The individual journal volumes are handled in a library with lots of intricacies. Many a time these issues have to be taken out of the display area for Xerox work. There are also chances of their shelving in wrong cabinets.

These problems are tackled by using a control number for the current journal issues and barcoding them accordingly. A database of journal issues can thus be generated so that their management through cards can be avoided. If the parent institution also has a computerised accounting system, all the bills can be routed after barcoding so that their follow up and processing are done efficiently. Barcoding has come a long way and it is here to stay for faster and efficient library work.

AUTOMATED LIBRARY STOCK VERIFICATION WITH BARCODE AND LIBSYS

The modern technology has enabled automation and integration of the various processes of libraries and information centres to reduce or avoid human intervention and to increase the efficiency and speed. As the libraries provide open access service to make the holdings available to the users, the loss, damage, and misplacement of books are inevitable. To know and replace the lost books, and to maintain balance between various subjects, and to take adequate precautionary measures, it is necessary to do periodical inventory and accounting of the library collection of the library.

The term stock verification thus came into existance with regard to libraries. It is also referred as stock taking, physical verification or checking, stock inspection, and inventory, taking meaning physical checkup of any article on record.

Libraries of Govt. of India and its other organisations has to do a mandatory physical verification of all their holdings as per the following guidelines:

- Complete annual physical verification of books should be done every year in the case of libraries having not more than 20,000 holdings and not fewer than one qualified library staff. In case there is only one qualified staff, the verification may be done as per sub-para.
- Complete physical verification at intervals of not more than three years should be done in the case of libraries having more than 20,000 but not more than 50,000 volumes.
- Sample physical verification at intervals of not more than five years may be done in the case of libraries having more than 50,000 volumes. If such sample verification reveals unusual or unreasonable shortage, complete verification shall be done.

Libraries traditionally perform the periodic stock verification by adopting any one of the following methods: Verification by accession register; using a separate register with accession numbers; slips containing accession numbers; numerical counting; and shelf register cards or shelf list cards. The methods are cumbersome, time-consuming, and error prone as these are done manually.

The automated stock verification procedure adopted at Raja Ramanna Centre for Advanced Technology (RRCAT) library by employing barcode and LibSys facilities library stock verification could be performed easily with less manpower; one person scanned the barcode label (accession number) of documents and other person marked the documents by putting month and year stamp at the inside back cover to ensure that the document was physically verified.

Besides, identification of damaged and worn out documents for repair, binding of obsolete volumes, and rearrangement and cleaning can also be done simultaneously. During the stock verification period, the returned (check-in) documents were also verified before shelving. Once the data capturing was over, the verification and generation of report with LibSys could also be done in a short period of time.

IMPLEMENTATION OF BARCODE TECHNOLOGY AND LIBSYS AT RRCAT LIBRARY

To improve the library service and to have an efficient control over the entire operation, the LibSys, which is a commercially available integrated multi-user library automation package, was implemented at RRCAT in 1995. To improve the services further, the barcode technology (print-related automatic identification technology) was implemented in 2000. The hardware installed to implement these technologies at RRCAT are: Laser barcode scanner for reading labels (at circulation counter); portable data capturing terminal with build-in laser scanner for inventory (stock verification); and accessories such as cradle, cable, battery and other items. The softwares for interfacing the data capturing terminal with computer are: PowerGen, SysTools and Label Works for Windows for label designing.

BARCODE AND BARCODE SCANNER

The barcodes are being used effectively to speed up, avoid human error, and automate the processes in industry for production planning control, materials management, purchase/ sale, and inventory control. In libraries, barcode is being used to automate the data-capturing process, for stock verification, and in the circulation counter for issue/return of documents.

A barcode is a sequence of dark bars on a light background or the equivalent of this with respect to the light-reflecting properties of the surface. The coding comprises in the relative widths or spacing of the dark bars and light spaces. A barcode scanner is an optical device that reads the code by scanning a focussed beam of light, generally a laser beam, across the barcode and detecting the variations in reflected light. The scanner converts these light variations into electrical variations, which are subsequently digitised and fed into the decoding unit programmed to convert the relative widths of the digitised dark/light spacings into numbers and/or letters.

BARCODE LABELLING

Each document in a library should be uniquely identified for barcode labelling purpose. Most of the libraries in India use accession number for this purpose. RRCAT has also used the same for printing barcode labels. The labels designed using Label Works for Windows, which supports major barcode symbologies. Code 128, a high density linear symbology that can encode text, numbers, several functions and the entire 128 ASCII character set was selected for designing the labels. Figure shows the barcode label design specifications.

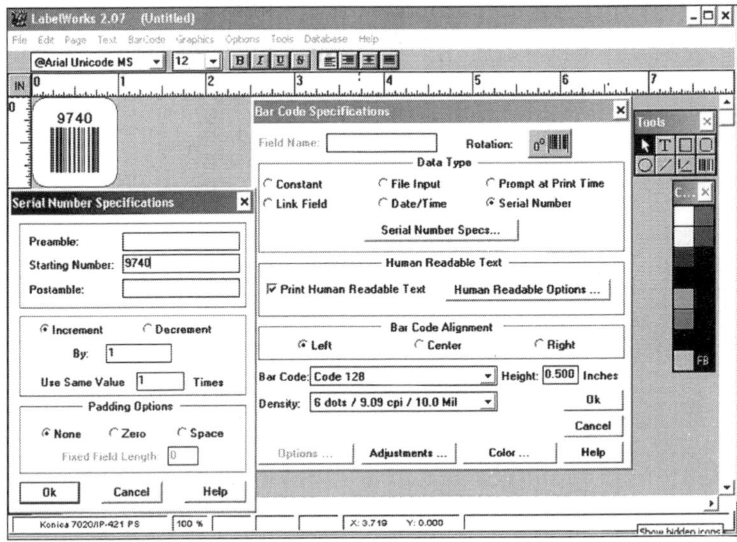

Fig. Barcode Label Design Specifications

DATA CAPTURING, MODIFICATION AND UPLOADING

The datalogic formula 732 wizard terminal was used to capture the data. The portable data collection laser scanner terminal scans the encoded data and automatically decodes and stores up to 128 KB of data in the memory. As the accession number differs from one to other, the terminal stores approx. 2500 accession numbers. The data was downloaded into the PC using Systool's (software utility for data exchange) and was saved in a data file (*.dat). Later downloads were also appended to the same file. The PowerGen was the other software utility used to build personalised settings as per the requirements.

Each document was scanned and stamped (month and year) manually at the inside back cover to avoid duplication. During scanning, the terminal stores the accession number of each document and automatically displays the document number for a moment. If a data scanned is wrong, it can be manually updated or rescanned, and if a document has been inadvertantly scanned multiple times, the terminal simply stores the documents with duplicate accession numbers.

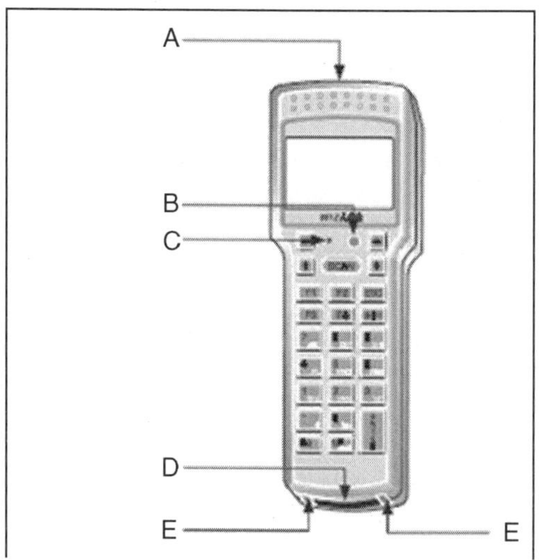

Fig. Datalogic Formula 732 Wizard Terminal

Notes:

A. Laser beam output window
B. Two colour LED
C. Reset key (shielded)
D. Cradle communications window
E. Contacts for battery recharging

The downloaded data in the PC shows a vertical bar '|' (pipe) character after each accession number. The '|' characters were manually removed from the file using the windows text editor. The comprehensive file was then moved to LibSys work file ('wfilexx' directory).

DATA PROCESSING

As the entire collection of RRCAT was catalogued in the LibSys, the data analyses and report generation was carried out through the LibSys cataloguing stock verification module. The initiation of stock verification function is executed at once. This operation sets the system for the big exercise on inventory entails.

Data Analysis

The LibSys provides data verification in two ways; accession numbers one by one, and list of accession numbers in a file. All accession numbers are stored in a file. The system registers accession numbers for verification in the database. After matching the accession number from the file, the LibSys automatically generates an exception case file with extension '*. exp' and saves it in the work file path, i.e., in the wfilexx directory. This file enlists the list of mis-matching accession numbers and wrongly scanned numbers.

Report Generation

As the term stock verification implies only on stock, a list of missing accession numbers is generated against the captured data file. After several cross checkings, the final verification report is prepared in a text (*.txt) file. The flow chart is presented in figure.

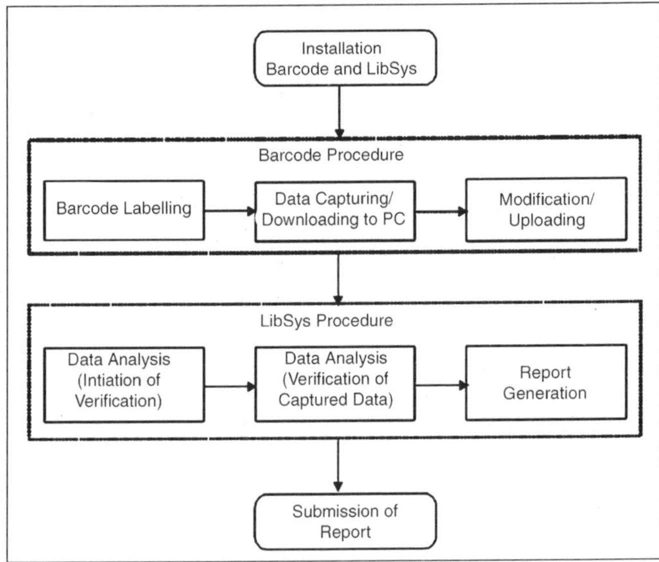

Fig. Flow Chart of Automated Stock Verification

CONCLUSION

Barcode technology is reliable and easy to use. It improves accuracy and accelerates the processing time, eliminates the typing errors, decreases the costs and improves the services. During the stock verification period, routine library activities can be carried out without any disturbance. Data-capturing terminal is handy and portable, and there is no problem of scanning the data multiple times. The only disadvantage being like libraries assign simple accession numbers 1 to n for books, R1 to Rn for reports, and S1 to Sn for standards (R and S are the accession series of specific publication type). If libraries carry out stock verification for books alone LibSys has no option to carry out stock verification by an accession series wise. It process as the data and generates a report for all records available in the cataloguing module. Overall, the technology is beneficial for carrying out stock verifications in libraries. Since, there is no human intervention, the verification report generated by the system is perfect and accurate.

9

Furniture and Shelving Care: As a Librarians' Duty

The timely arrival of furniture, equipment and shelving, which serves its function, meets quality requirements, and is within the project budget can put the finishing touches on a building project or be a disastrous ending to an otherwise successful project. The primary goals of furniture and shelving procurement are to insure the on-time arrival in a facility that is ready to receive furniture and equipment. The products must be of satisfactory quality and finish, meet performance standards, be priced within the project budget and fit in the desired location. The tasks involved include preparation of furniture and shelving programme and product specifications; evaluation of purchase options; implementation of selected bidding method; and delivery, installation and punch list.

Planning for furniture and shelving cannot occur too early in a project. The amount of furniture and shelving required to support a library's programme will drive the amount of space and funding required to complete the project. Many planners begin to identify furniture and equipment needs during the programming phase. Planning for the furniture and equipment for a library project requires careful scheduling and budgeting and the assistance of a design professional with experience in the selection, evaluation, and procurement of specific items. Furniture that is an after thought is frequently unavailable, mismatched to the architecture, or ill suited for the intended location or purpose.

WHAT IS A FURNITURE PROGRAMME

A furniture or shelving programme establishes the standards and requirements for all furniture, equipment, shelving, and sometimes millwork for the library project. It should list all of the furniture and equipment items to be placed in each area of the library, along with preferred dimensions, quantity, equipment to be housed, and any electrical and data requirements. It should also incorporate any staff workstation standards that are to be used. The programme may be adjusted as the furniture and shelving plan and building design develops, since, it provides the basis for the final furniture list and specification. Existing furniture to be reused should be noted indicating any refurbishment required.

Table. Sample Spreadsheet format for Preliminary Furniture Programme.

Item #	Item Name	#	Location	Ex./New	Description	Finish	Note
T4	Reader Table for 4	12	Ref. Room	New	36″ × 72″	Wood	
T4 A	Reader Table for 4	12	Ref. Room	Ex.	54″ Round	Wood	Refinish
C1	Reader Chair	48	Ref. Room	New	Armless	Wood	(Match existing)
C2	Reader Chair	48	Ref. Room	New	With Arms	Wood	
C3	Task Chairs	6	Ref. Room	New			OPAC
A1	Atlas Stand	1	Ref. Room	Ex.		Wood	Refinish

A simple furniture or shelving programme can be prepared using a spreadsheet, which can be sorted by any number of fields; *e.g.*, Location, Item Name, Finish, or Note. Each unique furniture item can be given an alphanumeric code or a sequential numbering system can be used. The spreadsheet can contain an unlimited number of fields, but would most likely include some of those suggested as well as a notation regarding power or data requirements, specific equipment dimensional requirements, and an estimated cost.

WHEN IS IT NEEDED

The furniture and equipment programme should be developed in the programming phase of a project. The building programme often contains the essential elements of a furniture programme. This early input assists the space planner in providing adequate square footage to accommodate the required furniture. It also assures that realistic budget figures can be developed.

WHO PREPARES IT

The library director and/or the library consultant might initiate the furniture or shelving programme, listing quantities, dimensions and location by individual item. Other elements, such as design, finish materials, and electrical and data requirements, can be included or developed with the interior designer in the design development phase of the project when architectural and millwork design are being formalised. The interior designer's scope of services may include specification of furniture and shelving, coordination with other design consultants, and installation observation, supervision and punchlist.

There are a variety of methods available to procure furniture and shelving. These include competitive bidding, sole source, proprietary specifications, government contracts, or a combination of the above. Frequently, the governing agency will determine which method is required, and frequently, this is determined by the dollar value of the purchases. The procurement method can also be determined by the owner's expertise, available assistance, or the time available to order and receive the furniture. All options should be explored to assure the best pricing and highest quality of service. The interior designer and the purchasing agent, if there is one, can pool their knowledge to produce the best buying situation for the client.

COMPETITIVE BID METHOD

This commonly used method of procuring furniture and equipment, requires a pool of qualified, interested bidders and clear, detailed specifications in order to achieve the desired result. Since, the paperwork required is substantial, it calls for more effort by the bidding agency, and sometimes discourages prospective bidders. The open advertisement policy, typical of competitive bidding, can attract bidders who lack the experience, expertise, and financial stability required for this highly specialised type of project. The primary purpose for following a bid procedure when procuring furniture or shelving is to be able to make the purchase at the lowest cost possible. Competitive bidding has merit for most initial purchases and for almost all large installations.

Specifications can be either generic specifications or one-manufacturer specifications. Almost all manufacturers will publish descriptive literature and written product specifications which can be a useful starting point for developing a specification. By specifying a particular product, or a one-manufacturer specification, the Owner can be certain of receiving exactly the desired product.

A generic specification, which opens the process to more potential bidders and other products, can be written using specific manufacturers' product descriptions as a starting point. Comparison of competitive products can be hard to dissect in terms of quality and design nuances without specific performance criteria for product comparison.

Writing specifications for shelving and furniture is a task that requires product familiarity and a great deal of experience, and the use of a consultant or purchasing agent is highly recommended. Although the idea behind competitive bidding is to allow the client to purchase the furniture at the lowest price possible, while maintaining the integrity of the design concept, frequently similar but unequal products are bid. This requires time-consuming evaluations by the client and the designer before the contract can be awarded.

This can be very difficult if the furniture is of a unique or custom design, in which case requiring samples with the bid is an important safeguard of quality and the ability to produce the product. Competitive bidding can open the door to potential claims and suits related to the bid award. If the price difference among bidders is great, the client often feels pressured to accept the lowest bid, which may not meet the design criteria. This possibility makes it extremely important to eliminate all unqualified vendors during the bid process.

Competitive bidding is often required for orders above a specified dollar amount. Its success depends greatly upon the integrity and depth of the specifications and the effort given to evaluating the bids as well as the bidder's qualifications and past experience. The use of bid and performance bonds also elevates the quality level of the prospective bidders.

SOLE SOURCE METHOD

This method involves specifying and purchasing a particular product without the bidding process. Proprietary specifications are developed which cite the product and materials by manufacturer name and model number. After requesting pricing from a qualified dealer who sells and installs the product, the client then prepares purchase orders that are sent directly to that dealer. No alternates are accepted, and no competitive bids are requested. The advantage of this method is that much fewer construction type details are required in the specifications, and the detailed and lengthy bidding process is avoided entirely.

The client and designer can be certain that they will receive what they want and that the design integrity of the project will be preserved. They can also take an active role in selecting the dealer who will provide the product. The disadvantage of this method is that the client does not have the opportunity to compare pricing, and may pay more for the product than he would in a competitive bid situation. Few governmental agencies permit this method unless the monetary value is quite small and under the minimum that requires public bid.

PROPRIETARY SPECIFICATIONS

This type of specification describes the product by manufacturer name, model or part number, and finish material designation. This product may be used as a "base bid", meaning that all bidders must base their bid on that particular product, or it may allow for substitutions with an "or equal" clause. The "base bid" proprietary specification is a closed specification; while the one that allows "or equals" is an open specification. Proprietary specifications provide more assurance that the actual product that was planned for and envisioned will be provided.

Therefore, it ensures a higher level of design control and makes the bidding and evaluation process easier, particularly when it is a base bid. The "or equal" clause, however, does allow the element of uncertainty to arise, as discussed under the Competitive Bid Method. One way to address this is to require that requests for substitutions be submitted prior to close of bid.

Brochures, samples, and other detailed information may be made part of this request. Suppliers or manufacturers can qualify as "Or equal" only when the specifier chooses to waive specifications or permit those suppliers or manufacturers to bid. The burden is on the supplier or manufacturer who has not been specified to convince the specifier that their product is equal for the purpose of a particular project.

GOVERNMENT CONTRACTS

If the governing agency does not require competitive bidding, the client may sometimes purchase the product directly from a government contract that has been set up between particular government agencies and the manufacturer. Contracts exist with the Federal government and various cities and counties, which can be accessed by other cities and counties. In addition, some states have set up a programme (CMAS in California) that allows client agencies to purchase off the Federal contract (GSA) or other multiple award contracts.

Working with these contracts allows the client to purchase products directly from the manufacturers at the greatest discount available. Storage, delivery and installation services must be purchased separately from an authorised office furniture dealer, and may be bid. This method also requires separate purchase orders for each manufacturer, rather than one order or contract with a dealer for the entire project. Most major furniture manufacturers have GSA contracts in place, although many smaller manufacturers who do not typically deal with government agencies do not. Some library furniture manufacturers also have GSA contracts. Not all of a manufacturer's product may be on GSA contract, so some research needs to occur before this method is selected.

WHICH TO USE WHEN?

Frequently the governing agency will determine whether competitive bidding is required, and whether substitutions may be allowed. If that is not the case, the interior designer should research the product and status of available government contracts with manufacturers to determine the feasibility of buying from these. Other options of sole sourcing or requesting proposals from several office furniture dealers can be explored to assure the best pricing and highest quality of service. The interior designer and the purchasing agent, if there is one, can pool their knowledge to produce the best buying situation for the client.

To prepare for a competitive bid process, the Owner, Owner's purchasing agent, or consultant must identify appropriate vendors for the product to be purchased. These vendors will receive a bid package including requirements for submitting a bid; a scope of work including quantities, detailed specifications, and a furniture or shelving plan; and general conditions. Frequently the bid form required for submitting a bid is included. Bidders may be required to attend a mandatory walk through (or pre-bid conference) to familiarise themselves with the site, field conditions, coordination issues and any obstacles that might complicate delivery or installation.

Typically when potential bidders have questions, they are answered in writing and the response is shared with all potential bidders. Additionally, the Owner may issue an Addendum or clarification prior to the bid's due date. The entire process from the issuance of the bid to the receipt and punch list of the furniture or shelving can take from six months to one year. Most library planners begin the process of procuring furniture and shelving simultaneous to the commencement of construction. The actual bidding should conclude approximately eight months before the product is needed.

This allows an appropriate amount of time for each of the phases to take place. At least two to three weeks should be allowed for the evaluation of the bids and any samples. Two to three weeks will be required for the issuance of the purchase order(s) or contract to the successful furniture vendor(s). Shop drawings and finish material submittals and approvals will require an additional three to four weeks. Typical production time for standard library furniture is sixteen weeks; custom would probably take longer. An additional two weeks for shipping is needed, particularly if the manufacturer is on the East Coast. The final installation can take anywhere from one week for a very small library, to up to four weeks for a large one. In total, the amount of time required after the receipt of bids can be twenty-six to thirty-two weeks.

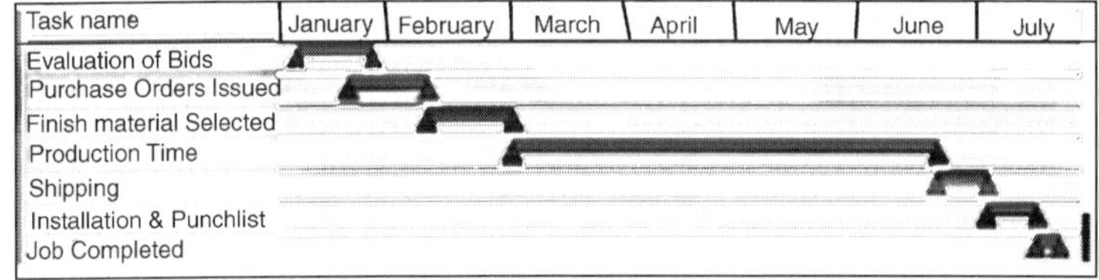

Fig. Timeline from Bidding to Punch List.

BID DOCUMENTS

A bid document must clearly establish the procedures, expectations and penalties involved when a Vendor wishes to submit a binding bid for a project. Such documents will most likely be issued on standard forms originating with the Architect, State, or other government agency, or any institutional purchasing department. These forms must contain criteria pertaining to date and time of bid closure, clarification of type and amount of bid security, and usually, a statement as to whether the opening and reading of bids will be an "open" or "closed" procedure.

The document should contain statements as to the anticipated time allowed for bid review, and the expected official award date on resultant contracts. The bid should be clearly noted to either "include" the applicable state sales tax, or, the bid should advise that sales tax will be "added" to the final contract amount at time of invoice. In either case, the bid should clarify that the sales tax is to be paid by the shelving Vendor (or Bidder) not the Owner. In the case of shelving, the requirement that the successful Bidder be responsible for structural engineering drawings and calculations must be made clear, as well as if they are to also be responsible for submitting and retaining approvals by pertinent authorities.

Instructions to Bidders

This section of the document will contain the outline rules for submitting a bid.

It should include, at a minimum, the following information:

- Brief summary of project.
- Governing agencies and applicable codes.
- Specific labour and other requirements.
- Who is qualified to bid.
- When are bids due and to whom, including date, time, and location.
- Where are questions to be directed, including telephone number.
- Who is the Owner's Representative.
- How are bids to be submitted and which forms are required.
- Are alternates acceptable.

Bidders' Responsibility

This section of the bid document outlines the bidders' responsibilities.

It might include some of the following:

- Bidder shall carefully examine the specifications and any drawings that might be made part of the specifications. All quantities and locations must be verified by the bidder.
- Bidder will be required to visit the site, because claims of misunderstanding as to either materials to be supplied, or work to be performed, will not receive consideration.
- Bidder will be required to visit the site and familiarise himself with unloading facilities and site conditions and take all necessary measurements.
- Bidder will request any alternates or substitutions in writing before the bid is due.
- Bidder will supervise all subcontractors.
- Bidder will become fully informed as to the nature and extent of the work required and its relation to any other work in the building.
- Any modification of a product needs to be clearly stated as a mandatory aspect of the specifications and Contract. For example: Will the successful bidder's standard product paint colour choices be acceptable, or, will a custom colour match be necessary to satisfy Contract requirements?
- Bidder will have all necessary permits and licenses.
- Preparation of any drawings and details in a form presentable to the *NAME OF YOUR CITY* Building Department and other governing agencies (DSA in California).

- Obtaining all necessary permits from authorities having jurisdiction.
- Bidder will have liability insurance and Workmen's Compensation insurance.
- Bidder will be bonded.
- Bidder will be required to submit shop drawings and finish samples as required by the owner.
- Bidder will provide information on storage fees if there is a delay clause in the contract.

Strategies for Eliminating Unqualified Bidders

These additional requirements can keep unqualified bidders from submitting a low bid for a product representing a product that does not meet specific requirements:

- Bid and performance bonds are required.
- Five references for similar projects must be submitted.
- A product sample or mock-up installed on site, typically no less than a three section range of shelving, or prototype table or chair, must be submitted.
- The bidder must have a minimum specified number years of experience.
- A lengthy product warranty is required.

Scope of Work

This section, which will identify specifically what the bid price must include, might include the following:

- These specifications, together with the shelving or furniture plan, will cover the complete installation of furniture. Unless otherwise specified, bidder shall be responsible for the furnishing of all materials, labour, and apparatus necessary for the proper installation of all shelving units and accessories called for in the Section "Shelving" or "Furniture" and/or the drawings.
- Installation is to include prepaid transportation.
- Bidder will coordinate with the Owner, Project Manager and/or General Contractor all dates involving arrival of materials at site and a staging area designation, and verify installation date with completion schedule.
- Bidder will deliver all furniture or shelving components to final building destination including movement to and from staging area.
- Bidder will set all items in place, leveled, aligned properly with adjacent units and in accordance with the layout provided Bidder will attach all units to the building where required, as part of the installation and provide any bracing as specified which is a part of this contract.
- Bidder shall install all units plumb and aligned properly with adjacent units and in accordance with layout provided.

- Bidder will leave the premises in clean condition with all packing materials and debris removed and all items free of dust and lint.
- Bidder will furnish written guarantees from the manufacturers.
- Bidder will be responsible for immediate minor repairs, paint touch up, or replacement of any damaged items.
- Bidder will be responsible for all claims against manufacturing defects or freight Damage.
- Bidder will instruct the client in the operation or adjustment of any items installed.

Workmanship

The minimum acceptable standards will vary depending on the product. *Some suggested standards covering workmanship includes the following*:

- Only top workmanship shall be acceptable.
- Framing parts shall be straight, all parts properly aligned and securely fastened, and all fittings neat in every respect.
- Any connections requiring bolting, welding, or riveting shall be neatly done.
- Any exposed surface of the installation that may be exposed shall be smooth and non-abrasive. Components with chipped paint will not be accepted.
- Wood with excessive graining will not be accepted.
- Other conditions as relate to the specific product.

ALTERNATE BIDS

Some bid documents are also used to produce a shopping list of alternates and possible additions to the base bid by including project desirables as alternate "ADD" or "DEDUCT" costs which the Owner may choose to fold into a contract resulting from the bid.

BID ALTERNATE

The City of ______________ may elect to additionally purchase any of the following:

OPTION A. LUMP SUM "**ADD**" For substituting sloped base shelves on Items F-45: F-46: F-50: 5-51. three (3) faces of three (3) sections only.
$______________

Fig. Bid Alternate Option.

CHANGE ORDERS

Frequently the bid document will require the Vendor to prepare and submit shop drawings for the work along with guidance in determining rough-ins for related services, and then accurate field checks of same before fabrication. This can avoid costly change orders during the fabrication or installation process due to "unforeseen conditions." When the field check points to unascertained building changes requiring non-standard product or installation considerations, a change order may be required to cover the additional cost.

ITEMISED BIDS

Occasionally the Owner may request a bid based on a per unit cost rather than a turnkey operation. An example of this procedure might be asking for prices for individual shelving units by type. Itemised bidding is not necessarily economical bidding. This procedure places a burden on Bidders to cost out their bid using single item cost basis for shipping, handling and installation, etc. While a bidder may price the item being bid with a "gambler's hope" that they will be awarded some accumulation of items being item bid, there is never the economy of scale and project control that turn-key project bidding affords.

USE OF LIBRARY FURNITURE

Planning for furniture cannot occur too early in a project. The amount of furniture and equipment required to support a library's programme will drive the amount of space and funding required to complete the project. Many planners begin to identify furniture and equipment needs during the programming phase. Planning for the furniture for a library project requires careful scheduling and budgeting and the assistance of a design professional with experience in the selection, evaluation, and procurement of specific items. When furniture is an afterthought it is frequently unavailable, mismatched to the architecture, or ill-suited for the intended location or purpose.

WHAT IS A FURNITURE PROGRAMME

Furniture is an essential element that makes a space functional. Without it, people cannot work, customers cannot be served, and the equipment and tools of the business cannot be housed. It typically supports all of the functions and services that must occur on a daily basis. Often, however, little attention is paid to it until just before it is needed. When it is addressed early, an adequate budget and production and delivery schedule can be built into the project.

Additionally, with pre-planning coordination issues, such as architectural design and electrical and data placement, can be discussed and resolved. A furniture programme provides a formal method for establishing the standards and requirements for all furniture, equipment, and sometimes millwork for the library project. It should list all of the furniture items to be placed in each area of the library, along with preferred dimensions, quantity, equipment to be housed, and any electrical and data requirements. It should also incorporate any staff workstation standards that are to be used. The programme may be adjusted as the furniture plan and building design develops, since, it provides the basis for the final furniture list and specification. Existing furniture to be reused should also be noted indicating any refurbishment specific items might require.

A simple furniture programme can be prepared using a spreadsheet, which can be sorted by any number of fields; *e.g.*, Location, Item Name, Finish, or Note. Each unique furniture item can be given an alphanumeric code or a sequential numbering system can be used. The spreadsheet can contain an unlimited number of fields, but would most likely include some of those suggested as well as a notation regarding power or data requirements, specific equipment dimensional requirements, and an estimated cost.

WHEN IS IT NEEDED

The furniture programme should be developed in the programming phase of a project. The building programme often contains the essential elements of a furniture programme. This early input assists the space planner in providing adequate square footage to accommodate the required furniture. It also assures that realistic budget figures can be developed.

WHO PREPARES IT

The library director and/or the library consultant will initiate the furniture programme, listing quantities, dimensions and location by individual item. Other elements, such as design, finish materials, and electrical and data requirements, can be included or developed with the interior designer in the design development phase of the project, when architectural and millwork design are being formalised.

The Interior Designer can be employed directly by the Client (Owner) or by the Architect as a member of the design team. The primary benefit to employing the Interior Designer directly is having an independent and objective advocate whose only focus is the function and aesthetics of the interior space. The main benefit to having the Interior Designer under contract to the Architect is enhanced communication and closer project coordination. In either case the Interior Designer's activities will be closely coordinated with both parties.

The Interior Designer's scope of services may include space-planning, development of the furniture programme and budget, design of custom millwork and furniture, selection of interior finish materials and design motif, interior signage design and specification, specification of furniture and shelving, coordination with other design consultants, and installation observation. At the minimum the scope should include several meetings to discuss the function of the interior spaces and the furniture requirements and several meetings to present layout, selection of specific items, and presentation boards of proposed colours and finish materials. The Interior Designer's fee can be a flat fee for a specific scope of work, an hourly rate for consultation services, a percentage of the furniture and equipment to be purchased, or a dollar per square foot cost of the total construction project, although the latter is not common.

Qualified designers belong to professional interior design associations, such as ASID or IIDA, are certified in the State of California by CCIDC, and will have references for previous work available. Interior designers who specialise in libraries and public facilities will have a better understanding of the requirements of a public library.

There are a variety of methods available to procure furniture. These include competitive bidding, sole source, proprietary specifications, government contracts, or a combination of the above. Frequently the governing agency will determine which method is required, and frequently this is determined by the dollar value of the purchases.

The procurement method can also be determined by the owner's expertise, available assistance, or the time available to order and receive the furniture. All options should be explored to assure the best pricing and highest quality of service. The interior designer and the purchasing agent, if there is one, can pool their knowledge to produce the best buying situation for the client.

EVALUATING EXISTING FURNITURE

The reuse or refurbishment of existing furniture is sometimes desirable, particularly when furniture is high quality and relatively new. Evaluating the furniture requires an assessment of its condition, quality, age and projected life span. The cost of refurbishment is also a consideration. An inventory of the items should be compiled, as well as a cost evaluation comparing the use of the existing furniture versus the cost of buying new. The interior designer or furniture dealer, who has expertise in this area, should provide the evaluation.

Some items are easily refurbished, while others require labour-intensive attention that may make this process almost as expensive as new. Typically, wood case goods and metal items must be taken off-site to be stripped and refinished or electrostatically painted. Minor touch up may be done on site. Seating is typically not worth refurbishing, as the cost of pick-up, refinishing, reupholstery, and delivery may total more than the cost of a new chair.

An exception would be if the chair were of very high quality or a recent purchase. Another element to be considered is whether the design of the existing furniture will fit into the new or remodelled library, particularly in the public areas. Ideally, the furniture will enhance the architectural design. New furniture can be selected or designed so that this goal is achieved, while existing furniture may not contribute to the desired effect.

A final critical factor to consider relates to quantity and availability. Is there a sufficient number of the existing item available for reuse to fit the new plan? If not, is the item still on the market and easily obtained? If not, what is available on the market that will match the existing item in the new library?

TIMELINE

The selection and budgeting of furniture is typically done during the design development phase of a project, while the specifications and any required drawings are produced during the construction documents phase. Because of the electrical and data coordination required, this must occur early in the project. The actual bidding should conclude approximately eight months before the product is needed.

This allows an appropriate amount of time for each of the phases to take place. At least two to three weeks should be allowed for the evaluation of the bids and any samples. Two to three weeks will be required for the issuance of the purchase order(s) or contracts to the successful furniture vendor(s). Shop drawings and finish material submittals and approvals will require an additional three to four weeks.

Typical production time for standard library furniture is sixteen weeks; custom would probably take longer. An additional two weeks for shipping is needed, particularly if the manufacturer is on the East Coast. The final installation can take anywhere from one week for a very small library to up to four weeks for a large one. In total, the amount of time required after the receipt of bids is twenty-six to thirty-two weeks.

Counting forwards from furniture programming, design review, and the lengthy decisionmaking process that needs to occur before the specifications are written and the bids issued, one can assume that the entire process requires approximately 14 to 16 months and should begin before the groundbreaking. During the six to eight month period prior to the issuance of bids, the owner and the Interior Designer will review furniture layout and specific furniture items, "test drive" certain pieces of furniture, and make final decisions on the style and motif for the project.

Many libraries have underestimated the length of time it takes from the issuance of bids until the new furniture is in place, particularly the subtle difference between the date the manufacture of the furniture is completed and the actual date the furniture arrives on site.

COORDINATION WITH MILLWORK

In a well-designed project, the public area millwork and furniture are an extension of the architecture and complement the over-all theme of the library. The ultimate coordination is achieved with custom furniture, which can be designed to replicate millwork details and finishes providing a totally cohesive design throughout the facility. If this is not an option, standard (catalog) library furniture can be selected with careful attention to shapes, details and finish materials that are compatible with the millwork.

CUSTOM VERSUS CATALOG

The architect and interior designer often prefer custom designed furniture. It brings a unique look to the project that complements the architectural statement and avoids the standard, cookie-cutter approach of manufactured library furniture that is so prevalent. It also permits custom sized pieces that are designed to fit unusual spaces and the equipment that is housed in them. The quality of custom furniture can be much higher than that of catalog furniture. Local craftsmen, employing time-honoured techniques for building furniture by hand, may be available to produce custom furniture. Joinery and other detailing will be superior.

There is no limit to the types and combinations of materials that can be used, unlike catalog furniture, which usually permits only a few wood species, standard laminates, and a small range of colours for metal trim. Custom furniture can often be a good value, with pricing that may be competitive with higher end catalog furniture, depending upon the complexity of the design and the materials used. In addition, if it is locally made, there are no freight charges from the East or Midwest, where most library furniture is manufactured.

Depending upon the manufacturer's workload, production time may be shorter, and if it is local, the two weeks of delivery time are shortened substantially. Standard library furniture manufacturers have fixed production schedules and are rarely open to negotiation unless the project is large. The challenges with custom furniture occur when replacements or additional pieces are required. New items that are not identical to the original furniture will require professional design drawings. The cost of producing a few custom pieces may be more than when they were part of a large order.

Typically custom manufacturers are small firms, and may be less stable than the larger vendors. It may be necessary to find another manufacturer if the original one is no longer in business. Catalog furniture, on the other hand, is generally available for as long as the manufacturer is in business, so it is easy for library staff to simply order another piece that will match, even when many years have passed. There is a consistent level of quality of construction and finishing with a given manufacturer, and typically, product samples can be reviewed before ordering, either via individual samples or visiting a similar installation. Project references should also be furnished to verify comfort and durability.

Because the furniture is massproduced, engineered and manufactured, the pricing at the low to mid range of product is typically lower than that of custom furniture. There is also a fairly broad range of product styles to fit most budgets, ranging from low to very high end. Many library furniture manufacturers will customise their standard product by changing dimensions, wood species, finish colour, minor design details, or create a new piece to match standard product. Warranties are easily obtained from standard furniture manufacturers, and they usually have the history and stability to make them meaningful.

ALTERNATIVE FURNITURE

Office furniture can be used in place of standard library or custom furniture, particularly when budget is of primary concern. Although office furniture is not constructed for the heavy usage and frequent abuse that library furniture experiences, ergonomic task chairs and modular systems furniture can have a place in the library. The latter is most often used for staff workstations but may substitute for the traditional wood carrel or study station. The acoustic properties make it especially suitable for that usage. Manufacturers who supply chairs for restaurants are also a viable source for study chairs, as long as the construction is extremely durable and incorporates the use of stretchers with wood chairs. They offer a much wider variety of styles and materials than the library furniture manufacturers. Steel framed chairs made by office furniture manufacturers may also make durable reader chairs.

PERFORMANCE STANDARDS

There are many points to consider when selecting library furniture, with functionality and durability being primary. Whenever possible, performance standards should be reviewed prior to making a decision. Although there is no universal, comprehensive set of furniture standards, there are some standards available for individual items.

It currently lists the American National Standard for Office Furnishings (ANSI) standards for the following products: General Purpose Office Chairs, Lateral Files, Vertical Files, Lounge Seating, Desk Products, Panel Systems, and the BIFMA Ergonomics Guideline for VDT (Visual Display Terminal) Furniture. Static electricity generation standards are available for floor covering products, but not for furniture, even though it may be a contributing factor.

Because static electricity is typically the result of the contact of two dissimilar materials, one being clothing or shoe soles, it is difficult to predict when it will occur. When computer use dictates minimal static electricity, metal and vinyl should be avoided.

TECHNOLOGY INTEGRATION

The importance of integrating technology requirements into the furniture at an early stage cannot be stressed strongly enough.

BUDGETING

Early and accurate budgeting of the furniture will aid in achieving a successful project and prevent unpleasant surprises later. Once the furniture programme and an initial furniture plan have been prepared, a preliminary budget can be estimated. It is important to use realistic itemised costs at this point rather than general cost per square foot figures typically used by cost estimators and others who have no expertise in furniture selection and specification. Allowances should be included for freight, delivery, installation, relocation and sales tax. A contingency amount should be included for unforeseen items and unanticipated price increases, particularly if the project timeline is a long one. The budget should be updated as the furniture plan is revised and more decisions are made about furniture style and materials. Life Cycle Costing is sometimes a factor in budgeting and specifying furniture.

This method includes elements other than the acquisition cost to determine the actual cost over time. Initial costs may include discounts, shipping, delivery, handling, assembly, storage, installation, personnel training, etc. Other elements to be considered include service life of the product, recurring operational costs such as electrical power required, recurring maintenance costs, etc. A lengthy checklist is prepared and thoroughly evaluated by the design professional in this approach. Life Cycle Costing adds another dimension to the budgeting process and provides additional quality control by analysing the cost of the product over its lifespan, with the added potential for operational and maintenance cost savings that may be realised by the library.

Since, the labour cost of these items over a period of time is often more than the initial product cost, the savings can be substantial and more than make up the difference between a low and high bid. Because this is a complicated procedure requiring a great deal of information and analysis, it may not always be warranted. However, including the option for using Life Cycle Costing in the furniture specification puts the bidders on notice that the bid evaluation may include much more than initial cost and leaves the door open for its use if desired.

OPTIONS AND COMPARISONS

The variety of materials that can be used in furniture, particularly custom furniture, is practically limitless. It includes all types of metal, wire mesh, vinyl, glass, stone, fabric, lightweight concrete, Plexiglasè, plastic laminates, molded plastic, solid surface materials, tile, Formicaè, linoleum and, solid wood or wood veneer. Standard furniture typically limits itself to a few of these materials with less variety of colour and finish.

SELECTION CRITERIA

In addition to functionality and cost, appropriateness to the over-all design concept is one of the first criterion used in selecting furniture finish materials. If the furniture is custom, then some of the materials used in the millwork and architectural backgrounds should be used in the furniture. Careful attention should be paid to matching materials and stain colours and sample submittals for all products should be scrutinised and compared. Standard (catalog) library furniture can often be customised through the use of special stains, wood species, or paint colours sometimes at an increased cost.

In this case, extra care is needed to provide samples to the manufacturer for matching and to check submittals for accuracy. Some manufacturers have a difficult time achieving satisfactory results, and others will not attempt custom work. Durability is an important criterion in selecting materials. If a material won't stand up to heavy use and wear or can't be easily repaired, then it probably shouldn't be used. Often, longevity depends upon the choices made within a material category. For example, some woods are harder than others, natural, matte finishes show fewer scratches, some paint methods are superior to others, some laminates have special coatings or embedded metal particles to increase their lifespan, etc.

Table. Hard Wood Species and Pressure Required to Mar (in Pounds).

Wood Species	Pressure to Mar	Wood Species	Pressure to Mar
Hickory	1820	Walnut	1010
Maple	1450	Maple	950
White Oak	1360	Cherry	950
Beech	1300	Gum	850
Red Oak	1290	Elm	830
Yellow Birch	1260	Sycamore	7.70
Green Ash	1200	Alder	590

To minimize static electricity generation in sensitive computer areas, wood or other non-conductive materials should be used rather than plastic coated or metal furniture. Vinyl upholstery can also contribute to the problem. Wool or wool nylon blends would be a better choice. Colour and texture are other aspects of material finish selection that impacts the appearance and durability of the product. Very light or very dark solid colours, particularly with no pattern, can be poor choices, regardless of the material, as they provide little or no soil or abuse hiding properties. Very heavy textures can be problematic, as they tend to attract dirt and bacteria.

A design professional can find the perfect material to fit the aesthetic as well as the durability criteria. Upholstery fabric requires another level of knowledge in order to select the best product. Different yarns and constructions react in a variety of ways to the heavy wear experienced in a library. In addition, they have varying flame resistance. The Association for Contract Textiles (ACT) has established minimum standards and test results for fabrics. Most commercially used textile samples have a card attached bearing the ACT symbols indicating compliance with these minimum standards.

The tests and standards cover such things as abrasion resistance (how many "rubs" the product can sustain before it begins to wear), flame resistance, colourfastness (how many hours of sunlight a product can endure before it begins to fade), breaking strength, pill resistance, seam slippage, and mildew resistance.

The American Society for Testing and Materials (ASTM), a non-government group, develops fire safety codes and standards and is involved in developing testing procedures. The greatest variety of upholstery fabrics is now made of nylon or nylon blends, and they are at the top of the durability ratings. Wool has long been a top quality upholstery fabric, known for its durability and higher price.

Polyolefin fabric has also become more popular due to its ability to be cleaned. When comparing the ACT or ASTM ratings, however, nylon fabrics will typically have outstanding results. Where a fabric is located in the facility with regard to exposure to sunlight is a factor which should be considered particularly in regard to fading. State fire safety rules also apply to upholstery fabrics.

The minimum California standard for this product is TB 117. It is mandatory that all seating products comply with this technical bulletin. Another, more stringent State bulletin is TB 133, which applies to upholstered seating in public assembly areas without sprinklers. It is important to scrutinise all of the test results for proposed fabrics and assess the usage conditions before making a selection.

MAINTENANCE ISSUES

Even the most carefully selected and highest quality furniture materials must be maintained. However, these are usually the items most often overlooked or carelessly cleaned by the custodial staff. Maintenance instructions should be requested from each manufacturer and kept together in a file for reference. Often the life of a material is determined by the care it receives. Wood, for example, can retain its appearance indefinitely if the finish is renewed periodically. Many materials, particularly laminates and vinyl molding or finishes attached with a specific gluing compound, are actually harmed by improper cleaning compounds or excessive pressure. Correct cleaning procedures will help preserve the value of this significant investment.

COORDINATION

In addition to the focused attention on individual furniture pieces, the over-all theme of the project must be kept in mind. All of the disparate materials should produce a harmonious, cohesive entirety. Having a myriad of resources from which to choose, and being able to visualise the end result are attributes, which the professional can bring to the project.

CHAIRS

Several different types of chairs are found in the library, among them the lounge chair, reader chair, and task or ergonomic chair, which is on casters, adjustable, and scientifically designed to support the body. Stools, benches, rocking chairs, and sofas are used as well.

Chairs in the public area can be upholstered, solid wood, metal frame with molded plastic shell or upholstery, or a variety of other combinations of materials. Upholstered chairs are usually more comfortable, give a more residential, home like feeling to the space, and provide the opportunity for colour and pattern accents.

Non-upholstered chairs may be easier to maintain and more durable, although plastic and wood show scratches and handprints. One of the more important factors in considering a chair is its scale in relationship to the intended user, the architecture and surrounding furniture.

Lounge Chairs

Lounge chairs are larger, upholstered chairs designed for casual reading or relaxing. Some manufacturers will produce children's size lounge chairs also. The dimensions of the chair are an important consideration so that the chair itself is not too large to move, the pitch of the back is comfortable, and the seat is not so deep as to make it difficult to stand up or prevent the occupant's feet from touching the floor. The height of the back and the arms also impact the chair's comfort. There is no substitute for sitting in a chair to determine its suitability; catalog photographs cannot tell the story.

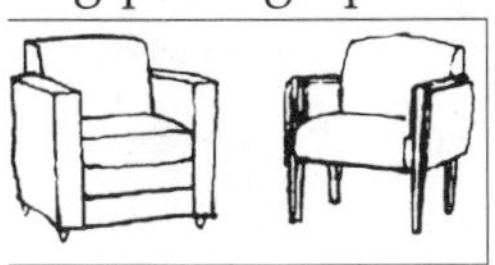

Fig. Lounge Chair with Upholstered Side and Arms (Left), and with Wood Cap on Chair's Arms (Right).

The chair's construction is also important, particularly the structural materials used, type of upholstery filling and fabric covering. Ease of recovering and cleaning should also be factors.

Because of their scale, large patterned fabrics are often used to make these chairs focal points. In this case, a COM (Customer's Own Material) may be specified providing a wider range of fabrics over and above the manufacturers' own sometimes limited offerings.

Fig. Lounge Chair With Wood Arms and Sides and Footstool.

For durability, consider elimination of piping on upholstery seams, using tight or fixed seat and back cushions, and selecting a wood cap on the chair's arms where the wear is likely to be the heaviest.

Reader Chairs

Reader chairs receive more use and abuse than any other piece of furniture in the library. They seem to present a challenge to patrons who have discovered many creative ways to occupy them. Since, these chairs must be comfortable and durable, much care should be given to their selection. Different sizes should be used for young children, juveniles and adults. Standard wood reader chairs are seen in many libraries, some with a few new design elements to update them. The seats and backs may be upholstered or non-upholstered. In addition, there is a wide range of other wood chairs, metal-framed chairs and thermoplastic molded chairs manufactured by contract furniture companies that may be appropriate. Many of these have been manufacturer-tested for performance, and the results should be reviewed before a decision is made. Samples should also be requested for evaluation, which should include investigation of the type of joinery used for the various parts, the size and placement of the rails and stretchers, the size of structural members and whether they are continuous, type of fastening hardware used, the diameter of metal frame tubing and other details.

Fig. All Wood Sled (or Sleigh Base) Reader Chairs, Armless (Left) and with Arms (Right), With Side Table and Table Lamp.

Styles may vary from four-legged, sled based, steel framed, and with or without arms. When arms are selected for reader chairs, it is critical that the arms fit under the tabletop or carrel work surface. This should be tested on the specific table or carrels intended for use since, the addition of a skirt or panel to a table can lower the under-table clearance. The chair's weight is also a factor in the ease with which it can slide in and out under the table. Sled based chairs can be quite heavy and difficult to move, but with glides attached, they can extend the life of a carpet in a way that chair legs being pulled in and out over the finished carpet can not. Many libraries prefer heavier chairs, which are less likely to migrate around the building.

Fig. Reader Seats, with Legs, With Upholstered Seat and Back, Armless (Left) and with Arms (Right), Floor Lamp, and Side Table.

If upholstered, fire and life safety code requirements apply to the fabric and filling used. It is always a good idea to ask the manufacturer if the chair is appropriate for this type of heavy use facility, or if it has been used in other libraries. Checking actual references is time well spent.

Task Chairs

Task chairs are often found in both public and staff areas of the library. These chairs are ergonomically designed to adjust to the user's body via mechanisms ranging from simple seat height to a multitude of sophisticated adjustments. The back and seat may tilt or be fixed, back tension may be increased or decreased, the back and arms may lower or rise, etc. Casters are attached to the base, which facilitate easy movement. A particular style of chair may come in a variety of overall widths, depths and heights, with or without arms, so that the right size can be tailored to the appropriate use.

Armless chairs are often used when the space is confined or when the occupant is in and out of the chair frequently. People who spend significant time in the chair working at a computer or completing other seated tasks often prefer chairs with arms. When specified for staff areas, samples should be requested for trial.

The ease of adjustment is especially important so that the user doesn't need to vacate the chair in order to adjust it. The pneumatic lift mechanism is favoured for that reason. Since, these chairs receive heavy usage, strong warranties are advisable.

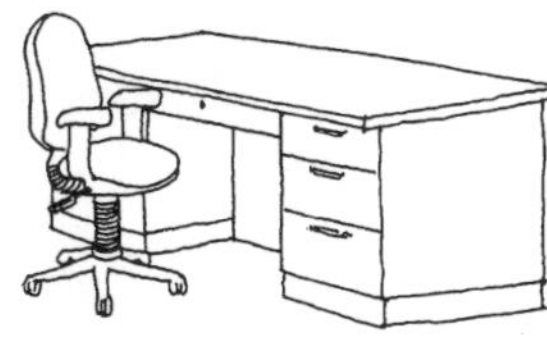

Fig. Ergonomic Task Chair at Standard Double Pedestal Desk

Criteria for evaluating an ergonomic chair include:

- Arm rests which adjust independently and are short enough so the occupant can get close to the work surface or which fit under the work surface.
- Lower back support.
- Stain and fire resistant or open mesh upholstery.
- Seat and backs units, which can be field replaced.
- Seat and back units which move independently; adjustable back rest height
- Adjustable tilt tension.
- Pneumatic seat lift for adjustable seat height.
- Stable base with five star pedestal support preferred.
- Heavy duty casters, hooded if available.
- Minimum five to ten year product warranty.
- Electrostatic discharge rating.

Other Reader Seats

Other seating options include sofas, rocking chairs, benches, upholstered cushions, and stools. Sofas or loveseats are sometimes used in the preschool area so that a parent and child can read together.

They are rarely used in the other public seating areas since, people tend to want their own space and dislike sitting close to strangers. Benches are frequently used in waiting areas, such as the lobby to provide a brief respite. They also may appear in children's areas where picture book tables with sloped tops are used. Stools also can provide short-term seating in children's areas or at catalog computer stations. Upholstered floor cushions provide impromptu seating in the children's reading or story time areas and can be creative, whimsical elements when special shapes such as animals or bright colours are used.

TABLES AND CARRELS

Tables

Tables are an important component of the library furniture plan. The elements of a table must produce a balanced construction that will be strong and stable. Tables that are not designed to carry the load required of heavy usage will wobble, sag or tip under certain conditions. Review of performance tests and actual use experience is valuable.

The strength of a table depends upon its structural support (legs or base), the stability of its top and supporting rails and keels, and the quality of its joints and attachment hardware.

Tables may be constructed of all wood, wood and laminate, wood and metal, metal and laminate and other materials. The style may feature four wood legs with a variety of rail and stretcher placements, panel ends, metal legs, metal or wood columns and may have a rectangular, round, square or other geometric shape top.

Fig. Single Station Panel End Reader Table.

The panel end design presents an opportunity for added stability, additional design details and provides the maximum cable-hiding abilities. The panels, however, can become an attractive target for kicking and foot propping by the occupants. They also create a heavier appearance than the four-legged table.

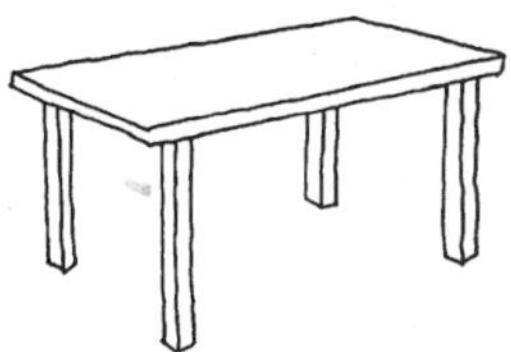

Fig. Standard Reader Table for Four with Legs.

The latter are lighter in scale, easier to move, and provide the most flexible seating. If current or future use dictates any electrical or data connections, the legs must be designed to house cabling, or a centrally located vertical chase can perform that function. The typical adult reading or reference table is a 36" x 72", or 48" x 72", rectangle that can seat four people, two per side. This provides suitable space for books, and writing materials.

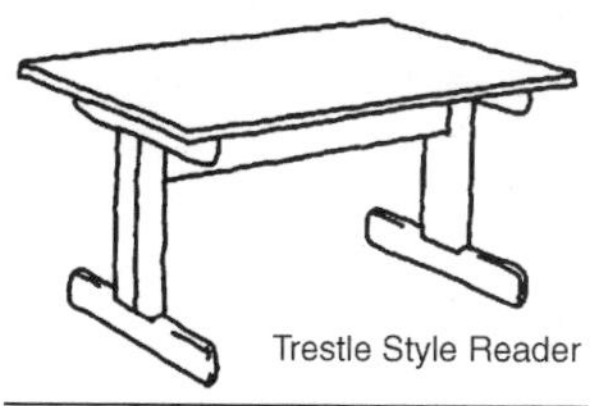

Fig. Trestle Style Reader Table for Four.

Small, square tables are sometimes used in informal reading areas, and round tables are frequently preferred in cafes, lounges, browsing areas, and juvenile and children's areas because of their body-friendly curves and egalitarian seating arrangement.

Fig. Single Pedestal Square Table for Four.

The material selected for the tabletop determines how well it maintains its appearance as it ages. Wood provides a classic, rich look and can be refinished, but it presents an almost irresistible temptation for carving and scratching. High-pressure laminate plastics are extremely durable and come in a wide variety of patterns, textures and colours. Some manufacturers produce laminates with metal or other particles on the surface to provide greater protection and longer wear.

Small patterns or textures will hide abuse better than solid colours, particularly dark ones. High gloss laminates, which can create glare, should never be used in horizontal applications. Solid surfacing materials, such as Corian®, may also be appropriate for tabletops, although they would be much more expensive, and are usually offered for custom furniture only. Appropriate sizes should be selected for young children and older juveniles, as well as adults.

The table design often will include task lighting and electrical and data components all of which should be integrated into the table and should provide wire management as well.

Criteria for evaluating a table include the following:

- Appropriate size for function.
- Scale for location.
- Stability and weight.
- Durability and mar resistance.
- Finish.
- Reflectivity of work surface.
- Ease of maintenance of item and surrounding area.
- Availability of accessible pieces (or compatible units).
- Ability to provide power and data at the work surface if required.

Carrels

Originally designed for quiet study, carrels are now used to house a variety of electronic equipment from computers and printers to television monitors, other video equipment, and audio listening devices. The style and materials selected should complement that of the other library furniture, particularly the tables. Smaller sizes and lower work surfaces should be specified for children. As with tables, the durability of carrels depends upon their structure.

They may have legs of wood or metal or panel ends, or may be part of a larger structure that forms a hexagon or other geometric shape. The typical rectangular shape may be single faced for one user, or double faced, where two carrels share a central panel in a face-to-face configuration. They may also be ganged or joined together using one dividing panel to form longer runs of single-faced or double-faced carrels. These are typically known as "starter" and "adder" units.

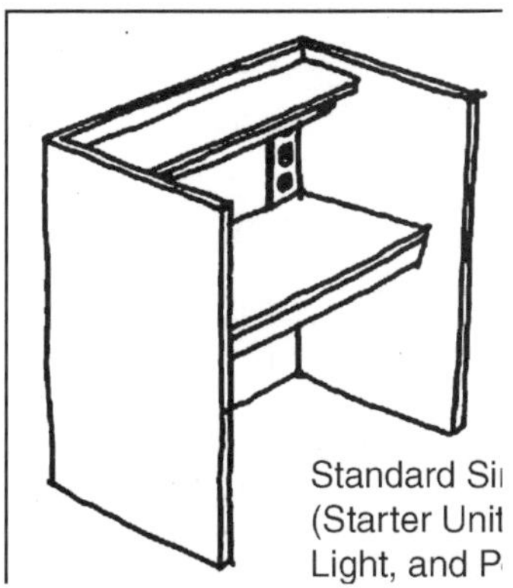

Fig. Standard Single Station Study Carrel (Starter Unit) with Overhead Shelf, Task Light, and Power and Data Strip.

Carrels joined together may share electrical and data cabling and connection up to a maximum determined by the equipment load. The manufacturer should install UL Rated electrical components within the carrel. Reader carrels can contain a shelf above the work surface for books and a fluorescent light under the shelf. If large equipment is to be housed, the upper shelf and light are removed to provide clearance. Custom carrels may be designed with storage units and shelves for the various equipment and media.

Because the vertical panels of the carrel define the dimensions of the work surface, it is important that sizes and placement of the equipment have been taken into account. Computer use may dictate a lower work surface or an adjustable one, or a keyboard tray. However, accessibility standards must be considered here as well.

At least five per cent, or not less than one, of each seating element in a library must comply with accessibility guidelines. Custom carrels can also be included in the general construction contract and be designed as built-in casework utilising the perimeter walls as the back or side of the carrel. This can reduce costs, but will also reduce flexibility, and may provide issues with replacement of work surfaces should carrels become damaged. If carrels are designed utilising a perimeter wall, the walls will quickly become marred and damaged by feet.

Application of a protective material, such as perforated metal, can protect the surface of the wall.

Technology Stations

Fig. Custom Six-station Technology Pod at University of Southern California's Leavey Library.

Technology tables, carrels, and counters to house electronic workstations in either the public or staff work areas, are available from systems furniture manufacturers, office furniture vendors, and library furniture vendors. They are available in as many shapes and varieties as other public and staff furniture, including single surface workstations, counters, side-by-side, or back-to-back, or in circular or hexagonal "pods" accommodating four, five, six, or more stations. Multi- station configurations, which are heavier and occupy a large footprint, should not be used if flexibility is a concern. They are difficult to relocate and are frequently hardwired to a power source provided through a floor box.

They are available as sit down stations, or stand up since, many libraries allocate a percentage of the technology stations to be stand up stations in the public area to discourage long term use. Of the many optional features available in a technology station, the most frequently included are a "sling" or lockable CPU cabinet, a built-in mouse pad, an articulated keyboard carrier that can slide under the work surface, and audio jacks or electrical outlets on the work surface. Of primary concern in selecting a technology carrel is the depth required to house the hardware and the width to accommodate both the hardware and paper materials if this is desired.

Of further consideration is whether or not a printer or scanner is required adjacent to the computer workstation, and the dimensions of this printer or scanner, and any other peripheral equipment that will be housed on the work surface. The required electrical and data components should be an integral part of the carrel. Recommendations for the minimum dimensions for a technology carrel are a depth of no less than 30" with 24" acceptable for a "dumb" terminal and a width of no less than 36" for a library catalog only station, with all others at 42", 48" or 60" wide.

Training Room Furniture

Training Room furniture shares many of the same characteristics and can be purchased from office furniture dealers or educational and institutional furniture dealers. Because different instructors frequently reconfigure training rooms, the tables should be light enough to be moved around and reconfigured frequently. Many vendors offer training tables on casters with locking brakes. Units are available in various shapes including semi-rounds, and curved trapezoidal pieces in order to configure the room in horseshoes, or concentric horseshoes. Smaller units, less than 24" wide, are available that can be interlocked between tables and can be used to house CPUs or printers. Tables that gang or attach together and that house all of the required electrical and data outlets are typically preferred. Close coordination with building outlet placement is essential.

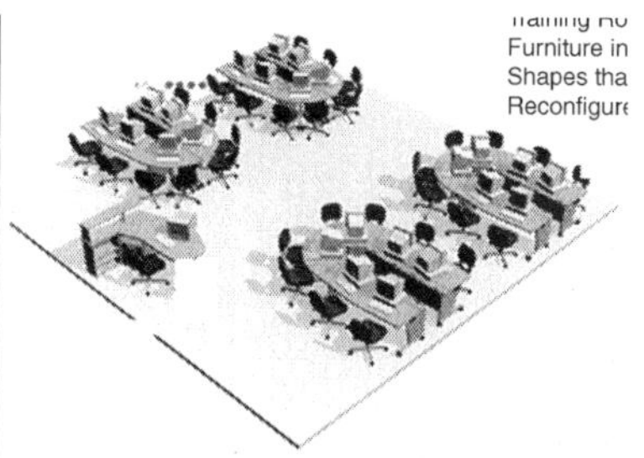

Fig. Training Room Furniture in Various Shapes that are Easily Reconfigured.

SYSTEMS FURNITURE

Other types of furniture are often used in the public areas of the library as well as in the staff areas. Modular office systems may be used for carrels or public staff desks. These systems consist of vertical panels of varying heights and sizes containing vertical slotted strips from which such components as work surfaces, shelves, and storage cabinets and files are hung (cantilevered or mounted similar to a bookstack construction.) The panels can connect together to form L or U shapes.

If electrical, telephone and data jacks are provided in accessible horizontal channels at the base or work surface height of the panel, they are known as "powered" panels. Other panels which provide simple slots or grommets for cord pass through are less expensive and more easily installed. The panel surface may be fabric, laminate or wood; the components are usually plastic laminate.

Fabric panels provide acoustical value that hard surfaces lack. A number of tests have been performed on panel systems relating to flammability, acoustic properties, stability and durability. Systems produced by different manufacturers are not interchangeable, so a detailed evaluation of products is important before locking into a long-term commitment. In some systems, additional space is required for the connecting posts, which may add up to a substantial increase if many workstations are joined together.

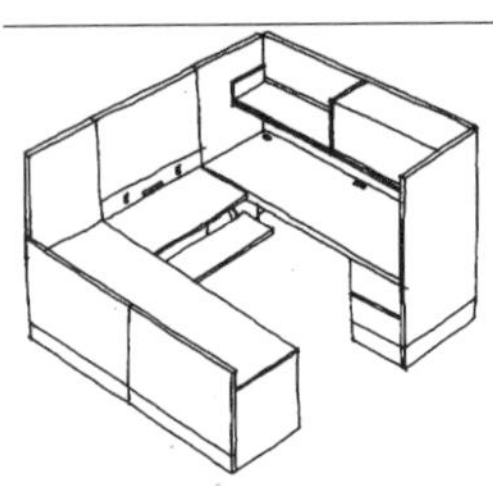

Fig. U-Shaped Systems Furniture Workstation with 60 High Panels and 42″ High Panels, Keyboard Carrier, Overhead Shelf, Overhead Storage, and Under Counter Pedestal Unit.

A variety of storage modules are available with systems furniture, including pedestals that fit under the work surface and cabinets and shelves that hang above it. Pedestal units typically house files and may contain a combination of file and box drawers. Some are completely mobile on casters, while others may be hung from the work surface or sit on the floor and support it.

The upper cabinet units typically have flipper doors that open up and slide over or into the cabinet. Open cabinets and shelf type units may also hang off the upper panels.

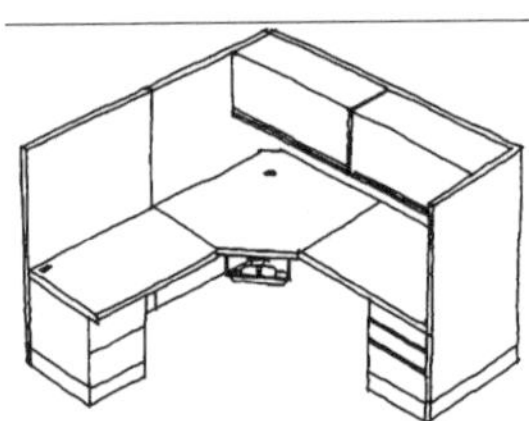

Fig. L-Shaped Systems Furniture Workstation with 60″ High Panels, 45°Corner Unit, Keyboard Carrier, Overhead Storage Units, and Two Under Counter Pedestal Units.

When systems furniture is used in large open areas, the freestanding panels form the workstations, and all components hang off vertical strips on each end of the panel.

When it is used in small areas or offices, panels may not be needed, and the components can be attached to wall-mounted strips. Additional legs or panel ends for work surfaces may be required. Using the wall strips saves a great deal of money over the use of panels.

However, since, the panels contain the cabling raceways, all equipment would now connect directly to the building power rather than the panel. The challenge of hanging cords and cables will need to be addressed.

While panel based workstations can be easily moved, wall-hung units are less flexible and require patching and painting when wall strips are relocated. In addition, walls must be clear of windows, switches, fire extinguisher cabinets, chair rails, thermostats, and exit signs.

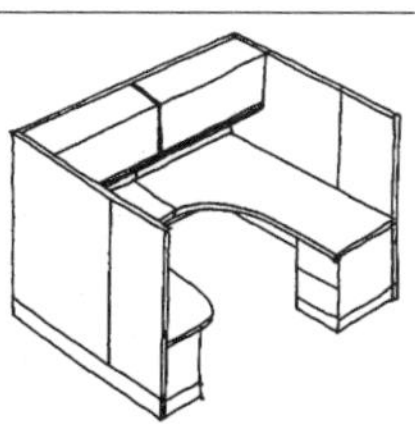

Fig. U –Shaped Workstations with 60" High Fabric–covered Panels, Under Counter Pedestal Unit, and Overhead Storage Cabinets.

Many grades of fabric are available for the panels, with the resultant price increase as the patterns become more sophisticated. Basic simple weaves in solid or heathered colours begin at grade 1, with several higher levels after that. In a large project with many panels, the choice of fabric can have a significant impact on the overall cost. If the system furniture manufacturer's fabric choices are not desirable, COM or Customer's Own Material may be specified. However, only vertical panel fabric (100 per cent polyester) may be used, and the furniture manufacturer must approve the fabric in advance. Specifying COM may increase delivery time as the fabric must be ordered separately and received by the furniture manufacturer before panel production can start.

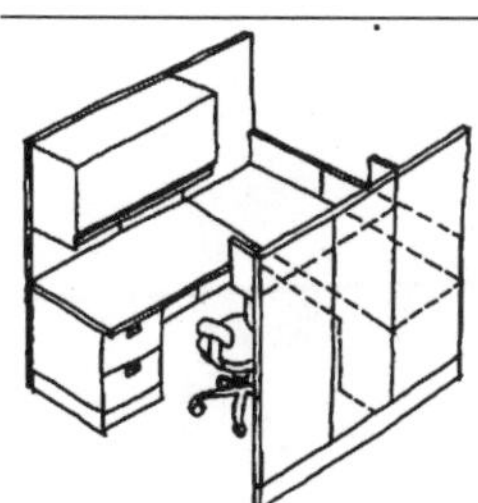

Fig. L-shaped Systems Furniture Workstation with Panel Mounted Work Surface, Wall Mounted Work Surface, Freestanding Panel, Under Counter Pedestal Units, and Overhead Storage Cabinets.

FILE CABINETS

File cabinets are frequently located in both public and staff areas. Available floor space often determines whether vertical or lateral files are used, although the latter are now the most common and consume less space since, they are typically 18" deep. Another consideration if the files form a walkway is whether adequate exiting space exists when the drawers are open.

The 30" deep vertical files often cannot fulfil this requirement. Files can be configured in many ways and for different media, and should have been tested for stability and strength. They are available in all steel, steel frames with laminate or wood cladding, all laminate or all wood. The use of a steel frame enhances the strength of the cabinet. Only quality file cabinets that are stable, weighted and balanced, and will not tip over when drawers are opened should be used in library applications. Many products that are available for the home office are inappropriate for library applications.

OFFICE FURNITURE

Freestanding office desks, credenzas, bookcases and workstations are also part of the furniture programme. These may be made of wood, laminate or steel and are available in a wide variety of qualities and price ranges. To ensure longevity and serviceability, the highest quality furniture that is affordable should be selected.

Items to be considered include the quality of construction details and how well the pieces fit together, an absence of any rough or sharp surfaces, the quality of the wood finish, operation of drawers, adjustability of glides on the legs or panel ends, etc. Grommets should be provided where needed for cord drops, and locks specified where required. Frequently accessories such as keyboard trays and task lights are incorporated into this category of furniture for additional cost. They can add greatly to productivity, however, particularly if the user spends a substantial amount of time at the computer. Standard desks are too high for ergonomic keyboard use.

MEETING ROOM FURNITURE

Meeting rooms, community rooms, and conference rooms of the library may require conference tables and chairs, lecterns, media carts, folding tables and stacking chairs and other multi-purpose furniture items. While there can be unlimited options in metal finish, wood, laminate, molded plastic, and fabric for these items, the style, finish and colour of all furniture items should be coordinated with the architecture of the building. Strength and stability are another important criteria for evaluation.

Fig. Sled Based Stackable Meeting Room Chair with Molded Plastic Seat and Back.

In any location where chairs with arms are used with tables, clearance for the arms must be provided. Stacking chairs require the appropriate dolly to facilitate their easy removal to storage areas. Meeting room chairs come in many different styles, upholstered or non-upholstered, with or without fasteners to gang them together in rows. Tablet arms can provide a writing surface, and under seat wire baskets can hold books or packages. Because people often sit for extended periods of time in stacking chairs, comfort is a prime focus. Some models feature a back that flexes as the occupant changes position, which can greatly enhance comfort. Chairs must be also be tested for pitch and depth of seat.

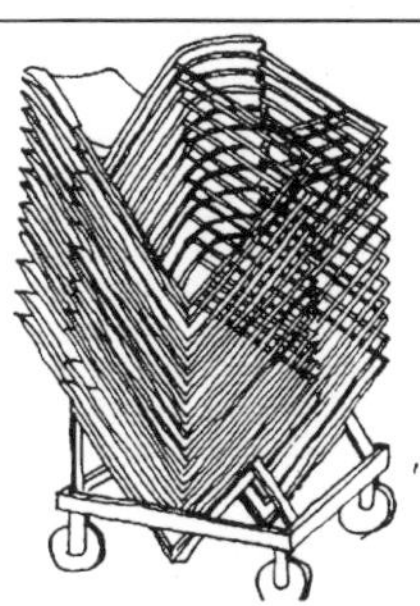

Fig. Stackable Meeting Room Chairs on a Dolly (20 to 30 Chairs Per Dolly).

Folding tables have dollies to facilitate their movement as well. These should be included in the furniture and equipment budget. Large tables are often too heavy and difficult for staff to handle. Thought should be given to the use of lighter weight but durable tables with a honeycomb top construction. They look like the heavier tables but are easier to fold and store. These tables also may have clamps for ganging them together in rows, and some models provide electrical and data capacity as an option. Folding tables should be coordinated with the overall design of the building, or be relatively neutral, since, they are likely to be used on a temporary basis in almost any location in the building.

Electrical and data outlets should be incorporated into any furniture piece that may potentially house equipment or need that flexibility. Meeting room tables that will be required to serve as training room furniture should be a minimum of 30" deep with a width allowance of no less than 36" per person. Shallower tables, 24" deep or less, often referred to as "ribbon tables," will accommodate the use of a laptop computer with the same width per person. Occasionally the requirement for fixed, auditorium style seating may arise in a large meeting room that is heavily used by the public. This is a specialty type of seating that is manufactured by only a small number of vendors.

The seats and backs are usually upholstered, and the outer back shell is often wood or laminate for durability. Wood or highdensity plastic arms are an added comfort feature. Because it is attached to the concrete floor, it is usually provided and installed by the general contractor. The floor is generally sloped, raked, or tiered to provide good sightlines, and the seat widths vary in order to conform to the width of the rows provided. After a preliminary plan is produced by the design professional, the vendor will develop an exact seating plan showing the various seat widths, and aisles. Many code issues come into play regarding aisle widths and exiting. In addition to furniture, meeting rooms will frequently require whiteboards, blackboards, projection screens, and presentation centers which combine these. The furniture and equipment budget should also include an allowance for blackout shades if there are windows, audiovisual carts, multimedia presentation equipment, media cabinets, and lockable storage for the equipment and the folding tables and chairs.

MISCELLANEOUS FURNITURE

The furniture programme for a library will typically include a variety of miscellaneous furniture and accessory items including footstools, coffee tables, end tables, literature racks, clocks, lamps, desk accessories, coat racks, dictionary stands, atlas cases, map cases, display cases and cabinets, book troughs for display, and information kiosks. These should be selected to coordinate and enhance the other furnishings in the project and specified at the same time. Among these items, lamps are likely to be the most problematic in this type of facility.

They must be UL listed, and should have a compact fluorescent lamp rather than incandescent. Table lamps should be bolted to the table surface so that they are not easily moved and the cord can be concealed. The shades for table lamps must be of a durable and relatively mar resistant material, frequently metal or glass are preferred over cloth, which can have a short life in a public building. Individual light switches may be provided, or the lamps may be controlled by main lighting switches.

Floor lamps must be stable and preferably bolted to the floor to prevent tipping over, which makes their location less flexible. Cords should be secured, shortened if necessary, and concealed. Careful thought must be given before using floor lamps in public libraries, and even then, they should be used only in adult areas where there is less likelihood of damage.

CHILDREN'S FURNITURE

Fig. Children's Juvenile Reader Table for Four with 27″ High Table top and 16″ High Reader Seat.

Scale is a primary factor in selecting children's furniture. Very few manufacturers make children's furniture, and of those who do, typically two sizes of children's tables and chairs are available unless the product is custom designed. Juvenile tables are typically 27" high and pre-school tables are typically 21-24" high. A few manufacturers have more options, with heights of 16", 18", 20" or 25".

The corresponding seat heights on chairs are typically 16" high for juveniles and 13-14" high for children. Whichever is selected, the table and the chair must be in the same scale and most critically allow a dimension of 9-10" between seat height and table height. If a chair designed for an adult is to be scaled down for children and juveniles, it is not enough to merely lower the seat.

The seat saddle should also be scaled down, as should the back height to provide comfortable seating for smaller bodies. This is also true of stools used as seating. Frequently children's chairs are available without a back, a feature that makes the chair more stable and less prone to tip over. Children's chairs should be designed not to rock or tip over.

Fig. Children's Slant Top Picture Book Table with Stools.

Several types of child-size lounge seating are available from library furniture and commercial seating manufacturers. Here, too, the overall size of the piece must be scaled down from adult versions in order to be appropriate for children. A great deal of the typical children's furniture seen in catalogs is poorly designed and badly made, so it is worth the effort to seek out those few manufacturers who regularly build well designed furniture for children. Children's furniture with sharp or squared edges should be avoided, as they are potential sources of injury.

FURNITURE FOR SENIORS

At the other end of the spectrum is the senior patron, who may also have specific furniture needs to consider. Lounge seating should be firm and not too low (18 to 181/2" seat height) so that it is easy to stand up. The seat depth should not be so great that feet can't touch the floor.

Typically 30 to 32" seat depth is advisable for medium sized people. Arms must provide a firm base for steadying the body as the patron attempts to stand. The chair should not have casters or be so light as to easily move out from under the patron when they stand up. Reader chairs should provide firm support. Arms are particularly helpful when attempting to sit down or stand up. The chair should be light enough to move easily back from the table but stable enough to be leaned upon.

FURNITURE FOR YOUNG ADULTS

Young Adults appreciate furniture that is fun and casual in style and facilitates their more informal style of interacting. They frequently do not use chairs in the intended manner, so they must be extremely durable and easily maintained. Modular armless lounge furniture may be appropriate in casual reading areas, particularly if it can be recovered on site when necessary. Reader chairs should be very sturdy; the two-position chairs, which rock back slightly, are popular with this group, which often balances chairs on two legs. Stand-up workstations and stools may be good choices for these active patrons, as well as furniture that facilitate interaction. Comfortable and roomy chairs and tables are needed for study and research activities, while carrels are often preferred for individual study.

ACCESSIBLE FURNITURE

A very important part of the library planning process is providing access to the disabled person, and making all areas of the library available and welcoming. The Americans with Disabilities Act (ADA) sets forth the requirements for reading and study areas, checkout areas, displays and stack aisles. At least 5 per cent, but not less than 1 of each element of fixed seating; tables or study carrels must comply. This means that tables, carrels, or other work surfaces must provide the 30" wide by 19" deep by 27" high clear knee space, and the tabletop must be from 28" to 34" maximum above the floor. At least one lane or portion of the checkout desk must provide a counter at least 36" long with a maximum height of 36".

Display furniture must provide reach height between the 18" minimum and 48" maximum for forward approach, or 54" maximum for side approach. There are several ways to achieve the optimum height for tables, carrels, and counters. One is to specify a design that does not incorporate an apron or other obstruction where the patrons will sit. Another is to select furniture that features an adjustable height mechanism to raise or lower the table as needed. Some manufacturers make tables and carrels that use hand cranks or electric motors to accomplish the adjustment. The hand crank is a much less expensive option than the electric motor, but may be more difficult to operate, particularly by someone with arthritis or impaired motor skills. Since, only 5 per cent of the furniture must comply, the additional cost of the electric motor would not greatly increase the over-all budget and would allow greater flexibility in height adjustment than the typical 29" high carrel work surface affords, particularly in the children's area, where tables and carrels are usually lower than the ADA standards.

COORDINATION

Coordination of all of the elements impacting the furniture must occur during the construction stage, particularly that of the placement of the electrical and data outlets. Verification of their proper location by the architect or designer should occur before the final slab pour so that any necessary adjustments can be easily made. Any dimensions critical to the placement of furniture are also taken at this time by the appropriate vendor and required modifications discussed with the designer and client. Many components from different vendors will be installed towards the end of the project, so it is critical that all of them be coordinated and scheduled so that they do not interfere with each other. The process must start before orders are placed, as once they are in production, shipping dates cannot be changed.

This often poses a challenge in new construction or extensive renovation, as the general contractor must commit to his completion date as a starting point to scheduling furniture. Ideally, all construction will be complete and the construction punch list corrections finished before any furniture is moved on site. Millwork and steel shelving should be in place before furniture installation commences, as these are large items that can easily damage furniture.

DELIVERY AND INSTALLATION

The furniture may be delivered directly to the site when it is ready to receive it, thus circumventing storage charges and double handling. The furniture dealer's installation crew must be on site and ready to receive the furniture when the truck(s) arrives. This is sometimes difficult to achieve. The alternative is to have the furniture shipped to the dealer's warehouse, where it can be inspected and scheduled for later installation. This allows more control over the date of installation but does incur storage fees. If more than one furniture dealer is involved in the project, as is often the case, they are scheduled so that one follows the other in a logical fashion, depending upon what areas should be completed first. Delivery of large amounts of furniture can create confusion, even when the installers have a furniture plan to refer to. It is essential to have the interior designer and a designated library staff member present during the installation(s) for guidance and to answer questions.

PUNCH LIST

After all of the furniture is set in place and wiped down by the installers, the interior designer and a staff member should inspect each item and note any incorrect product or finish, any damage, or defects, and any missing items. This punch list will be prepared by the designer and provided to the client and appropriate vendors. Vendors must address all items on the punch list to the client's satisfaction before their contracts are concluded. Vendors should also provide the client with maintenance and operating information and warranties on the product and arrange for a demonstration to staff of appropriate items, such as task chairs. Written information should be kept together so that it is available in the future. Any subsequent problems with the furniture should be addressed directly to the furniture dealer so that prompt action can be taken and replacements provided, if appropriate.

EQUIPMENT INSTALLATION

Even the most perfectly planned project can be compromised when the equipment vendors perform their installation improperly, particularly when they do so without using the wire and cable management devices provided within the furniture. The result is unsightly cords draped over furniture, spilling onto the floor and creating obstacles in areas designed for feet and knees. Aside from the aesthetic considerations, this lack of attention can create an uncomfortable and hazardous situation for patrons and staff. Since, these are usually the last vendors to perform their work, the library staff should make sure that the furniture and equipment installation is done correctly and that all of the cabling is properly stowed out of view. This extra attention will produce a project that is well planned and executed down to the last detail with nothing to mar the over-all result.

10

Role of a Digital Librarian in the Management of Dynamic Digital Library

This chapter describes a digital library architecture and implementation that is configurable, extensible and dynamic in the way it presents content and in the services it provides. The design manifests itself as a network of modules that communicate in terms of XML messages.

All modules characterize the functionality they implement in response to a "describe yourself" message, and can transform messages using XSLT to support different levels of configurability.

Traditional library values such as backwards compatibility and multiplatform operation are combined with the ability to add new collections and services adaptively. The paper describes the new design and shows how it can be used to build four different digital library systems.

We conclude by showing how the design fits existing interoperability frameworks. This chapter describes a digital library design that improves upon the Greenstone toolkit. First, it provides more flexible ways of dynamically configuring the run-time system and adding new services to it.

Second, it lowers the overhead incurred by collection developers when accessing this flexibility to organize and present their content. Third, it modularizes the internal structure and simplifies the addition of new modules.

The design is based on widely-accepted standards such as XML, current software practices such as simple protocols (like SOAP), cross-platform development strategies (Java), and contemporary schemes for software modularization and dynamic updates.

Most important of all, it is informed by our experience with the current Greenstone system and the problems and challenges faced by real users, international collection developers, and practicing librarians.

The structure of the paper is as follows. First we give some background out of which the requirements for the digital library software arose. Next we describe the new design, called Greenstone, and discuss how it meets the identified needs. Fundamental to the approach is the use of XML throughout for data representation, combined with XSL Transforms to provide a flexible mechanism for adjusting the functionality of the runtime system without having to modify and recompile the source code.

To promote cross-platform independence (which has consumed inordinate human resources in the present Greenstone system) and facilitate the dynamic loading of services and other modules, the implementation uses Java. Following this we describe four very different examples built using the new design.

The first demonstrates backwards compatibility, and, in addition, operates within a distributed environment. The second augments text at display time, using an established software tool for text mining developed elsewhere, to show how functionality can be enriched through the introduction of a new service.

The third is a map-based digital library that introduces two new services to support geographic functionality and, while still accessed through a web-based interface, is highly tailored to the specific domain of its source documents.

The fourth is a radically different interface for the interactive viewing of search results as a hierarchically organized cluster of documents, and illustrates the versatility of the design in coping with fine-grained interaction. We conclude with a commentary on how the design fits existing interoperability frameworks, from which many valuable lessons have been learned.

Background

Over the years the Greenstone digital library software has been employed by many users internationally to develop a wide variety of digital libraries. In addition to operation over the Web, an early application, and still a major one, is collections of humanitarian information in the form of CD-ROMs that run on any Windows computer (including Windows 3.1).

There are now over two dozen of these collections, and they have been distributed widely by the United Nations and other non government agencies. Many other styles of collection have been developed under Greenstone.

They range from numerous personal collections based around common document formats such as E-mail, photographs, Word, and PDF documents through to largescale bibliographic catalogs such as the BBC radio and TV archives.

There are mixed media collections involving text, images and audio drawn from data such as historic newspapers and oral history. Several demonstration music collections support direct content-based retrieval through "query by humming." Many customized and branded user interfaces exist, such as the New York Botanical Gardens, and many international collections in local languages created by institutions in China, India, Croatia, Russia and Israel. The software is distributed in source form, and for convenience binaries are available for Windows, Linux and MacOS X. The user interface is available in 30 languages. A recent addition is a graphical interface for collection design and construction which is also multilingual.

A portfolio of demonstration collections is available at www.nzdl.org, and selected example collections built internationally can be found at www.greenstone.org.

Weaknesses

Many experimental interfaces have been built for Greenstone, some of which make use of a CORBA-based protocol to support distributed client-server interaction. These include a Venn diagram tool for formulating Boolean queries graphically, and a bibliographic visualization tool that plots matching citations on an x-y grid based on publication year and ranked relevance score to the query terms.

However, while perfectly functional, some of these variants are implemented inelegantly, exposing limitations caused by certain aspects of the design.

For instance, the immutable nature of the index files generated during the building process makes incremental adjustments to a collection expensive. Another hindrance is the low level of functional customization supported by the runtime system.

Although minor presentation tweaks are easy, more extensive changes involve modifying and recompiling the source code. The strongly typed nature of the CORBA protocol was also found to be overly restrictive in many practical situations.

Requirements

From these and other considerations arose the following requirements for an improved design.

- *Backwards compatibility:* Naturally we wish to retain the existing system's strengths. This is accomplished by ensuring that the new design is backward compatible, which has the added benefit of providing existing developers and users with an easy migration path.
- *Levels of customization:* To match the different categories of people involved in constructing digital libraries, different levels of customization are required. For instance, a content developer may wish to include source documents in a new format; a collection editor may seek influence over diverse issues of presentation.
- *Software modularity:* To facilitate development and long-term management of the software, code modularization—a mantra of any software engineering approach—is essential. This is promoted by adopting off-the-shelf technology such as a database system, indexing tools, and page rendering software; and by the use of standards.
- *Service based:* Basing a digital library around a set of services is

another way to accomplish modularity—in this case, modularity of function.

- *Distributed architecture:* A rich digital library infrastructure can only be supported by a distributed architecture, and the addition of an open protocol helps to foster interoperability.
- *Future compatibility*: Libraries are long-term institutions with a mandate for preservation, and it is essential that old collections can be presented by future versions of the system. This is a more ambitious requirement than mere extensibility which, although an admirable quality in any design, does not necessarily ensure that future versions can safely interact with current ones.
- *Dynamic:* Many aspects of the library should be dynamic, for example content, whereby documents and metadata can be added, revised and removed while a repository remains on-line, and configuration, where presentational issues can be adjusted and services added at runtime.
- *Integrated documentation:* Large-scale software systems such as digital libraries benefit immensely from the use of an integrated documentation system.
- *Self-describing modules:* This goes a stage further than the previous item: modules describe themselves in a machine-readable format so that other modules can interact with them without the need for explicit control. Computer environment integration. A digital library should mesh well into a user's existing computer environment. Full integration makes a digital library become a seamless component of each user's work environment.

SOFTWARE DESIGN

The new software design has evolved from the requirements articulated above, our own experience of developing digital library systems, and studies of other open source software and research projects.

This section provides an overview of modularity and inter-module communication, and then works through a simple, stand-alone example. The next section describes four very different examples built using the new design, to illustrate the general applicability of the approach.

Modularity

We decided that the best way to meet the challenges posed by the list of requirements was to reimplement Greenstone using a modular topology. In the design, a digital library manifests itself as a network of modules, and communication between them is expressed through an instantiation of XML.

A mandatory requirement for a module—enforced through its base class definition—is that it handles "describe yourself" messages. What kinds of messages follow typically depend on the outcome of an initial "describe yourself". Modules have the ability to transform messages by applying an XSL Transform. This is a particularly useful mechanism for dynamically controlling levels of configurability—one of our requirements. Within the network of modules comprising a digital library, a set of services are defined that prescribe the functionality supported by that particular digital library configuration.

Communication

Modules communicate using synchronous request-response pairs. Figure shows an example XML exchange, where the Text Query module in a collection called "demo" is asked to describe itself. It does this, providing information about the structure of the service as well as fragments of text to be used for display.

These are returned in the language specified in the request. While the language used is structured and typed, it has been crafted in such a way that the information it contains can be open-ended.

For example the paramList structure allows other items to be included, such as whether stemming is on or off. In addition to supporting optional parameters, extensions can be introduced without having to update the protocol's API, thereby avoiding the need to propagate code changes to the entire distributed network (which may require taking it off-line while the changes are made).

Programming for a sample XML exchange as a request/response pair.

```
<request to='demo/TextQuery' lang='en' type='describe' uid='21'/>
<response from='demo/TextQuery' lang='en' type='describe'>
<service name='TextQuery' type='query'>
<displayItem name='name'>Search</displayItem>
<displayItem name='description'>Full text search</displayItem>
<displayItem name='submit'>Search</displayItem>
<paramList>
<param name='index' type='enum_single' default='stx'>
<displayItem name="name">Index to search in</displayItem>
<option name="dtx">
<displayItem name="name">entire documents</displayItem>
</option>
<option name="stx">
<displayItem name="name">chapters</displayItem>
</option>
</param>
<param name='maxDocs' type='integer' default='10'>
<displayItem name="name">Maximum hits to return</displayItem>
</param>
```

```
<param name="query" type="string">
<displayItem name="name">Query string</displayItem>
</param>
</paramList>
</service>
</response>
```

A Simple Stand-alone Example

The simple stand-alone example shown in Figure encapsulates many of the design's key features. It comprises a "back end" server, termed a digital library site in our design, coupled to a "front end" that provides the user interface. The modules' names were chosen to emphasize the roles they play.

The Receptionist's point of contact with the server is the Message Router (MR) module—all communication with the site occurs through this module. The configuration is designed to generalize to a distributed environment. The digital library back end in Figure contains two collections, demo and fao, and a cluster of collection-formation services.

Add Document is a service that adds a document to a collection. Import Collection imports into the system all documents associated with a collection, converting them where necessary from their original form. Build Collection builds all indexes and browsing structures that are associated with a collection.

Activate Collection makes a newly-built collection active, so that it can be seen by digital library users.

These services are all concerned with creating a digital library collection. Being related, they are grouped together into a "service cluster." In Figure the services just listed are accessed through the Collection Formation service cluster module.

As far as the digital library user is concerned, a "collection" is a focused group of documents with a uniform means of access. For the system, it is a service cluster that groups a set of services that are related by the data they work on.

For example, the demo collection towards the lower left of Figure contains three modules providing four services to the user.

The modules are called "Search," which provides a Text Query service, "Retrieve," which provides a document retrieval service Resource Retrieve and a metadata retrieval service Metadata Retrieve, and "Browse," which provides a metadata browsing service Classifier Browse.

The Web-based front end at the upper left of Figure centers around the Receptionist, which is the point of contact for the interface generator. A servlet (labeled "Library Servlet") takes HTTP commands in the form of URLs and arguments and translates them into XML for the Receptionist.

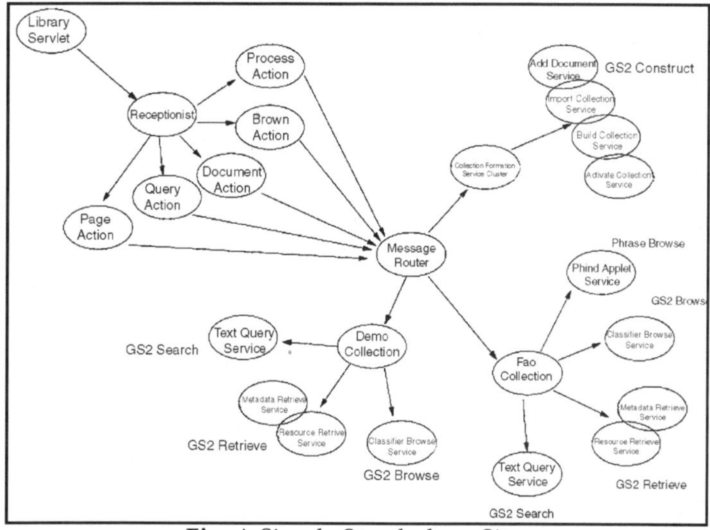

Fig. A Simple Stand-alone Site.

The Receptionist is capable of executing various different actions, each of which involves (usually) many calls to the digital library's Message Router. The builtin ability for Receptionist modules to transform XML messages using XSLT is used—in conjunction with a style sheet—to generate the HTML that is finally presented to the user.

Examples

For pedagogical purposes, the example configuration in Figure is rudimentary. The front and back ends (receptionist and site server) are compiled together into a single executable process with a single Message Router handling all communication between them.

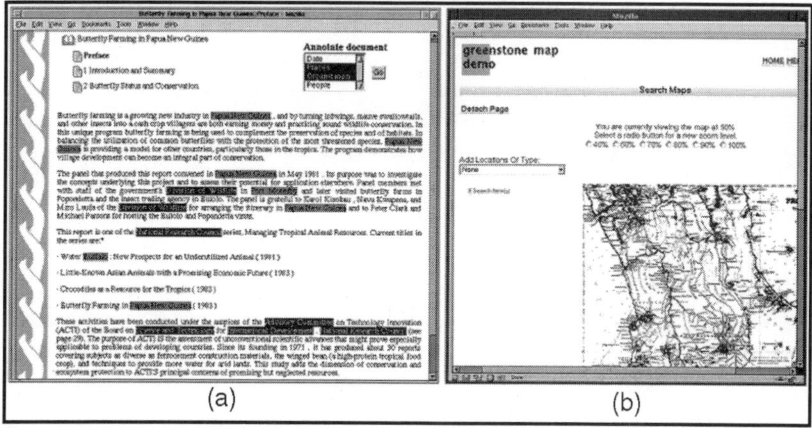

Fig. Additional Services to Augment run-time Functionally (a) text Augmentation of place names; (b) a novel map-based Interface.

However, the design supports a far richer infrastructure than this. Message Routers have the capability to communicate across a distributed network with other Message Routers and with Receptionists.

Different implementations of the same service can be switched in and out to give a digital library site different algorithmic behaviour (such as incremental building); and new services can be introduced and brought on-line, dynamically if necessary. The library can also have many different user interfaces.

We now describe four more interesting scenarios. The first emulates "classic" Greenstone to demonstrate backwards compatibility, with a distributed configuration a straightforward addition. The second augments text at display time, to show how functionality can be enriched through the introduction of a new service.

The third and fourth utilize novel interfaces to enrich the interaction: the former is specialized for geographic maps, and the latter for text based collections.

Classic Greenstone, with collections on remote sites

To provide backwards compatibility, a set of Greenstone services have been implemented that access index and database files generated by a Greenstone system. Indeed we have already seen these in Figure.

Moreover, using Cascading Style Sheets (CSS), the look and feel of the traditional interface has been matched one-for-one, so that the user's experience of the digital library remains the same. Of course with the more versatile design, more sophisticated internal structures can be built within the digital libary.

For instance, because of the design decision that all communication be XML based, it is straightforward to arrange for the XML messages sent between modules to be seamlessly streamed across remote machines.

For this we employ the Simple Object Access Protocol (SOAP), but any protocol that can process text can be used. To the user there is no disernable difference accessing collections this way. Backwards compatability is not the sole aim, however, and the structure allows increasingly interesting digital library designs—ones that do provide a distinctly different expierence for the user. We discuss three such examples next.

Dynamic Text Mining

The next example shows how a new Greenstone service can be provided that enhances documents for the reader, based upon the open source GATE system for text mining. The motivation is that highlighting selected items in documents can make it easier for users to scan them for particular pieces of information. In this implementation, digital library documents, once located, are mined on the fly marking up entities such as keywords and place names before presenting them to the user. Figure shows a section of a book on Butterfly Farming in Papua New Guinea (from the Humanity Development Library at www.nzdl.org) that the user is reading.

The Annotate document menu at the top right calls the display time text mining feature. When items on this menu are selected, text of the selected type is highlighted in the document displayed. In this case the user has selected Places and Organizations, and these are highlighted wherever they occur, in different colors (simulated by white-on-grey and black-on grey in the illustration).

The selectable items in Figure were identified and extracted by ANNIE, GATE's information extraction system. Whenever an annotation type is selected from the menu, Greenstone calls the information extraction module dynamically to identify items of that type.

This incurs a delay that depends on the document's size but is usually short: the system processes text at the average rate of 15 Kb/sec on a typical workstation. In order to achieve this the software is loaded when the Greenstone server is executed and remains resident in memory thereafter, to avoid a start-up delay (of about 10 seconds) in which all the text processors are initialized and prepared for use.

In Greenstone3, GATE is encapsulated in a module as just another service. It takes messages with two parameters, the type of annotation and a document, and returns the document with relevant items marked up with XML tags.

A style sheet in the server module chooses the colors in which the items are displayed. In order to generate the menu in the figure, a "describe yourself" message is sent to the GATE module, which returns a list of the annotations that are available. Apart from this one module, the rest of the digital library system knows nothing of GATE.

However, it does know about a general class of services, Enrich, that take a document and return the same document with some elements marked up. To add this text-mining ability to an existing Greenstone site dynamically the Java class files for the new service need to added to the correct folder on the DL site's file system, the site's configuration file updated to name the new service, and a "reconfigure" signal sent (which can be initiated through a web browser) to the DL site server.

Geographical map based interface Figure is taken from a site configured to support map searching based on a small collection of New Zealand maps drawn between 1770 and 1953, part of our university library's special collections.

It shows the result of searching for "Rangiriri"—a township in the North Island of New Zealand and, on a hill nearby of the same name, the scene of a battle in 1863 between Maori and British soldiers. Two crosses (colored red when viewed online) have been overlaid on the map showing the position of the township and hill, and can be seen slightly above the centre of the map.

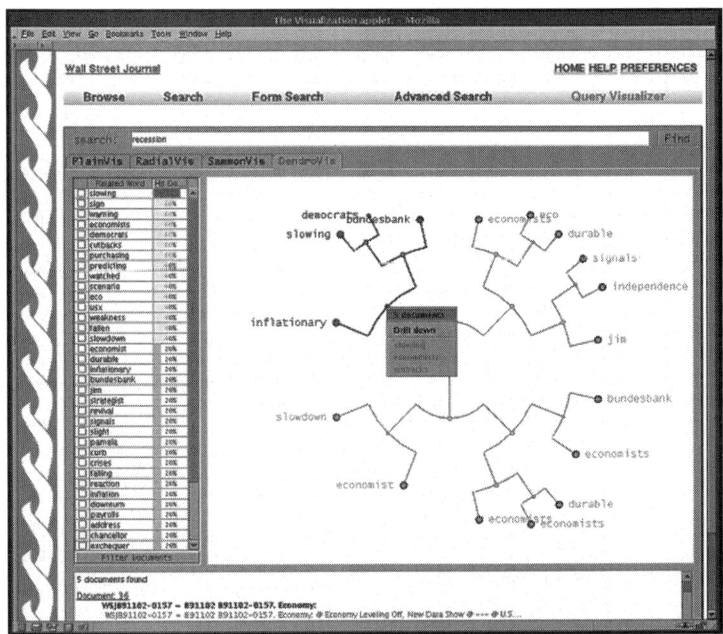

Fig. Applet based Dendro Visualization of Clustered Documents Matching query.

The query interface and presentation of the results is similar to the traditional interface, except that against each matching item a thumbnail of the map containing the place name is given.

Figure is the result of honing in on one such map appearing in the result set. Through the interface the user can change the level of magnification of the map and request that additional features such as cemeteries, bridges, and estuaries be marked.

This new functionality is provided by adding two new services, including geographic metadata with the collection's source documents (the maps), and a gazetteer of over 40,000 entries from Land Information New Zealand (LINZ). Searching is handled by the Map Query service. For each place name query term that is located in the gazetteer, its longitude and latitude are checked against each map to see if it falls within its boundaries.

Once all cross-referencing is complete, the list of maps with matching entries is sorted by the number of query terms on each map. Image manipulation and the results display are handled by the Map Retrieve service, which makes use of the open source Image Magick toolkit for copying, annotating (such as placing a cross at an x, y location) and resizing images.

Cluster Visualizations

Figure shows a web-based interface, but there may be other forms, ranging from standalone applications and applets that display documents in different ways to alert services that recognize when new information becomes available in one of the collections and formulate appropriate E-mail to users. Figure is one such instance: a Java applet that supports browsing result sets as document clusters through a multi-viewed, interactive interface.

To function it needs the addition of a new build-time service, Vis Construct, which is responsible for computing additional statistics about the collection necessary to perform subsequent document clustering operations, and a sub-classing of the Applet service, tailored for the HTML necessary to embed the visualization applet within a web page.

Besides this, the visualization can interact with any text-based Greenstone collection that defines keyword metadata. The distinctly different interface behaviour is achieved through fine-grained interaction with the existing Text Query and Metadata Retrieve services using SOAP. Derived from the query term entered, there are four views in the visualization.

The first is the standard result list format; the other three are based around a shared model of hierarchically clustered documents.

In Figure the user has entered the query term "recession" to a collection based on the Wall Street Journal and is viewing the result as a Dendro map—the circular arranged tree displayed in the main panel—which contains words like slowing, slowdown and inflationary around the circumference. The size of nodes in the tree represents the number of documents clustered at that point in the hierarchy, and for reasons of space only 5 levels of the tree are shown at a time. Clicking on a node shows a popup menu with the precise number of documents in the cluster and the option of "drilling down" as shown in the figure.

The consequence of choosing this option is for the tree to be redrawn with the selected node at the centre of the map, thereby exposing more of the detail in that part of the hierarchy.

While all this is going on, the left-panel displays the keywords relevant to the selected cluster, and the bottom panel lists the documents involved. Within the left panel, keywords can be activated or deactivated and the bottom panel dynamically filtered to reflect the changes.

INTEROPERABILITY FRAMEWORKS

This modular, service-based and dynamically configurable approach to digital library architecture can be found in other designs and systems. Two key examples are the Extended Open Archives Initiative protocol (XOAI) proposed by Suleman and Fox and the Open DLib system of Castelli and Pagano.

The XOAI protocol, based upon XML and related technologies, builds upon the basic OAI Protocol for Metadata Harvesting. It is a modular protocol which represents each service as a different type of OAI request. This service-based approach is readily seen in Greenstone's protocol, where each service has its own request and response format.

Like OAI and XOAI, Greenstone uses XML for representing requests and responses; providing a gateway between Greenstone and XOAI servers and clients should be readily achievable. The Open DLib system also takes a modular approach to service communication and library construction.

Many of its features are similar to those of XOAI and Greenstone, and the handling of requests to the library map as readily as for XOAI. However, Open DLib is centered upon a "manager" service that coordinates services, responding to the introduction of new services and alterations to existing ones.

Coordination is achieved through a communication protocol between the manager and each service. Individual services, including each library in a federation, acquire data from the manager.

The manager does not itself control or direct requests for searches, documents, and so on but instead coordinates between services to ensure consistency. Greenstone provides many of these features—for instance, service description requests—without requiring a centralized manager.

The similarity of protocols between Greenstone, XOAI and OpenDLib echoes experience with the previous generation of DL protocols and augers well for interoperability. Greenstone's widespread adoption and free availability allows others to adopt it as a platform for experimenting with the service-centered design approach.

It facilitates the addition of new digital library features which would have been hampered by the less open structures of Greenstone and its contemporaries. Greenstone retains and extends the lightweight configurability of its predecessor without requiring centralized management processes.

This chapter has presented a new digital library design which is significantly different from the present Greenstone, but strongly rooted in past success. To meet a broad range of requirements a modular based topology is utilized to provide a flexible infrastructure.

Written in Java to promote portability, dynamic loading of objects and internationalization, modules communicate by streaming XML messages between each other. Using SOAP this communication can be distributed across a network. All modules have the ability to describe themselves in a machine readable form, and to apply an XSLT to transform messages.

The latter is instrumental in providing different levels of configurability, an important ability given the different types of people involved in the life-cycle of a digital library. Several working examples have been given to convey the general applicability of the design.

The first example demonstrated backwards compatibility to collections built with Greenstone, and satisfies another of the identified requirements: to help minimize the migration path of existing developers and users. It also demonstrated the design functioning in a distributed environment. The second example augmented an existing DL site with text mining capabilities with the introduction of a new service. The third and fourth examples illustrated substantially different user interfaces: one specialized for maps that required two extra services to provide the necessary geographical functionality; the other provided an interactive visualization to search results through a Java applet that was applicable to a wider realm of text-based collections.

Numerous aspects of the design contribute to its dynamic configurability. The "describe yourself" feature allows receptionists to adapt to the facilities that a server presents. Through XSLT a corpus editor can exert significant control over the function and appearance of a digital library such as modifying the structure of a generated page, for example adding a transform that sorts the query results alphabetically by title rather than ranked score. Alternatively they may reformat the results according to OAI syntax in preparation for exporting.

Previously such changes required editing the source code and restarting the digital library software after recompilation. Implementing the design in Java has promoted dynamic attributes in the system, particularly through the ease in which modules can be loaded at runtime.

The re-reading of configuration files is also straightforward to arrange and adds dynamic abilities that a digital library administrator can take advantage of. In addition to integrating the documentation with the software using JavaDoc and other techniques, usability of the software also benefits from the development of self-documenting collections that both demonstrate and describe particular aspects of design.

The list of requirements is ambitious, however, and not all of them have been proven yet. For example, while none of the sample implementations demonstrate computer environment integration, the design is capable of supporting the idea through specialized receptionists. For future compatibility, more time is needed to establish if the design successfully meets such a criteria.

11

Knowledge Organization Systems and Librarians

KNOWLEDGE ORGANIZATION SYSTEMS: AN OVERVIEW

The term *knowledge organization systems* are intended to encompass all types of schemes for organizing information and promoting knowledge management. Knowledge organization systems include classification schemes that organize materials at a general level, subject headings that provide more detailed access and authority files that control variant versions of key information. They also include less-traditional schemes, such as semantic networks and ontologies. Because knowledge organization systems are mechanisms for organizing information, they are at the heart of every library, museum, and archive.

Knowledge organization systems are used to organize materials for the purpose of retrieval and to manage a collection. A KOS serves as a bridge between the user's information need and the material in the collection. With it, the user should be able to identify an object of interest without prior knowledge of its existence. Whether through browsing or direct searching, whether through themes on a Web page or a site search engine, the KOS guides the user through a discovery process. In addition, KOSs allow the organizers to answer questions regarding the scope of a collection and what is needed to round it out.

All digital libraries use one or more KOS. Just as in a physical library, the KOS in a digital library provides an overview of the content of the collection and supports retrieval. The scheme may be a traditional KOS relevant to the scope of the material and the expected audience for the digital library, a commercially developed scheme such as the Yahoo or Excite categories, or a locally developed scheme for a corporate intranet.

The decision of what knowledge organization system to use is central to the development of any digital library. The KOS must be applicable, either automatically or by human catalogers, to the resources included in the digital library. Once the material is included in the collection, the KOS must be meaningful to its users. This section outlines the characteristics of KOSs, describes the common types, and discusses their origins and traditional uses.

COMMON CHARACTERISTICS OF KNOWLEDGE ORGANIZATION SYSTEMS

It is often said that humans are inherent organizers. From an early age, children play sorting and matching games. We cope with our ever-changing world by comparing new objects or experiences with those with which we are familiar, identifying patterns and categorizing what is new into our existing frame of reference. The emphasis on developing comprehensive KOS's can be seen in the writings of our earliest philosophers, many of whom continue to influence our view of the world. For example, Aristotle's effort to categorize knowledge into groups is reflected in our language, our education, and our science.

The original classification scheme of the Library of Congress, used between 1800 and 1814, was based on the philosophical works of Sir Francis Bacon and inherited from the English tradition. Beginning in 1814, the influence of Thomas Jefferson can be seen on the Library of Congress collection. Jefferson, who reclassified the library, reflected a more humanist philosophy. There is no single knowledge classification scheme on which everyone agrees.

Michael Lesk speculates that while a single KOS would be advantageous, it is unlikely that such a system will ever be developed. Culture may constrain the knowledge classification scheme so that what is meaningful to one culture is not necessarily meaningful to another. Therefore, we live in a world of multiple, variant ways to organize knowledge.

Despite their diversity, KOSs have the following common characteristics that are critical to their use in organizing digital libraries:

- The KOS imposes a particular view of the world on a collection and the items in it.
- The same entity can be characterized in different ways, depending on the KOS that is used.
- There must be sufficient commonality between the concept expressed in a KOS and the real-world object to which that concept refers that a knowledgeable person could apply the system with reasonable reliability. Likewise, a person seeking relevant material by using a KOS must be able to connect his or her concept with its representation in the system.

TYPES OF KNOWLEDGE ORGANIZATION SYSTEMS

A review of some typical knowledge organization systems shows their scope and applicability to a variety of digital library settings. While there are specific definitions for many of these KOSs in the computer science and information science literature, and even in standards documents, there is debate over these definitions. Terms are often used, particularly in the popular press and in the book trade, in nonstandard ways. Reflecting the scope of this practice, a recent *National Information Standards Organization* (NISO) work shop on electronic thesauri emphasized the need to improve the definitions of "terminology relating to terminology".

The descriptions given here provide an overview of possible systems for organizing digital libraries. The descriptions are based on characteristics such as structure and complexity, relationships among terms, and historical function. The list is not comprehensive; nor are the definitions of these terms contained in specific standards documents. They are grouped into three general categories: term lists, which emphasize lists of terms often with definitions; classifications and categories, which emphasize the creation of subject sets; and relationship lists, which emphasize the connections between terms and concepts.

Term Lists

Authority Files

Authority files are lists of terms that are used to control the variant names for an entity or the domain value for a particular field. Examples include names for countries, individuals, and organizations. Nonpreferred terms may be linked to the preferred versions. This type of KOS generally does not include a deep organization or complex structure. The presentation may be alphabetical or organized by a shallow classification scheme. A limited hierarchy may be applied to allow for simple navigation, particularly when the authority file is being accessed manually or is extremely large. Examples of authority files include the Library of Congress Name Authority File and the Getty Geographic Authority File.

Glossaries

A glossary is a list of terms, usually with definitions. The terms may be from a specific subject field or from a particular work. The terms are defined within a specific environment and rarely include variant meanings. Examples include the *Environmental Protection Agency* (EPA) Terms of the Environment.

Dictionaries

Dictionaries are alphabetical lists of words and their definitions. Variant senses are provided where applicable. Dictionaries are more general in scope than are glossaries.

They may also provide information about the origin of a word, variants and multiple meanings across disciplines. While a dictionary may also provide synonyms and through the definitions, related words, there is no explicit hierarchical structure or attempt to group them by concept.

Gazetteers

A gazetteer is a list of place names. Traditional gazetteers have been published as books or have appeared as indexes to atlases. Each entry may also be identified by feature type, such as river, city, or school. An example is the U.S. Code of Geo-graphic Names. Geospatially referenced gazetteers provide coordinates for locating the place on the earth's surface. The term *gazetteer* has several other meanings, including an announcement publication such as a patent or legal gazetteer. These gazetteers are often organized using classification schemes or subject categories.

Classifications and Categories

Subject Headings

This scheme type provides a set of controlled terms to represent the subjects of items in a collection. Subject heading lists can be extensive and cover a broad range of subjects; however, the subject heading list's structure is generally very shallow, with a limited hierarchical structure. In use, subject headings tend to be coordinated, with rules for how they can be joined to provide concepts that are more specific.

Examples include:

- The Medical Subject Headings (MeSH); and
- The Library of Congress Subject Headings (LCSH).

Classification Schemes, Taxonomies, and Categorization Schemes

These terms are often used interchangeably. Although there may be subtle differences from example to example, these types of KOSs all provide ways to separate entities into "buckets" or broad topic levels. Some examples provide a hierarchical arrangement of numeric or alphabetic notation to represent broad topics.

These types of KOSs may not follow the rules for hierarchy required in the ANSI NISO Thesaurus Standard and they lack the explicit relationships presented in a thesaurus.

Examples of classification schemes include:

- The Library of Congress Classification Schedules,
- The Dewey Decimal Classification, and
- The Universal Decimal Classification.

Subject categories are often used to group thesaurus terms in broad topic sets that lie outside the hierarchical scheme of the thesaurus. Taxonomies are increasingly being used in object-oriented design and knowledge management systems to indicate any grouping of objects based on a particular characteristic.

Relationship Lists

Thesauri

Thesauri are based on concepts and they show relation-ships among terms. Relationships commonly expressed in a thesaurus include hierarchy, equivalence and association or relatedness.

These relationships are generally represented by the notation:

- BT (broader term),
- NT (narrower term),
- SY (synonym), and
- RT (associative or related term).

Associative relationships may be more detailed in some schemes. For example, the *Unified Medical Language System* (UMLS) from the National Library of Medicine has defined more than 40 relationships, many of which are associative. Preferred terms for indexing and retrieval are identified. Entry terms point to the preferred terms to be used for each concept. There are standards for the development of monolingual thesauri and multilingual thesauri. In these standards, the definition of a thesaurus is fairly narrow.

Standard relationships are assumed, as is the identification of preferred terms, and there are rules for creating relation-ships among terms. The definition of a thesaurus in these standards is often at variance with schemes that are tradi-tionally called thesauri. Many thesauri do not follow all the rules of the standard but are still generally thought of as thesauri.

Another type of thesaurus, such as the *Roget's Thesaurus*, represents only equivalence. Many thesauri are large; they may include more than 50,000 terms. Most were developed for a specific discipline or a specific product or family of products. Examples include the Food and Agricultural Organization's *Aquatic Sciences and Fisheries Thesaurus* and the *National Aeronautic and Space Administration (NASA) Thesaurus* for aeronautics and aerospace-related topics.

Semantic Networks

With the advent of natural language processing, there have been significant developments in semantic networks. These KOSs structure concepts and terms not as hierarchies but as a network or a web. Concepts are thought of as nodes, and relationships branch out from them. The relationships generally go beyond the standard BT, NT, and RT. They may include specific whole-part, cause-effect, or parent-child relationships. The most noted semantic network is Princeton University's WordNet, which is now used in a variety of search engines.

Ontologies

Ontology is the newest label to be attached to some knowledge organization systems. The knowledge-management community is developing ontologies as specific concept models. They can represent complex relationships among objects, and include the rules and axioms missing from semantic networks. Ontologies that describe knowledge in a specific area are often connected with systems for data mining and knowledge management. All of these examples of knowledge organization systems, which vary in complexity, structure, and function, can provide organization and increased access to digital libraries.

THE ORIGIN AND USE OF KNOWLEDGE ORGANIZATION SYSTEMS

In the physical library, classification schemes such as *Library of Congress* (LC), Dewey Decimal System, and the Universal Decimal Classification reflect, among other things, the need to store a single item at a single location on a shelf. To provide multiple access points beyond the limits of a single physical location, subject headings are applied. Libraries use subject heading schemes such as LCSH, Sears, or other specialized schemes developed for specific content or specific collections.

At the level of specific content, libraries have used authority files to control variant forms of personal, organizational, and geographic names. However, KOSs can be found in settings other than libraries. An awareness of the KOSs available from alternative sources is valuable when considering the development of digital libraries for a specific audience.

Abstracting and Indexing Services

Abstracting and indexing (A&I) services developed as an outgrowth of traditional bibliographies and the explosion of journal literature. In the sciences, the development of A&I services was spurred by the post-World War I concerns about inadequate access to scientific information. In the 1950s, investment in A&I services was fueled by the Cold War and Sputnik. Abstracting and indexing services in the humanities, such as the Bibliography of the History of Art or the *Modern Languages Association* (MLA) Bibliography, generally took a different growth path than did their scientific and technical counterparts, but they also quickly became important resources for scholarship in the online environment.

The scope of A&I services varies from broad discipline-oriented services to narrowly defined aspects of the literature and subdisciplines. Special KOSs, such as thesauri and subject categories, were developed to support A&I services and their specific products and audiences. These organizations applied increasingly complex schemes to provide subject access to the literature in a variety of subjects.

By the 1960s, A&I services were moving from the provision of printonly products to print and online services through large online vendors such as Dialog. Later, the products were distributed on CDROM and now, increasingly, on the Web. In many cases, the KOSs migrated from print to electronic media following the products they supported. While increased computing power, more sophisticated search engines, and more independent end-user searching have led to changes in some KOSs, most have retained their importance, even in the Web environment.

For many years, the KOSs related to A&I services were applied only by catalogers and indexers trained in using the KOS indexing for a particular product or products. The primary users of KOSs were librarians and other professional searchers. However, the proliferation of electronic data, the explosion of electronic publishing, and increasing concerns about the difficulty of locating information have led to a renewed interest in these KOSs for use not only by professionals but also by end users.

Publishers

As publishers have migrated to electronic composition systems, they have become increasingly involved in the production of A&I products. Large journal publishers such as Academic Press and Elsevier have developed their own systems to provide bibliographic records linked to the full text of documents. As the content of online journals has grown, it has become necessary to move from systems that provide browsing by table of contents and journal issue to systems that support searching by both free text and by KOS. Electronic journals have resulted in additional KOSs, particularly classification and categorization schemes. For example, Elsevier's Web site has a subject categorization scheme to provide access to individual Web sites of its more than 2000 titles.

Trade, Professional, and Governmental Organizations

A variety of authority files and classification schemes are used to support business and commerce. They range from the *Standard Industrial Classification* (SIC) code and the *North American Industrial Classification System* (NAICS), used in procurement and government statistics, to disease codes used to communicate patient illnesses and treatments among physicians, hospitals, and insurance companies. As more organizations develop Web sites, additional KOSs are being developed to support them.

Internal Projects

Organizations are among the most prolific creators and users of KOSs. Developers of corporate intranets and knowledge management systems have discovered hundreds of specific classification schemes, glossaries, categorization schemes, and other vocabularies in use within organizations. Many of these are geared towards specific tasks and are, therefore, very narrow both in subject scope and target audience. However, for these audiences, they can also be rich sources of information. For example, the *Department of Energy* (DOE), *Environmental Management Science Programme* (EMSP) and the Office of Scientific and Technical

Information are developing a digital library to support EMSP programme managers. Programme managers and researchers have developed "needs categories" and "science categories" to organize the *Environmental Science Network* (ESN).

The categories are used primarily to support the process of grant submission and award; however, the ESN also uses them to provide access to related material from within DOE and from other distributed databases from the EPA, the Department of Defence, and NASA. Vocabulary is currently being organized around these categories for use with a Web mining tool that will provide highly relevant Web resources for project managers in specific areas.

LINKING DIGITAL LIBRARY RESOURCES TO RELATED RESOURCES

This section emphasizes the ability of knowledge organization systems to link digital library resources to other related resources. The basis for this linking is the identification of information within a digital resource that can be extracted and used to search and locate information within a KOS. The KOS may then be used to expand codes to more explanatory full text, to provide more descriptive records, or to link entity names to resources of physical specimens.

EXPANDING CODES TO FULL TEXT

Practitioners of a discipline use coding schemes to facilitate communication within that discipline. It is often helpful to connect these coding schemes to the full names for which the code stands. The examples provided here include links between databank registration codes and the biological sequence data, and between industrial codes and the full name that the code represents.

Linking Sequence Numbers to Biosequence Databanks

The lengthy biochemical and genetic sequences that molecular biologists, biotechnologists, and geneticists identify each day are kept in databanks. Several databanks have been developed, for example, to cover protein sequences, nucleotides, and cell lines. One of the largest databanks contains information on the mapping of the human genome. As molecular biologists began to discover these sequences, they reported them in scientific journals. Difficulties in composing, proofreading, and printing the text soon arose.

Through an ad hoc standards process, major biomedical publishers agreed to require the inclusion of codes or databank numbers for these sequences in articles when they are published.

In addition, the sequence itself must be registered in a databank before the paper can be published. Some of the most frequently referenced databanks are listed on the Web site of the National Center for Biotechnology Information. They include GenBank and the Research Collaboratory for Structural Bioinformatics Protein Data Bank.

Each sequence number is different, but all begin with a persistent code identifying the databank. How can the link be made between the literature and the databank? Through a search profile, a text analysis programme, or keyword indexing, the text can be analysed and the sequence databank numbers identified.

An active link can be embedded. The active link consists of a search strategy to locate that sequence number in the databank where the actual sequence is stored. When the user clicks on the active link, the script is generated and launched from the user's browser.

The Web-enabled database is searched, and the sequence record is returned to the user. Depending on the services provided by the databank site, the user can analyse the sequence using a number of tools provided by the databank or download the sequence for local manipulation. This type of connection exists between the *National Library of Medicine's* (NLM) search service, PubMed, and GenBank at the National Center for Biotechnology Information. If a search in PubMed yields records that have GenBank numbers, the user can automatically search and display the sequence records from GenBank.

Linking Individual Industrial Codes to the Full Scheme

In business, classification schemes serve to communicate important facts about a company or product. These codes are generally controlled by a government, professional, trade, or international standards organization. They often serve as shorthand for users interested in material in a particular area of industry or a specific business sector. Perhaps the most familiar scheme is the SIC code, which was last updated in 1987. The SIC codes have been used by the U.S. government, economists, financial markets, regulators, and procurement offices to identify manufacturing, agriculture, and service sectors of the economy.

In 1997, a new scheme was approved for use within the United States. The North American Industrial Classification System was developed with Canada and Mexico as a means of providing an agreed-upon scheme for the collection, reporting, and analysis of information about the economy by sector, both within and across borders. Information about NAICS is available from the Web site of the U.S. Census Bureau. The digital library can provide related information by using the authority files for the coding schemes as a linked authority file.

If a company or economic sector mentioned in the digital library's collection can be linked to an SIC or NAICS code, the code can be searched against the official tables of definitions maintained by the U.S. Census Bureau. These files provide definitions of the codes and place each code in the classification scheme with other economic sectors. The digital library's content can be further enhanced by making a link between the SIC and NAICS codes. If the digital library resource has the SIC code, it can be extracted and searched against the Census Bureau's *1997 NAICS and 1987 SIC Correspondence Tables.* The table returns the corresponding code from the alternate scheme.

LINKING TO DESCRIPTIVE RECORDS

Linking the name of an entity, such as a personal name, organization, or location, to additional information about that entity was one of the first uses of hyperlinking. Knowledge organization systems such as dictionaries, glossaries, and classification schemes can be used to link the entities in one resource to richer descriptions of that entity in another resource. This is particularly helpful for users who are new to a topic and in cases where the additional information can make the user's task more efficient.

The examples that follow are from three disciplines. The first example links organism names to records that not only describe the species more fully but also put it in the context of the overall classification scheme for living organisms. The second example links chemical names to descriptive records and molecular structures. In the third example, proper names are linked to the biographies for the person.

Linking Organism Names to Taxonomic Records

Genus-species names are the Latin names for organisms—*e.g.*, plants, animals, and microorganisms. Taxonomists, who study and classify living organisms, create records for each of these organisms. Generally, these records are linked relationally to the other organisms in a hierarchy. Beyond the organism name and the information that it and its placement in the hierarchy convey, taxonomic records use other elements to describe the organism. These may include distribution patterns, the authority for naming and classification, and the date the organism was identified.

Scientists base the information on specimens that are retained because they serve as the physical evidence of the description. Natural history museums, private collections, and individual scientists number, or code, the specimens in their collections. Sometimes specimens are supported by photographs or line drawings, which may be digitized. By using a taxonomic authority file as an intermediate authority file, one can link a text or an image file containing a name or picture of an organism to additional related information.

By automatically processing the text or embedding a link from the organism name in the text or from the image to the taxonomic authority record, one can extend the knowledge conveyed by the text. The text can include the descriptive and historical information in the taxonomic record and, ultimately, link to a photograph, a drawing, or appropriate video or audio segments.

Because of the ambiguity in organism names, many examples of this type are now created manually. However, depending on the extent of the files involved, the ambiguity of the Latin and common names for organisms can be overcome.

An example of a taxonomic intermediate file is the *Integrated Taxonomic Information System* (ITIS). ITIS is a partnership of U.S., Canadian, and Mexican government agencies, private organizations, and taxonomic specialists cooperating to develop an online, scientifically credible list of biological names of North American plants and animals. It is used by many U.S. govern-ment agencies for consistent naming of plants and animals for regulatory and monitoring purposes. To link textual material in a digital library to the ITIS record, the organism name can be identified manually or automatically in the text and submitted as a query to the ITIS database. When a match is found, ITIS presents the ITIS record, which provides essential information about the organism. The information includes synonymous names, including some common names, and an indication of the placement of the organism in the larger taxonomic classification scheme.

Linking Chemical Names to Molecular Structures

The unique identification for a chemical substance is not its name but its molecular structure. However, chemical names are commonly used in research documents, project plans, catalogs, and directories, all of which may be resources in a digital library. There are competing systems of nomenclature as well as common and commercial synonyms. The ambiguity is resolved by providing links between the chemical names in the text and the molecular structure. This is done through a chemical registry number or code that is connected to a particular chemical name and an authority record that provides additional information about the chemical. This information includes the chemical's synonyms and some of its chemical and physical properties.

Most important in today's research environment is the link from this authority file to a chemical structure file. Structure files, used with the appropriate software, graphically depict the molecular structure. This sophisticated software allows for three-dimensional visualization, rotation, and substitution of the chemical bonds. An example of the use of the chemical registry number to link chemical names with molecular structures can be seen in the work of BIOSIS, the world's largest not-for-profit producer of biological and biomedical databases.

In 1993, BIOSIS began processing its bibliographic citations to automatically identify chemical names. BIOSIS assigns CAS *Registry Numbers* (RNs) to the chemical names identified in this process. In the STN International online system, hosted in the United States by CAS, a user of BIOSIS can select one or more of the records resulting from a search and extract the RN. The extracted RN can be applied against the CAS Registry File, which contains more than 21 million substances, including organics, inorganics, biosequences, metals, and alloys.

The registry file record for the chemical name, including the link to the synonyms for the chemical name and the structure file itself, can then be accessed. With special tools developed by CAS, the structure can be viewed and manipulated. It can be imported into modeling tools that allow the chemist to manipulate the structure and thereby envision new chemicals. Alternatively, the user can start with any database that contains CAS RNs and extract the resulting RNs to perform a search for complementary bibliographic records in the BIOSIS database. Linking chemical names to structures using RNs on a large scale is neither inexpensive nor easy. There are two approaches to identifying chemical names in text.

Some journal articles include the CAS RN for the major chemicals discussed. In this case, an analysis of the text for the terms "RN", "CAS RN", and variations preceding numerics can identify RNs that can be used as a link. Alter-natively, a programme to identify chemical names in text, similar to that developed by BIOSIS, could be devised.

Developing the identification programme, as well as searching chemical databases, is costly; however, if the digital library has license agreements for chemistry databases, this type of linkage may be possible. In addition, many organizations have small chemical files of their own that may include RNs and other information of particular relevance to the organization's research. It may be possible to link to these local databases using methods that are more direct.

Linking Personal Names to Biographical Information

A common type of authority file is the personal name authority, which controls variants of personal names. For example, the *Library of Congress Name Authority File* (LCNAF) is used to control variant personal names for authors, editors, artists, and others. The *Union List of Artist Names* (ULAN), developed by the Getty Vocabulary Programme, is another example. Name authorities serve as tools for catalogers and indexers. They ensure that the proper form of the name, rather than an unapproved variant, is used and bring together all works by or about the person.

A name authority file can also be used to link a biblio-graphic record or document containing the person's name to a variety of other related materials. If the digital library's resource has a standardized form of the name, it can be identified and searched against the authority file to locate variants. The standardized and variant forms can be joined in a search against a variety of other resources that can provide related information. For example, in the case of a digital library of images of artists' works or biographical or critical text, a name authority file such as the ULAN or the LCNAF can act as an intermediate file to provide additional information.

The file, which contains integrated variant names, can be searched by the name appearing in the digital library collection. When the record is found, the information about the artist can be displayed, providing a wide range of contextual material for the user. Citations to significant biographical or critical works about the artist, some of which may also be available on the Web, may also be provided in the name authority file. The variant names from a name authority can also be used to locate and provide automatic links from the personal name in the text to a biography, without requiring that the name be presented in the same fashion in the two resources.

One such resource that could be linked to for biographical information is Gale's Biography Resource, which contains more than 142,000 biographies and related citations from more than 1,000 periodicals. However, to produce this kind of link, there must be a mechanism for locating personal names in text. Several programs can do this type of text analysis; among those that have been developed commercially are NameFinder from the Carnegie Group and the Intelligent Agent from IBM. In addition, variant names can be extracted from the name authority itself, grouped, and run as a search against the text to locate name occurrences.

LINKING ENTITY NAMES TO PHYSICAL SPECIMENS

In some cases, it is possible to go another step and connect entity names in the digital library resources to physical specimens. The curation of physical specimens or artifacts is critical to the advancement of many disciplines. Exhibition catalogs describe the art objects in a particular exhibition. Museum catalogs provide inventories of the art, natural history, or cultural objects held by a particular museum.

These catalogs, increasingly available as computerized databases, are knowledge organization systems that not only provide descriptive records but also point to the location of the object in a museum, an archive, or another collection. For example, in biology, a physical specimen is particularly important when it is the result of the discovery and description of a new organism or of the reclassification of a known organism.

A type specimen is the example collected from the field by a taxonomist to serve as the prime example for the description of the organism and the validation of its taxonomic classification and naming. These specimens are held by natural history collections, and their deposit is required by the rules of various taxonomic societies. As part of the curatorial activity, the collections assign identification codes. While the primary use of identification codes has been to organize the physical collections, numerous projects are under way in the natural history community to digitize photographs of specimens and create database records for the specimens, including their identifiers, and thereby make them more rea dily accessible.

The degree of digitization varies from specialty to specialty. For example, in botany, virtually all significant research herbaria are digitally cataloging their type collections instead of maintaining paper records. Many are also making digital photographs of the type specimens available over the Web. The publication of identification codes in the journal literature is also changing. Historically, identification codes have been presented in the "Materials Used" sections of journal articles. The level of specificity of the identification code has varied, depending on the biological discipline. For example, botanical journals tend to list only the institution and the catalog, while vertebrate journals provide the code to the specimen level.

The current trend is to require lists of specimens that are more detailed. As the lists become longer and the printing costs increase, journal publishers are beginning to request links to independent Web sites maintained by the researchers or their organizations that carry all the specimens used in the study and provide some level of identification.

If the digital library collection contains resources that include the identification codes, these codes can be extracted and matched against the Web-based catalogs or databases. This link can provide users with location and contact information to allow them to access the physical object mentioned in the digital library resource. Curators or registrars of artistic, archaeological, and cultural history collections also assign inventory or accession numbers to items in their collections.

Identification numbers may also be found in scholarly catalogues raisonnés. Links similar to those described for natural history can be made between text related to works of art and the physical work in a particular collection. An article about a work of art can be linked to additional information about the physical specimen by linking the identification number in the text with an online catalog containing the number and additional information about the work.

As museums digitize their collections to establish a presence on the Web or to reduce the handling of the physical objects, KOSs that can link the digital library resources to the physical object are being developed. If there is a museum with a collection that complements that of the digital library, it is worthwhile to discuss ways in which the digital library and digital museum collections may "co-evolve."

MAKING RESOURCES ACCESSIBLE TO OTHER COMMUNITIES

Someone recently compared the Web with a large room filled with books that were scattered all over the floor. The Web is the world's largest mass of bits and bytes. It is a meeting place that brings together disparate communities. The "Internet Commons," as this meeting place has been called, requires connections between and among disparate communities in order for an "economy" to develop. This economy will provide the framework within which both commercial and noncommercial transactions can occur. KOSs are one means of connecting these disparate communities.

Knowledge organization systems can be used to:

- Provide alternate subject access,
- Add modes of understanding to digital library resources,
- Support multilingual access, and
- Supply terms for expansion of free-text searches in domains that are relatively unknown to the user.

PROVIDING ALTERNATE SUBJECT ACCESS

Alternate subject access refers to the provision of one or more additional subject orientations that make the resources of the digital library accessible to different audiences. This approach is particularly valuable when the digital library resources appeal to groups that do not share a common terminology. It can be a system of subject headings, a classification scheme, or any other subject-oriented system.

Alternate subject access can be provided by:

- Indexing or classifying the resources using multiple schemes,
- Retaining original schemes from organizations that contribute to the digital library, or
- Mapping between the primary scheme and an alternate scheme.

Indexing the Material with Multiple Schemes

The most direct method for providing alternate subject access to a collection is by classifying or indexing the resources with multiple schemes, but it may also be the most costly. This approach requires redundant cataloging or catalogers who are knowledgeable in both schemes. It may also require modifications to the cataloging tools and procedures. However, if the cataloging is at a high level or if the schemes are not difficult or detailed, it may be a reasonable approach.

Retaining Alternate Indexing from Contributors

If the digital library is being built through contributions from a variety of sources, the originating organization may have applied an alternate scheme that could be used. For example, the NASA database on aeronautics and astronautics receives relevant bibliographic records from other U.S. agencies, such as the Department of Defence and the Depart-ment of Energy.

The controlled vocabulary terms assigned by the contributing organization are processed through a machine-aided indexing process to create candidate indexing terms from the *NASA Thesaurus* for review by NASA's indexers. However, the final records contain both the *NASA Thesaurus* terms and the controlled vocabulary terms from the contributing organization, with the alternate indexing terms retained in a separate data element in the bibliographic record. The terms collected from other organizations can be viewed as an alternate access point, so that at least part of the collection is accessible through another discipline's terminology.

Mapping Multiple Schemes

The third method for providing alternate subject access is the most indirect, that of mapping one or more schemes. Several examples of this approach can be found among A&I services. Both BIOSIS, the world's largest private sector A&I service in the life sciences, and the NLM apply MeSH to

BIOSIS documents. The records that BIOSIS contributes to NLM's TOXLINE database are processed automatically to have appropriate MeSH terms added. This is based on a mapping of the natural language terms that occur in the toxicology literature and BIOSIS' normalized natural language keyword indexing with the MeSH terminology.

In the new BIOSIS relational indexing structure, BIOSIS builds and maintains authority files that connect natural language disease names to the MeSH-controlled disease terms. When the BIOSIS indexer assigns the free text keyword for the disease name, the appropriate MeSH term is also added to the record as an alternate access point. The assignment is based on the development over time of a mapping between the terminology used by BIOSIS and the MeSH-controlled terms. In addition to providing alternate access points to BIOSIS products, the inclusion of the MeSH terms makes it possible to perform cross database searching on the indexing field with MEDLINE and other databases that include MeSH terms. From 1999 forward, users can search BIOSIS databases using MeSH disease terms.

The disease terms can be extracted from the MeSH authority file or from a MEDLINE record and then used in a search against the BIOSIS files, or *vice versa*. This helps users find relevant records that are unique to either BIOSIS or MEDLINE. The inclusion of terms from an alternate KOS, such as MeSH, therefore supports the use of BIOSIS by medical librarians and practitioners who are familiar with MeSH terminology. A more extensive example of mapping variant schemes is the metathesaurus developed by the NLM's *Unified Medical Language System* (UMLS). This system has linked more than 40 separate KOSs from various medical specialties. They range from MeSH to coding and classification schemes used by insurance companies and physicians to describe treatments and diseases on patient records.

The UMLS is licensed by many other organizations for inclusion in applications that can bridge various health care communities. How can digital libraries use alternate indexing? While many digital libraries do not have the A&I resources of large database producers such as NLM and BIOSIS, the concept of applying alternate indexing can be scaled to fit. While the systems described deal with item-level bibliographic records, alternate indexing can be applied at several levels.

Alternate subject access can be applied only at the resource level, for the database, electronic book, electronic journal, or image collection, so that other communities can identify resources of interest that must then by searched or browsed individually. This concept is conducive to use with portals that provide access to the same resources with different views for different audiences. Alternatively, if the digital library has bibliographic records or metadata records at a very detailed level, it may be possible to develop switching programs that will translate concepts from the original organization of the digital library or resource to that of the alternate scheme.

ADDING NEW MODES OF UNDERSTANDING TO THE DIGITAL LIBRARY

People perceive the world through many modes, including textual and graphical. Some people comprehend information more easily in one mode than another. Most people benefit from a variety of modes that reinforce one another or that can be used when appropriate to the context. Many digital library projects remain text-based; however, this text-only dimension is changing as digital libraries become oriented more to multimedia and as other modes of information presentation become viable on the Internet. KOSs can be used to bring new dimensions to an information resource or a collection in a digital library.

In the digital library environment, these dimensions can be viewed as layers that can be added on top of one or more objects. Various tools and services can be developed that are geared to a particular mode. For example, the results of a text search can be presented in graphical or visual form, based on the number of occurrences of a term or concept or on the occurrences of documents from a particular country, journal title, or author. A more complex dimension that can be added is the geospatial dimension, which emphasizes access by place.

A "geolibrary" is defined as a digital library consisting of "geoinformation", or material that can be accessed by place. This so-called geo-referencing can be either direct or indirect. Georeferencing of textual objects is facilitated by a gazetteer, which brings together the place name and the spatial footprint for its location. Many gazetteers also include feature types for each footprint. The vocabulary used for the feature types varies among gazetteers, but may include terms such as "airport", "harbor", and "railroad station".

Although many organizations, including federal and state agencies, are currently required to provide geospatial referencing as part of the National Spatial Data Infrastructure Programme, the geospatial referencing is not readily available for older works. How can the data sets of today be integrated with the textual information of yesterday? The answer is by adding geospatial referencing to the text resource. Geospatial referencing requires that the text name for a place have an associated spatial footprint. This can be achieved by using a georeferenced, digital gazetteer that provides geospatial footprints for place names.

Through this type of knowledge organization system, place names in a library catalog or bibliographic database can have footprints assigned. If one or more of the library's resources have latitude or longitude coordinates in the catalog record or in the full text but no place name, the coordinates can be extracted and submitted to the gazetteer service. The service will return the place name for the footprint.

Alternatively, the resource may have a textual place name. This place name can be extracted and searched against the gazetteer, and the footprint can be provided to a mapping application. The latter search may result in more than one footprint, since place names may be ambiguous. Therefore, it is important that the user interface be designed to allow the user to distinguish the locations. Once the footprint has been determined, a user can access the text resource through a geographic mapping tool. Alternatively, a user of the text resource can find a set of results and have the place names displayed as footprints on a map.

In disciplines such as ecology, environmental science, and even public health and epidemiology, it would be beneficial to build a digital library with access to such a digital gazetteer service. Users could then access the system through the text mode or the geographic mode, depending on their comfort level and the type of information needed. Presenting the results on a map allows users to make new associations and analyse the results more easily. Through a geospatial KOS, they can see connections between disparate data, because the data are presented in an alternate mode.

PROVIDING MULTILINGUAL ACCESS

A third way that KOSs can support the use of digital libraries by disparate communities is to provide multilingual access. A variety of sources, including multilingual dictionaries and multilingual thesauri, can support this type of access. One of the most extensive multilingual thesaurus efforts is the *Generalized Multilingual Environmental Thesaurus* (GEMET) from the *European Environment Agency* (EEA), produced by Italy's research council, the *Consiglio Nazionale delle Ricerche* (CNR).

The GEMET is available in 12 languages, and plans for a global environmental thesaurus in many more languages were recently announced. GEMET is available by agreement with the EEA. The European Topic Centre on Catalogue of Data Sources in Germany is developing a system that will link data sources and metadata information in a virtual library. GEMET will be used to convert a search in one language into searches for the same concepts in other languages. Users will retrieve documents not only in their native language but also in other languages. This will allow data systems from throughout the EEA and beyond to be accessed as a virtual library collection with both controlled vocabulary and free-text term searching in multiple languages.

EXPANDING FREE-TEXT SEARCH TERMS

Free-text searching is the main method of searching on the Web. Only a small percentage of Web resources have metadata, and an even smaller percentage have controlled vocabulary assigned. However, variations in natural language make free-text searching problematic. Even a knowledgeable user may not know all the terminology that can be used in the literature to express a concept. The problem is exacerbated when the user is unfamiliar with the topic or is interested in an interdisciplinary area. How can the user expand his or her search to overcome these terminology differences? One possibility is to use KOSs as aids to the selection of free-text keywords. The Getty Vocabulary Project emphasizes support for searching as a significant application of its vocabularies. Harpring reports that the vocabularies are increasingly being used in search engines to look for different terms that refer to the same concept.

The Getty vocabularies are particularly rich in equivalence relationships. "When these equivalence relationships are exploited in search engines, there are typically two possible scenarios: the user may be allowed to first query the vocabulary database, locating appropriate terms, and then applying those chosen terms in a query across target databases; or there may be little or no user interaction with the vocabulary, when the vocabularies are used behind the scenes..."

Getty developed a prototype called *a.k.a.* to experiment with the use of equivalence terms to broaden or narrow searches across databases on the Web. In addition to expanding routine search queries, KOSs can be used in Web mining tools. Northern Light has developed a Web mining tool that reportedly returns a high degree of relevant hits. The KOS that supports the Northern Light site was built by ingesting large existing vocabularies and thesauri.

The result was then organized under an extensive classification scheme developed by Northern Light. The terms can be used to extend a user's search or to distinguish between multiple meanings of the terms supplied by the user. The results of a search are organized into "folders" based on the classification scheme.

These high-level categories, represented by the folders, help distinguish multiple meanings of the same term. For example, an ambiguous word such as "pitcher" might result in two folders being presented to the user. One folder would be titled "Sports", the second "Decorative Arts". The user who chooses only the Sports folder will be presented with only those Web resources that use "pitcher" in the baseball sense.

The user who selects the folder called "Decorative Arts" will be presented only with those resources that are related to water pitchers. KOSs can be very powerful in supporting free-text searching within digital libraries and in integrating Web resources into existing digital libraries. However, these systems must be used with caution. KOSs have generally been developed for a specific discipline, task, or function, or for the indexing of a specific collection or database.

Therefore, depending on the domain in which the KOS is being used and the complexity of the system, it may or may not suggest relevant free-text terms. Expanding a search with related terms, rather than pure synonyms, may return hits that are only peripherally relevant to the user.

PLANNING AND IMPLEMENTING KNOWLEDGE ORGANIZATION SYSTEMS IN DIGITAL LIBRARIES

This section provides general guidelines that may be useful for an organization that wants to use knowledge organization systems to organize a digital library. The framework described is applicable for KOSs of any type or subject.

PLANNING KNOWLEDGE ORGANIZATION SYSTEMS

Analysing User Needs

Of primary importance to any digital library project is an analysis of its users' needs, in terms of content and functionality. Many volumes have already been written about needs assessment, and providing detailed guidance on this subject is beyond the scope of this chapter. However, when analysing how a KOS might be used with a particular digital library, it is essential to thoroughly understand the environment of the user.

One must look not only at the needs for organizing the digital library materials but also at possible links between content within and outside the digital library walls.

This is particularly important for KOSs that are acting as intermediate authority files, because in such cases the links may not be readily apparent. It is important to consider other views that might be valuable for users and peripheral communities that might benefit from the digital library's content were it accessible to them through a KOS.

Locating Knowledge Organization Systems

Once the user's needs have been analysed, it is necessary to locate KOSs to meet the need. While an alternate system can be built locally, it is preferable to find an existing KOS for several reasons. First, it is costly and time-consuming to build a KOS. Second, KOSs often benefit by having been built over time.

Many of the systems described in this report have been built over decades; some existed in paper before digitization. The value of a KOS comes from its acceptance by the user community; sources built by noted authorities such as learned societies, trade associations, or standards groups will be viewed as more trustworthy than those built internally.

Finally, the networked environment has resulted in both an explosion of primary materials, including documents, electronic journals, and Web-based databases, and in an equivalent explosion of KOSs on the Web. There are several ways to identify KOSs that may be of interest. Many users are already aware of KOSs on the Web within their discipline. Developers may also turn to directories, librarians in the field, and reference sources, or they may perform a general search of the Internet.

Planning the Infrastructure

It is necessary to make decisions about the architecture of the KOS in the context of the digital library setting. The physical location of the KOS is important. Will the system be held externally or internally? There are pros and cons to either approach. If the system is available on the Web, it is possible to consider linking to the KOS as an external system. This architecture requires a script or some search query to locate the resource. One must then launch a query against the resource to obtain the piece of information that will serve as the key between the two files. This key could be a *universal resource locator* (URL) or input to another search query.

A query may be necessary if the KOS is stored in a database. The script may transfer log-on information from the digital library system to the external KOS, in order to provide access to the Web-enabled database. In the case of a more direct link, the access may be by URL. However, the use of a URL as the link has the same problem with persistence as does direct access via a URL from a browser. The organization may move the KOS, thereby changing the URL that is being used as the key. It is important to determine how often the URLs in the KOS change, whether there is a means of notification of these changes, and whether it is possible to consider an alternative that would be more persistent.

Schemes such as the Digital Object Identifier and the Persistent URL have been devised to enable resources to be physically moved among servers without having their names changed. Another alternative is the use of other Uniform Resource Identification (URI) schemes and the *Uniform Resource Name* (URN), which can be sent from the newer Web browsers. The benefit of linking to a remote resource is that the resource will always be upto-date. The maintenance of the KOS is in the hands of the owner, not the digital librarian. It may also be more apparent to users that the KOS is not owned by the digital library.

Linking to a remote KOS also has disadvantages. Persistence and unexpected changes in the organization and content of the system may cause problems. The software or telecommunications route between the digital library server and the KOS may be unreliable. In systems requiring fast response time or large amounts of data transfer, and, therefore, high bandwidth, the fact that a connection must be made between the digital library and the external KOS may make the system unacceptable to the user. Alter-natively, the KOS may be obtained from the owner and loaded locally.

In many cases, this requires licensing that may not be required when the KOS is accessed remotely, because a copy of the whole resource is being provided to the digital library. Loading a KOS locally also requires that one consider issues such as maintenance, local system administration, and disk storage. If the KOS uses special software, such as a database management system, loading the KOS locally will require a copy of that software, which may require additional purchase or licensing. Other considerations are the need for firewalls and interface design.

On the positive side, the KOS is under more local control. Therefore, it may be possible to improve the response time by not accessing the KOS over the Internet. If the KOS is to be used behind the scenes, concerns of speed and integration become more important. If additional modifications need to be made to the KOS to integrate it with the digital library, it will also be necessary to load the KOS locally. If the digital library intends to incorporate numerous secondary KOSs, it is important to consider the degree to which the architecture is scaleable.

The National Library of Medicine's UMLS incorporates more than 40 different sources. While its main purpose has been to develop a metathesaurus for moving among these vocabularies, the management of the systems, regardless of the mapping issues, has been a major consideration. Ingest has been a major concern, with the need to develop a system that can handle a variety of input formats-from ASCII text files to highly structured database output.

The architecture must also accommodate the character sets of the incoming sources. This is particularly important if a mark-up language has been used to represent special characters and diacritical marks. Systems that have been developed in Unicode, which extends ASCII to accommodate diacritical marks and non-Roman character sets, cannot be handled by systems that deal only with ASCII or extended ASCII sets. Since many digital library systems are being built as extensions or applications of existing *integrated library systems* (ILS), it is important to consider how the KOSs will integrate with the library system.

Unfortunately, many ILS vendors have not considered links to external files or databases in their system designs. In some cases, the vendor may require that the information be stored in the proprietary format of the ILS. The system may require that the files be on the same directory or server as the accessing ILS. The fields that can be linked to the Web or searched may be limited. Outside communi-cations may require Z39.50 client-server connections. With relatively closed systems, ILSs may be a difficult environ-ment in which to implement alternative and nontraditional KOSs.

Digital libraries that are interested in using KOSs should consider this integration when developing requirements for the procurement of a system to support them. Vendors should be encouraged to support relatively open architectures and to consider the extension of traditional library systems to support broader digital library functionality.

In addition to these immediate concerns, it is important to consider the incorporation of future KOSs. Initial success may spur the desire for integration of additional KOSs or enhanced functionality for the existing KOS.

Success may breed additional requirements and increase the strain on hardware, software, and network architectures.

Maintaining the Knowledge Organization System

For a digital library, an outdated KOS can be more of a hindrance than a benefit. Maintenance, both of content and of the system, should be considered when planning a KOS. This is particularly important if the digital library is to be self-supporting or revenue generating. Version control of the KOS is extremely important.

Reloading a new version from the system provider is one way to accommodate changes; however, this may not be acceptable if the locally held version differs substantially from that held by the system's provider. If there has been significant transformation or processing of the original KOS, it may be difficult, or impossible, to reload the original and recreate the changes that have been made.

A transaction-based approach, whereby only changes are transferred between the KOS provider and the library, is also possible; however, this requires that the system provider have the infrastructure, both machine and human, to produce these transactions. It also requires that the changes to the original KOS be identifiable in order to create change transactions. For example, Stuart Nelson of the NLM's UMLS Project recently reported that many systems can create annual transaction records to inform the UMLS about the changes that have occurred to the original system.

However, the changes are often not indicated with enough detail to support automatic change transactions in the UMLS. If a change date, for example, is recorded only at the level of the concept record, it is impossible to tell whether the term has changed or if the relationship between this concept and another concept has changed. Since the UMLS splits the incoming terminology and its relationships into a variety of files, it is often difficult to tell how the UMLS files must be change based on the changes made during the maintenance of the original KOS.

Presenting the Knowledge Organization System to the User

In addition to deciding which KOS should be used and what functions it should serve, the digital library will need to determine how to present the KOS to its users. A KOS may be exposed to the user or made relatively transparent. The KOS can be exposed to the user in different ways. Material can be grouped into KOS-related themes or categories on the digital library's Web site.

The KOS may be used at a higher level to identify specific portals for different uses or users. If the content of the digital library includes metadata records, the KOS may be displayed as index terms on the records or in its entirety as a navigation aid to searching. In other cases, the KOS may be transparent.

For example, a thesaurus can be used behind the scenes to extend the user's search to include synonyms, to connect the digital library's resources to other information and resources, or to filter or rank the information obtained.

IMPLEMENTING KNOWLEDGE ORGANIZATION SYSTEMS

Acquisition and Intellectual Property Issues

It is critical to properly handle the acquisition of knowledge organization systems. The first question is whether the KOS is under copyright. If so, the copyright holder should be contacted concerning the KOS. It is important to ensure that the apparent contact is the official one. Many references have been reprinted or put on the Web without proper acknowled-gment of the real owner.

Once the contact has been made, there are several points for discussion:

- If the provider maintains the KOS, how will the digital library find out about any changes that may be made in it? Is there a notification mechanism in place? How frequently must the information be updated to be of benefit to the digital library's users? Will the maintenance be self-evident, or must the agreement include notification requirements? What will the owner do if the maintenance can no longer be performed?
- What will happen if the provider discontinues the product or sells or transfers it to someone else?
- What uses can the digital library make of the KOS under the proposed agreement? As with other licensing, it is advisable to aim for the broadest permissions and the longest term possible. At a minimum, the library should be able to renegotiate the terms of the agreement relatively easily.
- In a networked environment, it is beneficial to develop mechanisms for linking to online versions rather than to maintain a local copy of the resource. This ensures that what is presented is up-todate, and acknowledges more clearly the ownership of the KOS. However, there are numerous factors to consider. Will the KOS be used on an intranet or behind a firewall, where access to the outside or information coming into the organization might be prohibited? Does the KOS service use "cookies" or require knowledge of the user's Internet provider address? Does it require a user ID and password?
- If the KOS is to be accessed remotely, are there service issues? Is it likely to be accessed with bandwidth, model, and computer speeds that are adequate for outside connections of this type? Is the use of such a critical nature that unreliable service on the part of the KOS or the Internet connection will cause the digital library itself to be viewed as less useful? Does the KOS require a specialized search engine or search query formulation? Can the digital library system properly

display the results, or would the results be better displayed through the KOS system? Will the resulting information be used in its native form or must it be extracted or transformed? If the KOS is to be loaded locally, in what formats can the content be received?

- If the KOS is not available electronically, can it be digitized? Is the owner interested in a cooperative venture, and are the human and financial resources for such an effort available?

Making the Link

There are two parts to establishing the link between the digital library and the KOS. The first is locating the key anchor information in the digital library's resource. The second involves the look up against the target file. The creation of this link may be more or less automatic, depending on the particular situation. The characterization of this activity is meant to be general and to allow both "on-thefly" links and embedded links.

Regardless of what function the KOS is going to serve in the digital library, the essential information contained in the digital library resource from which the link is to be made must be identified. The mechanism for doing this depends on the type of object from which the link is being made and on the information that is expected to be identified in the digital library's resource. The first step is to review any metadata related to the digital library resource. Do the metadata carry the term that is needed to make the link? If this information is included, the level at which the metadata are assigned should be reviewed.

If the metadata indicate the subject matter of the specific resource in which the user will be interested, the metadata can be used to make the links. However, in some cases, the terms that appear in the title or description at the resource level may not be indicative of the subject at the individual item level. Automatically making a link on the basis of the content description for an entire book may misrepresent the content of a chapter. Whether or not the metadata can be used will depend on the amount and type of information given in the metadata and the level at which the metadata are assigned.

If a text resource in the digital library provides no appropriate metadata, the procedure for identifying the key information may involve text analysis. A programme to perform simple string searching or a search engine that can preserve hit locations can be used if the text string has distinguishing characteristics, such as a database acronym, or a specific structure, such as a latitude and longitude coordinate. If the text string has no such cues, text mining or more complex textanalysis tools may be necessary. These tools use a variety of semantic and syntactic algorithms to locate key information.

There have been significant advances in commercially available text-mining tools, such as IBM's Intelligent Agent, which includes specific algorithms for identification of names of places and persons. The second step of the linking activity is to make the connection to the KOS. The methods for doing this vary, depending on whether the system is being loaded locally or is referenced remotely. If the system is loaded locally, it is possible to perform a significant amount of processing to match the two files, assuming that computer resources of this type are available to the digital library organization. If the system is only available remotely over the Web, the interaction will require knowledge of scripting and various Web-based access techniques.

Scripting should be considered in both local and remote approaches, since the more integrated the linking is with the resource, the more maintenance may be required if there are changes in either the resource or the KOS. Regardless of the approach that is taken, making the link requires an analysis of both the information in the original digital library material and the corresponding information in the KOS. If the KOS is being used as an intermediate file to bridge between the digital library's resource and another resource, it is also important to understand the data and the process whereby the search is performed and information returned from the target resource. If the KOS must return a value to the original digital library resource, the data and process must be evaluated in a bidirectional sense.

Choosing the linking mechanism is equally important. The link may be fixed or "on-the-fly." In the case of a fixed link, a specific URL is embedded at the link point in the digital library material. However, as stated before, problems of persistence are inherent in this approach. Alternatively, a URN can be used. The URN requires the creation of a namespace on the point of the target file, and the search is to this namespace rather than to a specific URL. Persistent locators and *digital object identifiers* (DOIs) can also solve this problem. These schemes are sufficient if the material is an HTML document. Content in databases is more difficult to retrieve.

The National Library of Medicine now supports the searching of a variety of its databases through its *Internet Grateful Med* (IGM) URL function. IGM users can create URLs that will actually perform searches against the databases. Information on the syntax for creating such a URL is provided on the NLM Web site. While the intent is that the search URL will be bookmarked by an individual user, the same concept can be used for creating an active link at the anchor point for the link. With additional scripting, the creation of the term *pneumonia* can be automatically replaced with an active link that picks up the term where the link has been made.

THE FUTURE OF KNOWLEDGE ORGANIZATION SYSTEMS ON THE WEB

As online databases moved to the Web, they began to provide their products, including vocabulary aids, in this environment. *Portable document format* (PDF) versions of printed vocabulary aids are common, since PDF can be easily produced from a Postscript file and it retains the look of the printed product. With Adobe's tools for indexing and searching, the PDF file can provide some level of support for linking. Many of these aids, however, remain in the form of HTML files only—there is no database structure to easily support the linking and searching.

In some cases, the full structure of the KOS is not made available on the Web; the only format for a Web-based thesaurus may be an alphabetical list of terms that does not enable the user to navigate easily the hierarchical structure. As unique ways of using these resources are developed, it is hoped that more KOS providers will be encouraged to provide their systems in formats that are conducive to such networked uses. Some of the requirements for such electronic KOSs were identified at a workshop entitled "Electronic Thesauri: Planning for a Standard" and sponsored by NISO. While the focus of this meeting was digital thesauri, consideration was also given to other KOSs in digital form.

The identified requirements include persistent identifi-cation at the concept level, the need for a simple protocol for the distributed querying and response from a KOS, and the development of a standard set of metadata attributes for describing a remote KOS. To facilitate the search and display of information from a previously unknown KOS, the system must have unique and persistent identifiers for each of the concepts in the system. For example, the California Environmental Resources Evaluation System and the U.S. Geological Survey have developed a system for remote querying and response. It requires that each concept in the thesaurus have a unique identifier.

In the case of the previously described ITIS, which is accessed remotely by the CERES system, the ITIS record number is used as the identifier. Other unique identifiers could include the DOI, or a classification notation that has been made unique by appending the scheme name or the URL to the notation. The second requirement is a protocol for the distributed querying and response of KOSs. This is particularly critical for highly structured systems such as thesauri, semantic networks, and ontologies. Work has been done in this area within the Z39.50 community.

A profile has been proposed by the Zthes Working Group to tailor the Z39.50 protocol to operate on thesauri that follow the Z39.19 standard. A similar effort is under way at the CERES Project. Instead of a Z39.50-based protocol, CERES has developed a structure that is based on the *Resource Description Framework* (RDF) and the HTTP protocol of standard browsers.

The RDF's concept of containers is a natural for managing the hierarchical structure of complex systems such as thesauri. The structure proposed by CERES is likely to be encoded using XML, a mark-up format that lends itself to structured information. This protocol for linking distributed vocabularies will support both searching and cataloging.

The user will be presented with remote vocabularies that can be displayed and navigated by a local client. The third major finding from the NISO workshop was the need for a metadata content standard for the description of KOSs. Such a standard is key to provision of knowledge organization services over the Internet. The metadata identify the Web resource as a KOS and provide important information to allow an application to use it remotely without prior knowledge of its content or structure.

A draft set of attributes for describing KOSs available in a networked environment has been developed by a task group of the *Network Knowledge Organization Systems* (NKOS) Working Group, an ad hoc group of terminology experts from organizations that are interested in issues related to the use and interoperability of KOSs over the Internet. The draft attributes are based on work originally done by Linda Hill and Michael Raugh.

The attributes describe the KOS so that content from the system can be transferred over the Internet and handled by a remote browser or client application. The attributes include the depth of hierarchy, the types of relationships included, the subject, storage format, copyright and rights management, and contact information.

To facilitate the transfer of information, the attribute set also includes information on character set and file size. To facilitate the acquisition and licensing of the KOSs, the draft content description includes point of contact information. During discussions about the metadata content standard, workshop attendees identified three methods for storing the metadata for a KOS. First, the metadata could be stored with the KOS, as metadata elements for that resource. Second, the metadata could be stored in a physically separate knowledge organization registry.

The third possibility is a hybrid approach, where a minimal set of metadata elements is contained in a central registry. The more detailed information would be stored with the KOS itself. There is significant interest in the use of KOSs to organize and search material on the Internet. It is hoped that this interest will result in knowledge organization services that will make these sources more readily accessible to a variety of software applications and to a variety of users. As services and enabled software proliferate, it will be easier to integrate these KOSs into digital libraries.

12

Care and Handling of Library Material: Librarian Duty

INTRODUCTION

What are the main threats to library material?

- The nature of the material itself
- Natural and man-made disasters
- The environment in which it is kept
- The way material is handled

Traditional library collections contain a wide range of organic materials, including paper, cloth, animal skins, and adhesives. Such organic substances undergo a continual and inevitable natural ageing process. While measures can be taken to slow this deterioration by careful handling and providing a sympathetic environment, it is impossible to halt it altogether. The chemical and physical stability of library material also depends on the quality and processing of the raw products used in their manufacture together with the design and construction of the final artefact.

Over the centuries, the pressures of mass production have reduced the material quality of what is received in libraries. Much of the paper stock manufactured after 1850 is highly acidic, is becoming brittle, and will self-destruct in time.

Binding techniques have been abbreviated for the sake of automation and many textblocks are now held together solely by adhesive. In fact, all books and, in particular, leather bindings, are far more susceptible to damage than most people appreciate.

Modern media such as microforms, optical and magnetic disks, digital formats, photographs, and audio and visual media, all have inherent preservation problems and need to be stored and used carefully if they are not to perish prematurely.

It is commonly difficult to accept is that a large amount of library material is reaching the end of its natural life, and the few years that it has left can only be prolonged by careful handling and storage.

WHY PRESERVE

- The type of library and how it is used reflect the preservation needs of its collections. The preservation requirements of a local public lending library are obviously different from those of a national library. However, both are obliged to maintain and keep accessible their collections, whether for a few years or indefinitely.
- Economically, libraries cannot afford to let their holdings wear out prematurely. Replacing library material, even when possible, is expensive. Preservation makes good economic sense.
- It cannot be easily predicted what will be of interest to researchers in the future. Preserving current collections is the best way to serve future users.
- Responsible and professional library staff should be committed to caring for and preserving the material with which they work.

WHO IS RESPONSIBLE

Everyone is responsible. While preservation and conservation specialists can advise and carry out specific activities, it is the duty of all library staff, from the head of the library downwards, to safeguard the welfare of their holdings. Preservation measures have to be endorsed, supported, and encouraged from the most senior level to the most junior in the library.

Those who are responsible for managing the library and maintaining the external and internal fabric of the buildings must liaise closely with those who are responsible for the welfare of the collections. For example, if money has been set aside to rewire and replace the lighting of a building, then the opportunity should be used for ensuring not only that energy-saving lighting is used but also that it meets particular preservation lighting requirements. When plumbing is being installed or replaced, all concerned should be working towards ensuring that risks to the collections are reduced, and not increased by having pipes running through areas where library material is present.

In such instances clear communication is the key. The preservation needs of a library have to be considered in line with the social and political climate in which the organisation operates. The organisation's purpose, collecting policies, and available resources also have to be taken into account.

Consequently, preservation policies must be made in consultation with various departments for the following reasons:

- The acquisitions and collecting parts of a library should be prepared to purchase additional copies of heavily used material, like reference works, when the cost of repairing such items is greater than replacing them. It is also necessary to calculate whether surrogate copies (*i.e.,* microform or electronic versions, and the machines to read them) are a more economical and effective way of providing access to heavily used material than 'hard' copy.

- A policy should be agreed with the cataloguing and record-creating activities of the library together with readers' services to direct users to surrogates rather than originals and to the most appropriate copy.
- Departments should plan for sufficient, good-quality accommodation for acquisitions.
- Reading room staff should be kept informed of any restrictions concerning the use of original material and briefed on limitations to photocopying.
- Resources should be provided for training staff on security for themselves and for library material, on how to handle library material correctly, and on how best to pass this knowledge on to users.
- An exhibition policy should be drawn up which ensures that items will not come to harm while on exhibition, whether within the library or on loan to other institutions. Librarians and conservation staff should agree on whether items are fit for display. Adequate support and security, and suitable environmental conditions for material to be exhibited, should be enforced.
- Preservation staff and those responsible for the collections, whatever their level of experience, should not only have some technical and scientific knowledge, but should also be familiar with the history of collections, the material they are made of, and the contents of the documents – so as to be able to understand better the preservation problems. Librarians, library staff at all levels, and students of librarianship should be acquainted with the importance of preservation within a library's overall function and policy.

WHERE TO BEGIN

Part of the process of formulating a preservation policy is to define whether, and to what extent, the library will acquire and retain material. There can be no general guidance for libraries on what material should be selected for acquisition and future preservation; this will depend on each individual library and its policy. However, national and regional libraries should cooperate in sharing the responsibilities of what to preserve and retain.

In order to be able to care for its holdings, a library must make a comprehensive and honest assessment of the physical state of the institution, the collections, and their preservation requirements. Moreover, to care for collections with a limited budget and limited resources, it is important that decisions are made on a clear and rational basis. Such an assessment can be done internally, by the library itself, or by independent consultants, whose expertise is established-both have advantages and disadvantages. Consultants are expensive and take up a lot of staff time. However, the final assessment should reveal the stark truth of the facts. An internal assessment will probably be cheaper but might be influenced by staff politics.

Unfortunately, it is also usually easier to accept recommendations from a body outside than from within. Such an undertaking must be a cooperative effort of all the departments and be endorsed at the most senior level. An assessment without authority is likely to be ineffectual.

The final report is obviously critical to the success of any 'needs' survey. It should clearly identify the risks to the collections and be realistic in its proposals.

HOW TO BEGIN

It is important to have a clear idea of the objectives of the study before investigations into the state of the institution and its collections begin. Details on policies, operations and procedures may be found in written documents, the most likely sources will be through interviews with library staff at all levels, observations on how material is cared for and handled by staff and users, and risk assesments on the buildings and collections. Identifying major and immediate threats to the library's holdings or particular collections should be of primary concern.

Such threats will vary for different institutions, from renewing a fire and smoke detection system, through setting up an integrated pest management programme, to moving an important collection of photographs to an area with a more stable environment. Surveys are a fundamental tool for developing a library's preservation policy. However, while they should be comprehensive, they do not necessarily have to be too detailed.

Surveys can often result in enormous amounts of information being accumulated which later become very difficult to put into order and analyse. Short questions and answers are the key to successful surveys. The ensuing chapters will provide more ideas on what to look out for when planning the surveys.

Building

Building to identify any security or environmental threats that are posed by the location of the institution; to describe the history and use of the buildings; and to ascertain the condition of the external and internal fabric of the buildings.

Disaster Preparedness and Response

Disaster preparedness and response to describe potential risks-man-made or natural-to the buildings and collections; to review present precautions against these risks; and to examine disaster preparedness and response plans.

Environment

Environment to report on what environmental measures are in place to preserve the collections; what are the good and bad points of these measures; and who is reponsible for maintaining them.

Collection

Collection to ascertain the current condition of the collection and identify potential problems. Describing the type and quantity of items in collections will help to create a picture of the library's holdings and age range.

Further points that need to be covered include:

- What is the overall condition of the collections?
- Which collections are in particularly poor condition?
- Which collections are most valuable/important?
- Which collections are most at risk?
- How fast are the collections growing?
- What direction is collecting likely to take?
- Is space available or allocated for future or expanding collections?

Knowing which material is heavily used will help to determine the preservation needs of particular collections. For example, a run of local history journals which is frequently in demand and in poor condition may become a higher microfilming priority than another run of journals which is also in poor condition but not often used. Other areas, which are highlighted in subsequent chapters, also need to be documented, such as the security of the collections; how material is stored and handled; the condition of storage areas; reading room practice; and level of staff training and expertise.

WHAT TO PRESERVE

Once a preservation needs assessment has been carried out, the next step is to prioritise the recommendations which have been made.

Because of both limited resources and the potential scale of the problem it is necessary to be selective in deciding what is to be done in terms of.

- Securing the fabric of the buildings
- Improving environmental control
- Improving the storage and handling of the collections.

Such selectivity needs to be an explicit part of a library's policy if its responsibilities towards future users are to be properly undertaken. It is important to understand that selectivity does not preclude adopting an holistic approach to caring for library collections. All library material may not warrant special attention in the way of boxing or being stored in specific environmental conditions, but all should be safeguarded against man-made and natural disasters, theft and mutilation, pest and mould attack, and poor handling practices.

Generally, selecting material for specific preservation processes such as reformatting or boxing is based on common sense. Boxing a collection which is in good condition and not used before attending to a collection which is in poor condition and heavily used is not common sense; neither is reformatting material which has been reformatted by an institution elsewhere.

WHAT ARE THE FINANCIAL IMPLICATIONS

Almost always, the amount of information held in libraries is greater than the resources available for carrying out their objectives with total success. It is not, and never has been, possible to save everything. A commitment to indefinite or permanent retention involves considerable financial expenditure on accommodation, special storage conditions, and possibly reformatting. Therefore, decisions have to be made as to what will be collected and preserved. Every library has a duty to ensure the welfare of its collections for present and future users.

There is no avoiding the fact that the maintenance and retention of collections costs money. For too long, libraries have spent a large proportion of their budget on acquisitions. Most libraries have no, or inadequate, funds set aside for preservation purposes. Spending time and resources on preventing damage to library material is almost always cheaper than repairing or replacing it. No library can afford not to take precautionary measures against fire, flood, theft, and mould and insect infestation, for salvaging material which has suffered from these disasters is extremely expensive in terms of human and financial resources.

The consequences of such disruptions are manifold. Serious disasters are often caused by circumstances which could have been avoided at little cost. Prevention is not only better but, more often than not, cheaper than cure. Caring for library material does not necessarily mean an excessive expenditure of library funds. There are many common-sense and economical solutions to preservation problems. However, all libraries must realise that preserving and maintaining their collections is as important as acquiring them, and that appropriate funds should be allocated accordingly.

WHY COOPERATE AND WITH WHOM

It is not simply sufficient for librarians to be aware of their responsibility for the preservation of their collections, although awareness is the first necessity. It is also important to raise awareness among the general public and those who are in a position to fund preservation programmes. Governments must play an active role in ensuring the welfare of a nation's heritage.

National preservation offices, financially supported either by government or private funding, are essential if a country's written heritage, in whatever format, is to survive. These establishments should be in a position to encourage all libraries and institutions to adopt sound preservation policies. Very useful services, such as supplying literature on disaster planning, photocopying, or security matters on request are not enough. Active training and education should also be provided. Furthermore, national preservation offices can sometimes be appropriate bodies for coordinating retention policies on a national scale.

There is also the potential for them to be the political mouthpiece for libraries on issues like the mandatory use of permanent paper in publishing. Enlightening the general public through poster campaigns in schools and public libraries about the respect for and care of library material is another useful responsibility that can be assumed by national preservation offices. If a nation's heritage is to survive, then the coordination of national, regional, consortial, and institutional preservation programmes is essential. It is unrealistic to expect libraries and archives to address individually and resolve successfully the technical and financial problems associated with preservation on a national level. For instance, in 1996 IFLA and ICA established the Joint IFLA-ICA Committee for Preservation in Africa (JICPA) to raise awareness of preservation issues and coordinate activities in the region.

Libraries should cooperate not only with archives but also with museums and galleries. Considerable savings can be made and duplication of effort avoided by institutions consulting with each other over areas such as environmental control, building and collection evaluation, and disaster preparedness and recovery plans.

SECURITY AND DISASTER PLANNING

SECURITY

It is the responsibility of the library manager to intitiate, coordinate, and implement the development of a security policy within the library. When drafting such a policy other libraries, police, and staff should be consulted.

Securing Perimeters and Buildings

- Library perimeters and grounds should be kept tidy.
- Building exteriors should be assessed for ease of access by criminals. An alarm and closed-circuit television system should be seriously considered. All areas should be well-lit.
- Close attention should be paid to doors and windows in respect of locks, security glass, or film.
- The interior of the building should be kept tidy. It will present an image of care and supervision which will deter the potential criminal.
- All entry/exit points and routes should be kept separate if possible and staffed at all times.
- Any staff areas should be locked when not in use.
- Expensive equipment should be chained or bolted down and marked with security markings.
- All contractors should sign in and out of the library and wear passes at all times.

- The need for an alert attitude should be instilled in staff.
- All storage areas should be kept secure and clear policy guidelines provided on who has access to what areas.
- Specific measures, like the use of vaults, should be taken for the security of rare/valuable material.

Preventing Criminal and Anti-social Behaviour

Criminal and anti-social behaviour ranges from the rowdy visitor to the determined thief. Staff, books, equipment, and personal property are all at risk.

Starting-points in deterring criminal and anti-social behaviour include:

- Having a calm and ordered library
- Creating an environment which the genuine reader regards as helpful and efficient, but in which the villain feels anxious and wary
- Having prominent notices which clearly define what is unacceptable behaviour
- Training staff in how to deal with an awkward or aggressive user or a suspected book thief.

Security in Reading Areas

Points to consider:

- How are loose items issued and how are they checked on return?
- How well are reading areas invigilated?
- Are security devices in place?
- Are bags allowed in these areas and are they checked on exit?

Security of Library Material

All library material should be stamped in a way that clearly identifies it as belonging to a particular institution. Library stamps should be fast-drying, non-fading, stable, and indelible. Security tagging systems, if present, should be regularly inspected.

Emergency Information Booklet

It is useful for all staff to have easy access to an emergency information booklet which lists only the immediate steps to be taken, key personnel, and how they can be contacted in the event of:

- Accidents to staff and visitors
- Vandalism, theft, and assault
- Incidents like power failures, lift failures, loss of security keys
- Emergencies which threaten the welfare of people, the collections, and the fabric of the buildings – *e.g.* bomb threats
- Hurricane, earthquake, and flood warnings.

DISASTER PLANNING

It is vital for any library, no matter what its size, to take every precaution possible to prevent the occurrence of an avoidable disaster. Of equal importance is having measures in place to cope with the consequences of disasters, whether they be natural or man-made.

Natural:

- Hurricanes
- Floods
- Earthquakes
- Volcanic eruptions
- Sandstorms

Man-made:

- Acts of war and terrorism
- Fires
- Water (broken pipes, leaking roofs, etc.)
- Explosions

Numerous resources have been published to aid institutions in implementing disaster avoidance measures and formulating a disaster response and salvage plan. Only the key points are listed here.

It should be mandatory for every library to have a written plan in which all these elements are fully developed. A 'phased' approach can be used in disaster preparedness (as it can in preservation activities in general). That is, it is acceptable, as a first phase, to begin with a few parts (even in outline form), particularly if the institution focuses first on those issues that are of greatest concern.

In a subsequent phase, the planners can gradually add more detail and other parts as they become better educated, have time to pursue the plan, and are able to develop consensus on how the institution should organize its preparedness activities.

Disaster planning usually involves five phases:

- Risk assessment ascertaining the dangers to the building and its collections
- Prevention implementing measures which will remove or reduce any danger
- Preparedness developing a written preparedness, response, and recovery plan
- Response procedures to follow when disaster strikes
- Recovery restoring the disaster site and damaged material to a stable and usable condition.

RISK ASSESSMENT

Try to identify any external and internal threats that might cause problems for the collections and assess any shortcomings of disaster prevention measures which are already in place. Consulting with fire departments will help to find any potential hazards which are not immediately obvious.

Identifying External Environmental Threats

- Describe the district where the collections are housed (residential, industrial, shopping centre, rural, recreational).
- Are there any major industrial or natural hazards very close to where the collections are housed (airport, railroad/motorway, natural waterways such as the ocean, lakes, rivers, natural vegetation or bushland, other buildings)?
- What are the immediate surroundings or perimeters to the building (fences and gates, natural barriers such as rivers, lakes, ocean front, dark corners, overhangs, areas providing cover)?
- Are the surroundings secure (regular patrols, effective lighting, gates secured and access controlled, separate access for staff and visitors/users)?
- Is pollution (dust, gaseous pollutants) from factories, traffic, or the environment a problem?
- How safe is the building from fire and flood – are there hazards in the vicinity, either natural as in woodland and river or man-made, as in petrochemical plants?
- Have any major incidents or disasters occurred in the past five years (bomb threats and bombing, civil disturbances, riots, wars, natural disasters – flood, earthquake, fire, dust storm, vandalism)?

Identifying Internal Environmental Threats

- What materials are used in the structure of the building?
- Is the external and internal fabric of the building fire-resistant?
- Are there fire-resistant walls separating parts of the building and are there fireresistant doors?
- Are collections stored at a safe distance from plumbing, electrical and mechanical installations-water pipes, radiators, air conditioning, kitchens, laboratories?
- Is the area where collections are stored susceptible to leaks or flooding?
- Is smoking allowed in any areas?
- Are large amounts of flammable material (like chemicals in laboratories) other than books stored on site?

Assessing Current Preventive Measures

- Has the building a smoke, fire or water detection system?
- Is there an automatic fire extinguishing system in the area?
- What sort of manual fire fighting systems are in the area (extinguishers – water, foam, CO_2, fire hoses etc.)?
- Are the fire detection and/or extinguishing systems inspected regularly?

- Does the building have lightning conductors?
- Are special precautions taken when potentially dangerous activities are undertaken, such as rewiring and refurbishing of the internal and external fabric of the building?
- Is the building security system (if there is one) connected to fire/police departments?
- Does a written disaster preparedness and response plan exist for the library? Elements it should contain: description of emergency procedures; disaster response outline; emergency supplies list; recovery priorities; conservation experts; supplies stored off-site; list of staff volunteers; other.
- Are staff trained in emergency response procedures (delegated officer-in-charge, regular training, emergency evacuations)?
- Is computer data backed up daily?
- Are manually accessed catalogues, registration and accession records duplicated and stored off-site?
- Are electronic catalogues and records duplicated and stored off-site?

PREVENTION

Once the risks have been assessed, take all the necessary precautions to make the library buildings and their holdings secure. Consult with the emergency services (fire, police, and hospital).

Fire Alarm Systems

All parts of the building should be provided with a fire and smoke detection system, which simultaneously alerts occupants and the local fire brigade. Smoke detection equipment can provide early warning of a developing fire, thereby giving an opportunity of manual suppression prior to the activation of a sprinkler system. Manually operated fire-alarm call points, which can be used by occupants to indicate the presence of fire or smoke, should also be present throughout the building.

Manual Extinguishing Systems

If an automatic fire extinguishing system is not present, the following should be installed:

- Hose reels or racks so as to ensure that all parts of the building are within 6 m of the nozzle of a fully extended hose.
- Hydrant systems or rising mains on all buildings more than 30 m in height or where a single floor exceeds 1000 m^2.
- The hydrant or rising mains should be located so as to permit the fire brigade to pressurise the pipework from outside the building.
- Portable fire extinguishers should always be available, even if an automatic fire suppression system has been installed. There should

be a suitable number of hand-held extinguishers (CO_2, water, or foam according to the likely cause of fire, *i.e.*, electrical or chemical) strategically placed.

Automatic Extinguishing Systems

Consideration should be given to the benefits offered by an automatic fire extinguishing system.

- A CO_2 gas system is only suitable for smaller compartments, *i.e.*, spaces which can be made airtight and which are not normally occupied by people.
- Halon gas systems are no longer produced as they are environmentally damaging, particularly towards the earth's protective ozone layer.
- Wet-pipe sprinkler systems are a reliable and safe extinguishing method and are relatively easy to maintain. Contrary to popular belief, the activation of one sprinkler does not cause all sprinklers to operate; and so danger of accidental discharge should not be over-estimated. The average sprinkler discharges 15-20 gallons per minute (90 litres per minute) while typical fire hoses release 120-250 gallons per minute (540-1125 litres per minute). It is important to remember that the environmental and human safety aspects of water are known, unlike the possible impact from various chemical agents. Furthermore, the recovery techniques for water-damaged material are also known.
- Dry-pipe sprinkler systems are essentially the same as wet-pipe systems except that the pipes in the protected area contain pressurized air. When the sprinkler is activated a valve opens allowing water to flow into the pipes. This lessens any threat of water leaking into collection areas.
- Micromist systems are being developed which discharge limited quantities of water at very high pressures, resulting in exceptionally efficient cooling and rapid fire control with significantly little water. Tests have proved that water saturation, often associated with standard firefighting procedures, is avoided. Other anticipated benefits include: lower installation costs, minimal aesthetic impact, and known environmental safety.

Routine Maintenance

Fire alarms and suppression systems, the building fabric, plumbing, electric, and gas supplies and fittings, etc., should be maintained and routinely tested. All reports should be kept and any maintenance work documented.

PREPAREDNESS

The following should be prepared, reviewed, and updated regularly:

- Building floor plans which indicate storage areas, windows, entrances, and exits; fire extinguishers; fire alarms; sprinklers; smoke/ fire detectors; water, gas, and heating pipes; elevator controls; electrical and water supply and cutoff points.
- Priority rescue lists made by departments, stating which items are to be salvaged from individual rooms. The fire services may allow entry into a building for salvage purposes for a limited time, and it is essential to know what items are to be saved and where they are located.
- Selecting and training an emergency response team comprising voluntary members of staff who live near the library. The team should be rehearsed in removing material and confident in making decisions about salvage techniques. It is essential for them to have participated in disaster workshops, where a disaster site is simulated and techniques can be practised.
- Detailed, step-by-step instructions on all phases of salvage operation, covering a range of incidents that are possible (*e.g.*, roof/plumbing leaks, flooding, and fire) and the various media included in the collections, such as books and journals, manuscripts/records, coated vs. uncoated stock, sound recordings, photographic media, computer/electronic media, etc.
- Instructions for long-term rehabilitation: procedures for activities including identification and labelling, smoke/soot removal, cleaning, sorting and rehousing, repair and rebinding, etc.
- A list of external contacts and names, addresses, and home and work telephone numbers of personnel with emergency responsibilities.
- Areas which could be used for recording and packing material.
- Locations for temporarily rehousing staff and material.
- Contracts with local freezer services.
- Contracts with vacuum-drying services.
- Arrangements with transportation services.
- Supplies for transporting, cleaning, and sorting material.
- *Record-keeping forms*: Multiple copies of all forms that may be needed in the salvage operation, including inventory forms, packing lists, requisitions, and purchase orders, etc.
- *Accounting information*: Description of institutional funds available in a recovery effort and procedures/authorization for access to them.
- *Insurance information*: Explanations of coverage, claim procedures, recordkeeping requirements, restrictions on staff/volunteers entering a disaster area, and information on state/federal disaster relief procedures.

RESPONSE

- Follow established emergency procedures for raising the alarm, evacuating personnel, and making the disaster site safe.

- Contact the leader of the disaster response team to brief and direct the emergency response team.
- When permission is given to re-enter the site, make a preliminary assessment of the extent of the damage, the equipment, supplies, and services required.
- Correct the environment, if necessary, to prevent mould growth.
- Photograph damaged material for insurance claim purposes.
- Set up an area for recording and packing material which requires freezing, and an area for air-drying slightly wet material and other minor treatments.
- Transport water-damaged items to the nearest available freezing facility.

Drying Wet Material

As part of the preparation for a disaster plan it is essential to be familiar with the various procedures for drying different types of library material.

The following drying methods all have advantages and disadvantages:

- Air-drying
- Dehumidification
- Freeze-drying
- Vacuum thermal-drying
- Vacuum freeze-drying

If time must be taken to make critical decisions, books and records should be frozen to reduce physical distortion and biological contamination.

Air-drying

Air-drying is the simplest technique for drying damp-not totally wet-material. A damp book can be stood on its end and its pages fanned out or interleaved with blotting paper. Although this is an effective technique which does not require expensive equipment or materials (fans and interleaving paper), it is labour intensive, time-consuming, and generally results in some dimensional distortion.

RECOVERY

- Determine priorites for conservation work. Consult with conservators as to the most appropriate methods for cleaning and repairing material. Obtain cost estimates.
- Develop a phased conservation programme when large quantities of material are involved.
- Select items to be discarded, replaced, or rebound from those justifying special conservation treatment.
- Clean and rehabilitate the disaster site.
- Replace treated material in the refurbished site.
- Analyse the disaster and improve the plan in light of the experience.

It is worth liaising with local and district authorities/councils about the availability of temporary storage facilities and other services they may be able to provide. Cooperating with other libraries, museums, and galleries in the area can save time, money, and resources.

ENVIRONMENT

The environmental factors of temperature, humidity, light, and atmospheric and particulate pollutants can all cause degradation reactions. The chemical, mechanical, and biological nature of these reactions may vary for different materials.

RELATIVE HUMIDITY (RH)

Relative humidity can be expressed as the ratio (in per cent) of vapour pressure in a sample of moist air to the saturation vapour pressure at the same temperature. Relative humidity is a difficult concept to comprehend and therefore warrants explanation. If the water vapour in one cubic metre of air, at normal atmospheric pressure, was extracted and weighed, the absolute humidity of the sample of air would be known and expressed as grams of water per cubic metre of air (g/m^3).

The hygrometric chart shows the maximum amount of water vapour a cubic metre of air can hold at certain temperatures. As air temperature increases, the amount of water vapour air can hold increases as well. At 10 °C (50 °F) air can hold no more than 9 grams of water vapour. The air is at its maximum absolute humidity and is said to be saturated. At 20 °C (68 °F) the saturation point is 17 g/m^3.

Therefore, if a cubic metre of air in a closed container at 20 °C (68 °F) contains 9 grams of water vapour, the absolute humidity is 9 g/m^3. If 3 grams of water is added to the container, it will evaporate and increase the absolute humidity to 12 g/m^3. If another 8 grams of water is added, 5 grams will evaporate and 3 grams will remain as a puddle on the bottom of the container because air at 20 °C (68 °F) can only hold 17 g/m^3. The relative humidity of the air in the container when only 9 grams of water vapour was present would have been:

$$\frac{\text{Absolute Humidity of Sample Air}}{\text{Absolute Humidity of Saturated Air}} = \frac{9}{17}\ 0.53, \text{ or } 53\%$$

The RH is temperature-dependent. If no additional moisture is added to the air, as the temperature increases, the RH decreases. So, if the air in the container is warmed to 25 °C (77 °F) – the hygrometric chart shows that at this temperature one cubic metre of air can hold 23 grams of water vapour – the RH would decrease.

$$\frac{9}{23} = 0.39, \text{ or } 39\%$$

Conversely, if the air in the container is cooled to 15 °C, the RH will rise, even if no more water is added. At 15 °C the air can only hold 12.5 g/m³ of water vapour:

$$\frac{9}{12.5} = 0.72, \text{ or } 72\%$$

If the air were cooled to 9 °C (48 °F), it would become saturated with water vapour, and the RH would rise to 100%. If the air were cooled any further, droplets would form on the side of the container because the air must give up some of its moisture as condensation. The temperature at which condensation first occurs (the temperature at which the air reaches saturation) is called the dew point. Indoors, in winter, the room air circulates to window panes, which are often cold enough to cool the air below its dew point. Drops of water then appear on the windows.

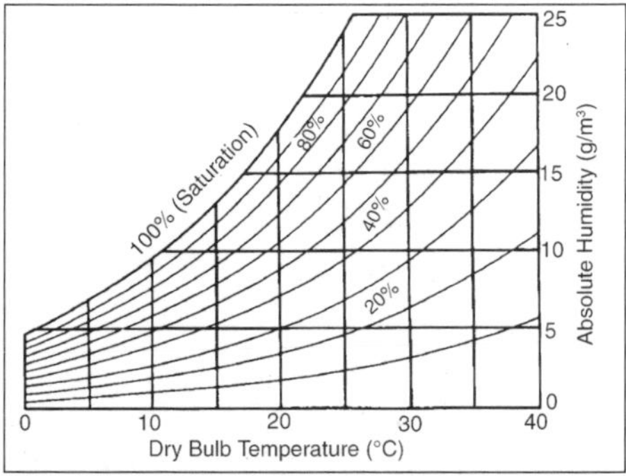

TEMPERATURE AND RELATIVE HUMIDITY

The following statements need to be kept in mind whenever temperature and relative humidity are an issue.

- The first point that needs to be understood about temperature and relative humidity is that there is no one ideal level for all types of library material – only values and ranges that minimize specific types of change in materials and objects. A temperature or humidity that is acceptable for one object may be disastrous for another. For example, photographic film, magnetic recordings, and digital carriers require low storage temperatures and relative humidity levels if their longevity is to be ensured; whereas parchment and vellum items require an RH higher than 50% if they are to retain their flexibility.
- There is extensive scientific evidence to suggest that paper will retain its chemical stability and physical appearance for longer at a constant, low storage temperature (below 10 °C/50 °F)) and relative humidity (30–40%).
- However, while the paper text-block in a leather or vellum binding may benefit from being kept at a low RH, the binding itself will

inevitably suffer. Leather and vellum need an RH of at least 50% if they are to continue to operate mechanically. The argument of chemical versus mechanical damage or content versus artifact has to be carefully considered when deciding what temperature and relative humidity ranges will have the most benefit for particular collections.

The Effects of Temperature

- It has been frequently stated that for every 10 °C (18 °F) rise in temperature, the rate of chemical degradation reactions in traditional library and archive material, such as paper and books, is doubled. Conversely for every 10 °C (18 °F) drop the rate is halved.
- Heat coupled with low relative humidity will eventually lead to desiccation and embrittlement of certain materials–leather, parchment/vellum, paper, adhesives, the adhesive binders on audio and video cassettes, etc.
- Heat together with high relative humidity encourages mould growth and creates an environment conducive to pests and insects.
- Cold (less than 10 °C/50 °F) together with high relative humidity and poor air circulation will lead to dampness and eventually mould growth.

The Effects of Relative Humidity

Organic matter is hygroscopic. It gains and loses water with increases and decreases in RH.

Consequently, materials expand and contract as moisture levels rise and fall.

- An RH of 55-65% minimizes mechanical damage as materials retain their flexibility.
- A sustained RH above 65% can eventually cause adhesives in both modern and traditional library material to soften and lose their adhesive strength.
- Above 70% RH, biological attack is a serious probability even if temperatures are low. In areas of poor air circulation RH should not exceed 60%; and even when air circulation is good RH should not exceed 65% in order to avoid mould growth.
- A low RH (less than 40%) minimizes chemical change but can cause materials to shrink, stiffen, crack, and become brittle.

The Effects of Fluctuating Temperature and Relative Humidity

- As has been stated, if the water content of a room is fixed, a sudden lowering of temperature will cause a rapid rise in the relative humidity, leading to condensation and possibly resulting in mould and other problems excess moisture causes.

- Moderate changes over a long period of time produce minimal stress in materials that are free to expand and contract.
- Fluctuations of temperature and relative humidity affect the dimensions and mechanical properties of organic materials and can lead to damage if they occur over a short period of time.
- Visible damage can take the form of flaking inks, warped covers on books, and cracked emulsion on photographs.

Measuring and Recording Temperature and Relative Humidity

Environmental conditions in all areas should be adequately monitored and recorded with reliable and regularly maintained thermohygrographic or electronic recording equipment.

Monitoring is very important because it documents existing environmental conditions; supports requests to install environmental controls; and indicates whether any climate-control equipment present is operating properly and producing the desired conditions. When monitoring equipment indicates notable changes in environmental conditions, reports should be given to authorities so that appropriate measures are taken immediately.

Recommended Levels of Temperature and Relative Humidity

- In general, library material should be stored and used in stable conditions which are not too hot, not too dry, and not too damp.
- Any attempts have been made to provide 'ideal' figures for temperature and relative humidity levels. However, it is now recognised that it is probably impractical and unrealistic to maintain a building or stack temperature at one setting throughout the year, especially in areas with extreme temperature variations, without incurring huge costs.
- If temperatures do rise above 20 °C (72 °F) it is vital that relative humidity levels do not rise or fall beyond acceptable levels.
- In institutions, temperatures are often dictated by what is deemed suitable for human comfort, around 20-22 °C (68-72 °F) for sedentary activities. Human beings are sensitive to changes in temperature but relatively insensitive to changes in humidity, while the opposite is true for most library material.

Setting relative humidity levels is always a compromise and is largely influenced by several factors:

- The nature of the collections
- Local climatic conditions
- Resources available to control the environment.

Taking into account these factors the following parameters should be observed:

- A level of moisture high enough to maintain flexibility

- A level low enough to slow deterioration of materials and control insects and mould
- A level that will do no structural harm to library buildings due to condensation in cold weather.

The Influence of Local Climatic Conditions on Relative Humidity

- In humid parts of the world, where relative humidity does not fall below 65% all year round and is much higher for long periods, it is unrealistic to expect a level much below 65%, unless the institution is air-conditioned day and night all the year round at great cost. In these regions good air circulation is imperative if mould is to be discouraged.
- In arid areas, where RH rarely rises above 45%, maintaining a level between 40-45% is all that can really be expected, unless great expense is incurred. Once again the key is to avoid fluctuations, to cool the air, and to keep certain materials like parchment and leather in an area where RH can ideally be maintained at no lower than 45%.
- Temperate regions with warm summers and cold winters often fare far worse than arid or humid areas. The RH in summer may be acceptable, but in winter, when central heating is used, it is often hot and dry during the day, and at night, if the heating goes off, it becomes cold and damp. Such fluctuations do far more damage than a constant high or low RH all the year round.
- In northern parts of America, Canada, and northeast Europe, maintaining 50% RH in winter without condensation is extremely difficult. Some institutions acclimatize their collections seasonally by gradually reducing levels of RH towards winter and increasing them towards summer.

ATMOSPHERIC AND PARTICULATE POLLUTION

Air pollution is to a large extent associated with towns and industry and is another cause of damage to paper and other organic materials. Air pollutants vary greatly in nature, from gases to particulates such as dirt and dust.

Gaseous Pollutants

Gaseous pollution is caused overwhelmingly by the burning of fuels. Pollutants such as sulphur dioxide, hydrogen sulphide, and nitrogen dioxide combine with moisture in the air to form acids that attack and damage library material. Ozone is a powerful oxidant which severely damages all organic materials. It is a product of the combination of sunlight and nitrogen dioxide from automobile exhaust; it may also be produced by electrostatic filtering systems used in some air conditioners, as well as by electrostatic photocopy machines. Smoking, cooking, and off-gassing from unstable materials (cellulose nitrate film, paint finishes, fire-retardant coatings, and adhesives) may also produce harmful gaseous pollutants. Wood, particularly oak, birch and beech, emit acetic and other acids, and vulcanized rubber releases volatile sulphides that are especially damaging to photographs. The composition of all equipment, materials, and finishes used for the storage, transport, and display of objects should be tested by recognised methods to ascertain whether they are likely to produce harmful emissions.

Particulate Pollutants

Particulate pollutants, such as soot, dirt, and dust abrade, soil, and disfigure materials. Dust and dirt that have absorbed gaseous pollutants from the air become sites for harmful chemical reactions when they settle on library material. Particulate pollutants can also aid mould growth. Modern library material, such as magnetic and optical media, are very sensitive to dust and dirt.

Dust is commonly a mixture of fragments of human skin, minute particles of mineral or plant material, textile fibres, industrial smoke, grease from fingerprints, and other organic and inorganic materials. There are often salts such as sodium chloride (carried in from sea spray or on skin fragments) and sharp gritty silica crystals. In this chemical mixture are the spores of countless moulds, fungi, and micro-organisms which live on the organic material in the dust (fingerprints, for example, serve as good culture media). Much of the dirt is hygroscopic, and this tendency can encourage the growth of moulds, as well as increase the corrosiveness of salts, hydrolysis, and the release of acids.

LIGHT

Light is energy and energy is required for chemical reactions to take place. All wavelengths of light-visible, infrared, and ultraviolet (UV)-promote the chemical decomposition of organic materials through oxidation. Higher-energy ultraviolet is the most harmful. However, light in all its forms, especially in the presence of atmospheric pollutants, leads to a weakening and embrittlement of cellulose, adhesives, cloth, and skin materials. Light can cause some papers to bleach and others to yellow or darken; it can also cause media and dyes to fade or change colour, altering the legibility and appearance of documents, photographs, art works, and bindings.

The following factors concerning light should be known by all those responsible for preserving library material:

- Chemical reactions initiated by exposure to light continue even after the light source is removed and materials are put into dark storage.
- Light damage is irreversible.

- The effect of light is cumulative. The same amount of damage will result from exposure to a strong light for a short time as to a weak light for a long time. 100 lux (the unit of measure of illuminance) on a picture for 5 hours gives it an exposure of 500 lux-hours, equivalent to 50 lux for 10 hours.
- Visible and infrared light sources, such as the sun and incandescent light bulbs, generate heat. An increase in temperature accelerates chemical reactions and affects relative humidity.
- Daylight has the highest proportion of UV radiation and therefore must be filtered.

Types of Lighting

- Incandescent lamps are the most familiar type of electric light source. Light is produced by passing an electric current through a thin tungsten wire filament. Incandescent lamps usually have less harmful UV radiation output than fluorescent lighting, but they generate more heat through infrared radiation. Tungsten incandescent lights also burn less efficiently and must be replaced more often than fluorescent lights.
- Tungsten-halogen lamps (also known as quartz halogen or just halogen lamps) also produce light by passing an electric current through a thin tungsten wire filament but with the addition of a halogen gas in the bulb, which enables the filament to operate at higher temperatures yielding a 'whiter', more efficient light source. Halogen lamps have three to five times the life and UV output of tungsten incandescent lights.
- Fluorescent lamps are low-pressure mercury discharge lamps which produce UV radiation which in turn excites a phosphor coating that emits visible light. The use of different phosphors is responsible for the various colour characteristics these lamps exhibit. Although fluorescent lighting is high in ultraviolet content, it is usually installed in libraries because it generates less heat and is more economical to operate.

Measuring Light and UV Levels

It is necessary to measure and record light and UV levels at different times of the year, as readings will change with the seasons. A light meter or lux meter measures the intensity of visible light in lux (lumens per square metre). A camera with a built-in light meter can also be used to measure light levels indirectly. A UV meter measures the amount of UV radiation (wavelengths less than 400 nanometers) in units of microwatts of UV radiation per lumen.

Recommended Light Levels

Lighting in museums, galleries, and exhibition rooms is usually left to specialists. This should also be the case for library reading rooms and storage areas. While 200–300 lux are acceptable levels for reading rooms, attaining such levels with a combination of natural and artificial light, which satisfy staff and researchers, is difficult. In stack and storage areas 50–200 lux is sufficient. However, to achieve these levels it would be necessary to exclude all natural light and rely entirely on artificial lighting. Light sources with ultraviolet radiation emissions above 75 microwatts per lumen require filtering.

Light Levels for Material on Display

In exhibition situations, the light level falling on the surface of objects on display must be kept low. No more than 50–70 lux during an eight-hour day for a maximum of 60–90 days, is often recommended for light-sensitive materials like coloured paper, newsprint, and certain bindings (*e.g.* textile bindings), and media like manuscript ink and watercolours.

MOULD

The spores of fungi that become mould are always present in the air and on objects and will grow wherever conditions are favourable. In general, moisture (above 65% RH), darkness, and poor air circulation are ideal conditions. Warmth is a factor, but certain moulds and bacteria will thrive in cold temperatures too (think of what can happen in a refrigerator). Mould can weaken, stain, and disfigure paper and photographic material. It is generaly recognised that 'foxing' may be attributable to mould reacting with trace elements in paper. Cloth, leather, vellum, and certain adhesives are also affected by mould.

Attending to an Infestation

- Mould can be checked to see whether it is active or inactive. Generally, active mould is damp, slimy, and smears if touched. Inactive mould is dry and powdery and can be brushed off with a soft brush.
- If mould is discovered in large portions of a collection, isolate the area immediately and do not attempt to clean up without first consulting a mycologist to determine if toxic moulds are present. Certain moulds commonly found in libraries can pose serious health risks, causing headaches, nausea, eye and skin irritation, and respiratory problems.
- A conservator may have to be employed or at least consulted on the treatment of infested items and on the return of the affected area to a suitable condition for housing material.
- If only a few items are affected, place them in a dry paper-based box until treatment. If possible, include a desiccant, such as

conditioned silica gel packets. This enclosure will prevent spores from circulating, but will not encourage the growth potentially created by the tightly sealed microclimate of a plastic bag.

- Alternatively, move the affected material to a clean area with relative humidity below 45%, separate from the rest of the collection, and allow them to dry.
- If immediate drying is not possible, or if many objects are wet, freeze them; later they can be thawed, dried, and cleaned in small batches. Material may also be freeze-dried and then cleaned.
- When dry, the items should be cleaned and stored under suitable environmental conditions. The storage environment is critical since even after cleaning, fungal residue will be present.

Cleaning Infested Material

- If the outbreak is small, and equipment limited, take the items outside – well away from the building – on a calm, mild day and brush them off with a soft white brush, away from you and downwind.
- Remove mould only with a vacuum cleaner that contains an HEPA (high efficiency particulate air) filter capable of retaining 99.97% of all particles down to 0.3 microns. Conventional vacuum cleaners have drawbacks: often the suction is too strong; as the bag fills up the efficiency decreases; the exhaust can be contaminated with fine particles not trapped by the bag, therefore redistributing them around the room. An HEPA vacuum cleaner is an effective way to remove mould because it does not spread the spores around. Vacuum cleaners designed to filter air through water are unsuitable for capturing mould's small particles. Even if a fungicide is present in the water, this will not prevent particles of mould from being discharged back into the air.

While certain treatments can kill mould that is active, they are far less effective with dormant spores, which are protected by relatively impervious cell walls. Proper conditions will insure that dormant fungi remain inactive and will prevent germination of accidentally introduced active spores. If the environment is favorable to fungal activity, mould will grow. Even if complete eradication were possible, it would not be a permanent solution in storage spaces without climate controls.

More spores are always being introduced and would sooner or later become a problem.

- If it is not possible to remove mould outdoors, work in front of a fan, with the fan blowing contaminated air out a window, or work in a ventilation hood. Make sure the ventilation hood uses a filter that traps mould. Be sure to remove the mould in an area well away from collection storage and other people. Close off the room. If the building has central/mechanical air circulation, block the uptake vents so that spores are not spread through the building via the airhandling system. Take care when disposing of solid cleaning materials such as vacuum cleaner bags or filters. These should be sealed in plastic bags and removed from the building.

- To remove inactive mould from paper or books, use a multiple-filter vacuum cleaner. Small brushes and nozzles used for cleaning computers are useful for this purpose. Papers can be vacuum cleaned through a plastic screen held down with weights. A brush attachment should be used for books. Covering the nozzle or brush with cheesecloth or screening will guard against loss of detached pieces. Remember active mould is soft and subject to smearing, and is easily rubbed into porous materials such as paper or cloth.
- Active mould is best removed from valuable artifacts with a small low-pressure vacuum cleaner. This delicate work is best done by a conservator.
- When fungal growth is visible on art objects or valuable items, it should be removed by a conservator. Staining caused by mould can often be removed or at least lightened. This is an expensive procedure and therefore most suitable for objects of significant value.

Treating an Infested Area

- It is important to find out what caused the mould outbreak in the first place.
- The room where a mould outbreak occurrs must be dried and thoroughly cleaned before the affected material can be returned to it. For moderate to large mould outbreaks contact a professional service that provides dehumidification or cleaning of the premises.
- If the RH is above 55%, it must be lowered before the collection is returned to the area. Adjusting the HVAC system or adding a portable dehumidifier may be all that is necessary. Also check for leaks or water condensation on outside walls. Inspect the heat-exchange coils in the heating/air-conditioning system, a notorious breeding ground for fungi, and clean them with a household disinfectant.
- Vacuum clean the shelves and floor with an HEPA vacuum cleaner, then clean them with a household disinfectant. Before returning the cleaned material to the area, monitor the RH for several weeks to make certain it does not exceed 55%.
- After the items are returned, check daily for new mould outbreaks.

Preventing Mould Outbreaks

- Check new collections or shipments for the presence of mould.

- Maintain moderate temperature and relative humidity (below 20 °C/ 68 °F and 65% RH).
- Circulate air.
- Vacuum clean regularly.
- Do not shelve books directly against an outside wall. Owing to temperature and humidity differences between inside and outside environments, moisture may develop along walls. Allowing air to circulate against the walls will enable the moisture to evaporate.
- Do not allow plants into the building.
- Waterproof basements and walls below ground level.
- Place or adjust outside gutters and drains so that water does not collect near the outside walls. Check gutters and drains regularly to avoid obstructions.
- Place lawn sprinkler systems so that they do not soak outside walls.
- Regularly inspect collections for mould so that any infestation is detected before it becomes serious.

INSECTS AND PESTS

Insects

Insects which most commonly cause damage in libraries and archives throughout the world are cockroaches, silverfish, book-lice, beetles and termites.

- They feed on organic substances such as paper, pastes, glues, gelatine sizing, leather, and bookcloth; birds nests are also a major source of food for insects, and bird droppings are corrosive.
- They prefer warm, dark, damp, dirty, and poorly ventilated conditions.
- Their damage is usually irreversible – text and images lost by insects eating and boring through paper and photographs cannot be replaced.
- Termites can devastate buildings and collections.

Pests

Rodents such as rats and mice can devastate collections:

- They will destroy books in order to obtain paper for their nests.
- They can cause fires by gnawing through electrical insulation.
- They will pare their teeth on library furniture and fittings.
- Their droppings are corrosive and can leave permanent stains.

Treating Infested Material

- Always look for the least toxic alternative. For example, when faced with a box of books with silverfish, avoid chemical treatments and simply hand-clean the volumes using a vacuum cleaner and a soft brush. When uncertain if pests are active, clean the item, bag it, and examine it later for signs of fresh activity. Be sure to segregate collections from new accessions or items with possible pest problems.

- The least toxic approach is not only the environmentally friendly approach, but for many collections it is the only responsible approach:
  - Most fumigants will likely affect the long-term preservation of at least some materials.
  - There is no one fumigant which is known to be safe for all collections.
  - Collections may be damaged through contact with the water- or oil-based spray.
  - Fumigation offers collections no resistance to future pest attack.
- It is essential that after treatment, steps are taken to prevent any new infestation from being introduced. This will probably mean segregating new (and possibly infested) collections, strictly isolating collections with any signs of pest activity, cleaning, and improving storage conditions.

Some institutions have selected freezing as an alternative to chemical fumigation. By rapidly lowering the temperature to at least –35 °C and holding it at this level for up to several days, most life stages of most insects can be killed. While some commercial freezers are adequate for pest control, others are not able to lower the temperature quickly enough. A slow reduction in the temperature allows some insects to go into a state resembling 'suspended animation' and survive the treatment.

Naturally, it is also important to ensure that the objects are not damaged by the low temperatures and that condensation is controlled.

Preventing Insect and Pest Infestations

It is now accepted that an integrated pest management (IPM) approach should form part of every preservation programme. IPM involves:

- Monitoring the building regularly for the presence of insects and pests
- Ensuring all staff, from cleaners to librarians, are vigilant and report any signs of fresh damage and activity
- Checking all material which is to be accessioned before it enters the library
- Using sticky traps. Traps have the advantage of catching insects before they can be found visually; they catch a wide range of species; they can be placed in areas which are difficult to inspect; trapped insects can be identified and counted; traps are good indicators of an increase in insect numbers in one area; they also highlight any failure of control treatment

- Understanding the biology and life cycles of insects and pests, which helps to know when and where they are likely to breed, what they are likely to eat, where they are likely to live
- Eliminating or containing all sources of likely infestation-ideally food and drink should not be consumed on the premises; flowers and plants should not be allowed in the building
- Maintaining an environment not conducive to pests and insects, which is clean, cool, dry, and well-ventilated
- Preventing pests and insects from entering the building-making sure doors close properly, installing mesh screens for windows and doors, etc.
- Using appropriate exterior lighting, such as sodium vapour, which is less attractive to insects
- implementing a cleaning and hygiene programme – rubbish should be safely and properly disposed of; attics and basements regularly checked and cleaned.

IMPROVING THE ENVIRONMENT

If the objective is to retain a collection or specific individual items indefinitely, then very close attention needs to be paid to the environment in which the items are stored. The ideal environment includes controlled temperature and relative humidity, clean air with good circulation, controlled light sources, and freedom from biological infestation. Good housekeeping practices, security controls, and measures to protect collections against fire, water, and other hazards complete the range of environmental concerns. Library buildings should be designed as far as possible to meet preservation requirements.

These requirements affect many aspects of planning: design and orientation of buildings; building materials (which can, under some circumstances, be used to produce satisfactory internal climatic conditions in preference to mechanical air control systems); internal building and furbishing materials; and materials used for furniture, including shelving as well as lighting, both natural and artificial.

Indigenous and traditional building methods and materials in subtropical and tropical areas often provide better storage conditions for library material than those that are imported. It is always worth considering constructing a sealed area within a building for material which needs tight temperature and relative humidity control.

Practical Measures to Improve the Environment

In many places heating, ventilating, and air conditioning systems (HVAC) may be too costly to install and maintain or may have to be restricted to specific collections. Nevertheless, there are many rudimentary measures and precautions that can improve a library's environment and protect collections. A first step in all efforts to improve the environment should be sealing the structure. This step alone will improve the physical condition of the building by reducing air infiltration, pest access, heating loss or heat gain, and air and particulate pollution.

Making the building watertight will also reduce the sources of moisture within the structure and may significantly reduce relative humidity levels.

- Use draft excluders and weatherstripping to make the building weathertight.
- Ensure windows and doors fit securely.
- Ensure good air circulation by appropriate use of fans and windows.
- Use dehumidifiers and humidifiers to reduce or increase relative humidity.
- Use insulation methods to reduce heat gain or loss.
- Use UV-filters on windows and fluorescent lighting.
- Use screens, blinds, shutters (preferably outside the windows, as this reduces solar heat gain), and heavy curtains to keep out direct sunlight.
- Ensure storage facilities are dark.
- Ensure buildings are properly maintained to keep out dampness during rainy periods.
- Use close-fitting enclosures (boxes and envelopes) wherever possible to protect important and valuable library material. These can create a micro-climate around the object, which delays the effects of changes in temperature and relative humidity. They also shield the item from light, and can act as a buffer against atmospheric pollutants and prevent particulate deposits.
- Paint the outside of the building with a pale-coloured light-reflecting paint in hot climates.
- Be aware that while trees and vegetation near buildings can reduce heat gain, they can also encourage insect and pest activity.
- Locate plumbing and heating pipes outside storage areas.
- Locate sanitary premises and sinks outside storage areas.

HVAC Sytems

If the institution has a heating, ventilation, and air conditioning (HVAC) plant, then the following questions should be answered as part of any environmental survey:

- Does the air conditioning provide constant climate control throughout the year?
- Is the air conditioning system kept at a constant level 24 hours a day?
- Is the air conditioning turned down or shut off at any time?
- At what temperature and humidity levels is the air conditioning set?

- Are monitoring devices for temperature and RH regularly used in the facility?
- If there is no air conditioning system or, areas not covered by the system, how are rooms heated and/or cooled?
- If there is no air conditioning system or, areas not covered by the system, how is humidity controlled?
- What sort of air filtration system is used?
- To what standard does it operate?
- Who maintains the air conditioning systems and how often?

House-keeping

To ensure the protection of the collections against particulate pollutants, a regular and sustained programme of cleaning should be maintained, undertaken with care and under supervision. Clean surroundings also discourage fungi, insects, and pests. The cleaning programme should include the examination of collections not only to provide early warning of biological or chemical damage but also to observe conditions throughout the area.

Cleaning the floors of storage accommodation and book stacks may be left to non-specialized staff under instructions to respect the collections and not to touch library material or shelves. Directions should be given to retrieve pieces of bindings, record slips, etc., from the floor (noting where they were found).

Library material on the shelves should only be cleaned by properly trained members of staff. It is important to provide appropriate materials and equipment which remove rather than redistribute dirt and dust. Cleaning cloths to which particulates adhere rather than dusters which merely spread them around in different places should be used to clean library fittings.

Floors should be vacuum cleaned (not swept) and damp-mopped once a week. Cleaning agents must be nontoxic and pose no threat to the collections from solvent fumes or abrasives. Products containing oil, chlorine, alum, peroxides, and ammonia should be avoided.

TRADITIONAL LIBRARY MATERIAL

PROCESSING LIBRARY MATERIAL

Written Notations

Written notations such as cataloguing and foliation inscriptions should be made as neatly and unobtrusively as possible with a soft (B) pencil, applying light pressure to prevent indentations. It is worth considering enclosing notations within brackets to indicate that the information was added by the institution. Inked notations (and accidental markings) are often permanent and cannot be removed. Many inks are acidic; others are water-soluble and will bleed and run when exposed to moisture, such as that encountered in a water-related disaster.

Shelfmarks (Call Numbers)

Shelfmarks should not be painted on books, nor should they be typed onto labels which are attached to books with pressure-sensitive tape or adhesive.

Paint is unattractive and disfiguring; tape and adhesive may discolour, stain or otherwise damage the binding. For antiquarian material, shelfmarks should be written on the first fly-leaf with soft pencil.

When using self-adhesive labels, care should be taken to ensure that the adhesive will remain effective over time. It is especially important that the adhesive does not desiccate, causing labels to come loose or fall off, and does not ooze, which will attract dirt and may damage other materials that come into contact with it. Ideally, labels should be on permanent paper.

Bookplates

If bookplates must be used in books, they should be made of low-lignin, alkaline paper, and should be attached with a stable, reversible adhesive, preferably riceor wheat-starch paste, or methyl cellulose; or polyester film jackets should be made and the bookplates attached to them. Circulation card pockets should be treated the same way, although books of special value usually should not circulate.

Inserts

All acidic inserts, such as loose bookmarks, scraps of paper, and pressed flowers, should be removed from books, assessed, documented, photocopied, and, if to be saved, then encapsulated in polyester. This is to prevent staining and acidity in the inserts from migrating into book pages and damaging them.

Fasteners

No attempt should be made to separate documents that are attached with lines or dots of paste or glue. If such items must be separated to allow for the safe handling, use, or filming of the records, a conservator should be contacted. Great care must be exercised when removing old fasteners such as staples, paperclips, etc.

Fasteners that have rusted or become strongly adhered to paper surfaces must be gently lifted; before removal, the line of contact between the paper and any encrusted rust must be broken. When removing fasteners, the document should be fully supported on a table, and one hand should be placed on the document to hold it in position and support the paper while the fastener is being removed.

If the procedure is conducted in mid-air, documents are likely to be torn and damaged. Staple removers should not be used on fragile or brittle documents, as they can easily remove an entire weak or brittle corner along with the intended staple.

READING ROOM PRACTICE

Reading rooms should have sufficient numbers of staff to ensure security against theft, mutilation, and vandalism.

Supporting Books When in Use

Books are complex composite objects which open in a variety of ways and require different methods of support when opened. Very few books can be opened at 180° without being damaged. It is strongly recommended that no book is opened more than 120°, and tightly bound volumes no more than 90°. Bindings are far more vulnerable and fragile than is presumed and need to be handled with great care.

Board attachments are often precarious, with extremely thin leather over the joints. Such books should always be supported when in use and boards should never be flipped back 180° from the text-block. The traditional wooden lectern or reading stand has caused many volumes to be damaged by presenting the book at a steep angle which strains the sewing and does not support the joints, which will soon weaken and eventually split. Moreover, such steep lecterns are not comfortable for readers to use.

For fragile and rare material, the foam book supports designed by Christopher Clarkson provide the most suitable way of supporting both tight- and hollowback volumes. A book can be set up at a comfortable reading angle of 20°, with an opening not greater than 120°, the joints fully supported, and the leaves restrained with strips of weighted fabric. As the reader progresses through the volume, the blocks can be adjusted to retain optimum support for the book's vulnerable joints.

With a thicker book, the reader should add or remove one or more of the flat pads to fit the volume's changing profile as it is opened in different places. A larger wedge may be placed beneath the two side-supports, to form the base of the book-rest and provide a more comfortable reading angle.

Notices to Readers

Reading rooms should have notices clearly directing readers NOT to:

- drink, eat, or smoke in the library except in designated areas
- handle library material with unwashed hands
- use ink of any kind
- use correction fluid or highlighters
- annotate texts, or write on paper placed on top of the pages of an open book
- lean on library material
- touch illuminations, painted images, manuscript or printed text areas
- insert slips or notes in the gutter of a book
- leave items in direct sunlight
- leave out items not in use

- have more than a limited number of items out at a time for consultation
- pile items on top of each other
- shuffle loose items to fit them in an enclosure, but to handle them individually (in order to prevent hidden edge tears from interlocking and causing further damage).

Assistance for Readers

Reading rooms should provide readers with:

- Information to encourage a regard for the welfare of library material
- Guidelines on how to handle library material
- Book supports and guidelines on how to use them
- Guidelines on how to remove and replace books on shelves
- Adequate space for the viewing of large items
- Cotton gloves for handling valuable material and photographs
- Clean work surfaces
- Polyester sheets for tracing maps
- Assistance with handling large items
- Clean, smooth weights to restrain unrolled plans.

Photocopying

Photocopying raises serious preservation issues. Flat-bed photocopiers and poor handling can cause severe damage to the structure of books and documents. Photocopy machines specifically designed for bound material and not office photocopiers should be provided. Overhead photocopiers, which allow a book to be copied face-up, are ideal but expensive. Ideally, photocopying should be carried out by the library's own fully trained staff, with each item being examined for its suitability. The criteria for restricting certain material and copyright regulations must be thoroughly understood by all staff members. Training parts in good handling practice and good copying practice should be mandatory for all new staff, with refresher parts for existing staff at frequent periods.

If it is not possible to allocate staff to carry out copying, there are some factors which can help to reduce wear and tear:

- Position the machines where they are within clear sight of staff.
- Post clear and concise guidelines on careful handling prominently by the machines. It is worth considering posters illustrating that the spine of a book should never be pressed down with the hand or the cover of the copier to ensure a good quality image.
- Make criteria for restricting material clear to users and discourage practices such as photocopying an item for the sake of a few sentences.
- Keep a record of what has been photocopied so that items which are frequently requested can be microfilmed.

The following material should not be photocopied:

- Fragile or damaged items
- Tightly-bound volumes
- Rare books and photographs
- Books stapled or stitched through the sides
- Fine bindings
- Vellum and parchment
- Items with seals attached
- Perfect bindings (books which rely on adhesive to keep the pages together and are not sewn)
- Oversize items that would have to be excessively manipulated to obtain a complete image.

STORAGE METHODS AND HANDLING

Storage methods have a direct effect on the useful life of material. While proper storage can extend life, slovenly, haphazard, overcrowded conditions soon result in damage to collections. Moreover, poor-quality storage enclosures can accelerate the deterioration of the material they are intended to protect.

Handling by staff and users also directly affects the useful life of library collections. Damage to books is cumulative. Repeated poor handling can quickly transform a new book into a worn one, and a worn book into an unusable book that requires costly repair, rebinding, or replacement. By following the guidelines presented here, the library can make significant strides towards improving the welfare of the collection.

Shelving and the Shelving of Books

- Shelving should be designed to provide smooth, secure, clean, and convenient support. Any protrusions and sharp edges should be attended to. Ideally, book cases should be constructed of steel with a baked enamel finish.
- Volumes should be shelved a minimum of 10 cm off the floor to reduce the risk of damage from flooding or passers-by. When possible, use shelving units that have a 'canopy' on top, as this will deflect water, dust, and some damaging light.
- Good air circulation should be maintained in storage areas and around shelving.
- Book cases should be at least 5 cm away from walls and the books another 5 cm away from the back of the book case. This is especially important when book cases are positioned against the outside walls of a building.
- When books are stored in steel cabinets, ensure the cabinets are adequately ventilated. Holes should be in the sides and not on the top of the cabinets to avoid dust and debris falling on the books.

- Books kept on mobile shelving must be shelved carefully to avoid any possibility of them falling off or being crushed when the shelves are moved.

For the maximum protection of books, the following rules should be enforced:

- Shelve books so that they are not difficult to remove or replace. Books which are tightly shelved will soon be damaged when they are removed or replaced.
- Use bookends to support books when shelves are not full. Allowing books to lean will distort and strain the structures and eventually cause their breakdown. Bookends should have smooth surfaces and broad edges to prevent covers from being abraded and leaves torn or creased.
- Do not let books extend beyond the edges of shelves into aisles because they can be damaged by passers-by and trollies.
- Shelve books by size whenever possible. Avoid keeping large books next to small ones because the large book will be inadequately supported.
- Box, or at least separate with a piece of card or board, bindings with metal furniture (clasps, bosses, studs, etc.), which are shelved next to unprotected books.
- Separate paper and cloth bindings from leather bindings. Acidity and oils in the leather migrate into paper and cloth and hasten their deterioration. Furthermore, degraded powdery leather will soil paper and cloth.
- Shelve small, structurally sound books upright.
- Move the books or rearrange the shelves if books are too tall to stand upright. Do not store books on their fore-edges as this will damage the structure of a book and loosen the binding.
- Store oversize, heavy, structurally weak, or damaged books horizontally to give them the overall support they require. Additional shelves may need to be inserted at narrow intervals to avoid having to stack these books.
- When oversize books that are stored flat are removed, the upper volumes should be transferred to an empty shelf or book trolley. The desired volume should be removed by lifting it with both hands, and the removed volumes should then be transferred back to the shelf. Replacing the book on the shelf is done in the same way.
- Avoid stacking books in piles on shelves or tables as the books can easily topple over. Ensure the stacks contain no more than two to three books.
- Take special care to ensure that shelfmark flags or titles of books that are stored flat are visible so the books can be identified without moving them.

- Do not place a large book on a small book.
- When the binding must remain on view, such as in a period room in a historic house, the use of book-shoes (supports that cover the sides but leave the spines of books visible) or placement of a piece of polyester film between the books.

Poor handling procedures can cause irreparable damage to books.

- They should not be pulled off the shelves by the headcap, a practice that causes the headcap to fail, tearing the spine of the binding.
- If there is room above the book, reach over the top of the book to the foreedge and then pull it out.
- If there is no room, push back the books on either side of the one to be retrieved, to expose enough of the spine to allow for a firm grip on either side of the spine with the thumb and fingers.
- The book should be removed, and the remaining books on the shelf and the bookends readjusted.

Carrying and Transporting Books

- Do not carry more books than can be comfortably held firmly in both hands.
- Pack books flat in tough boxes when moving them out of a room.
- If necessary, pad the box with polystyrene or foam so that the books do not slide around.
- Transport individual books in card boxes. Carry the box in a polythene bag when going outside.
- Use water-resistant polypropylene containers with securely fitting lids when moving books out of a building.
- Whenever possible use two people to move containers.
- Avoid leaving library material in vehicles.

Book Trollies and Books on Trollies

Use book trollies that:

- Have large rubber wheels, for this helps stability, and manoeuvrability, and reduces vibration
- Have wide shelves or protective rails to secure the items in transit
- Have bumpers on corners to minimize damage from inadvertent bumps.

When putting books on trollies ensure that:

- They are shelved upright on the trolley and are properly supported as in the stacks
- Volumes do not protrude beyond the edges of the trolley
- The trolley is loaded so that it has a low centre of gravity.

ENCLOSURES FOR BOOKS AND PAPER MATERIAL

Enclosures should be lignin-free, sulphur-free, alkaline buffered, and have a high cellulosic content (above 87%). Enclosures include boxes, envelopes, and folders and are available commercially in a range of shapes and sizes.

Enclosures are crucial to library preservation, for they:

- provide protection from over-handling
- provide protection in transit
- provide protection on the shelves
- provide protection against fire, smoke, and flood damage
- keep out light
- keep out dust
- act as a buffer against fluctuations in the ambient environment
- act as a buffer against atmospheric pollution.

Types of Enclosures for Books

- Tailor-made boxes of bookboard and cloth are ideal but are expensive and require time and skill to make. They can be justified only for extremely rare, unique, and valuable material. They have the advantage of being able to provide all round support and are more robust than other types of enclosures.
- Phase-boxes are a cheaper alternative, which provide adequate short-term (15-20 years) protection, and are much quicker and simpler to construct. They can be made in-house or commercially.
- Commercially made, archival-quality boxes and four-flap folders come in a wide range of sizes and can be purchased in small and large quantities.
- Book-shoes are appropriate for books that require structural support while being displayed on shelves.
- Slipcases should be avoided because they often abrade the surface of the binding and damage the text-block when the book is slid in and out.
- Envelopes are sometimes used for the storage of books. These generally do not provide the support books need and should be replaced with boxes.
- Wrappers of a permanent durable paper or card can be used to protect books that are infrequently used, if enclosures are too expensive or take up too much space on shelves.

Selecting Material to be Boxed

When prioritising books for boxing the following should be considered:

- Books with fragile and important bindings.
- Vulnerable and damaged books – books with loose or torn leaves, and books with loose covers.
- Books bound in vellum or with vellum text-blocks. Vellum responds readily to changes in relative humidity by expanding and contracting. This can result in warped covers and cracked joints. Boxing helps restrain vellum bindings and thereby minimizes warping.

Shrink-wrapping and Vacuum-packing

Shrink-wrapping and vacuum-packing, adapted from the food and packaging industry, are economical ways of protecting material. Both processes involve placing an item between sheets, or into pouches, of polyester/polyethylene film. The film is either shrunk using heat, as in shrink-wrapping, or a vacuum is created around the item and all air expelled, as in vacuum-packing. While they seem to be stable in the short term, further tests have yet to be carried out on the effects of long-term storage. Material which is to be moved and fragile items, in particular those with brittle paper, can be placed between boards and protected in one of the ways; the result is a rigid and strong enclosure. Shrink-wrapping and vacuum-packing are also being used as means of combatting insect and fungal attack and creating a stable micro-environment. Space can be saved as the process expels most of the air, thereby reducing the thickness of the item.

Newsprint

Commercially made, archival-quality boxes and vacuum-packing are both ways of preserving newspapers. However, because much of the newsprint produced after 1840 is made of short-fibred paper that contains lignin and other impurities, its long-term preservation is difficult at best and, consequently, microfilming has become the most common method of dealing with newspapers. Collections of newsclippings are usually important because of the information they contain and not because of the value of the clippings themselves. For this reason, again, photocopying and microfilming are the most practical preservation options. All photocopying should be done on low-lignin, buffered paper using an electrostatic copier with heat-fused images. Newsclippings that must be retained should be treated and then physically separated from better-quality papers in a folder or in an enclosure made of polyester film.

Periodicals and Pamphlets

Periodicals and pamphlets can be stored in boxes, folders, or card envelopes. Several items of the same cover size can be stored together in commercially made boxes. Items that differ in size can be placed in card envelopes and then boxed. If a single periodical or pamphlet must be shelved between books, it should be placed in a card envelope.

Scrapbooks and Ephemera

Many historical collections include scrapbooks and ephemera (*e.g.*, trade cards, valentines, patterns, paper dolls, etc.). These items pose challenging preservation problems because they often contain a variety of components and media. They may have raised surfaces, three-dimensional decoration, or moving parts.

They are frequently unique, fragile, damaged, and of significant associational value. They should never be interfiled with other categories of library and archival material because damage may result from the different sizes, shapes, weights, and materials represented. Scrapbooks that are of special historic value in their original form should be individually boxed. Unbound ephemera should be grouped by size and type (*e.g.*, photographs, printed material, manuscripts, etc.), individually enclosed to protect items from acid migration and mechanical damage, if needed, and stored in a way that will support them structurally.

Single-sheet Material

- For paper collections, only objects of the same size and category should be stored together.
- Differences in bulk and weight are potentially damaging, so it is not advisable to store single sheets in the same box with books or pamphlets.
- Generally speaking, heavy objects should be stored separately from lighter ones, as should bulky objects (which cause uneven pressure inside boxes).
- As acid migrates from paper of inferior quality to any other paper with which it comes into direct contact, it is important to separate poor-quality papers from those that are better. Newsclippings and other obviously inferior-quality papers must be removed from direct contact with historical documents and manuscripts on better-quality paper.
- Documents and manuscripts should be unfolded for storage, if this can be done without splitting, breaking, or otherwise damaging them. If unfolding may result in damage, a conservator should be consulted before proceeding.
- Documents should be stored in file folders. Ideally, no more than ten to fifteen sheets should be placed in each folder.
- Folders should be placed in document-storage boxes.
- All folders inside a box should be the same size and should conform to the size of the box.
- Boxes should not be overfilled because this can cause damage when items are removed, replaced, or reviewed.
- Boxes can be stored flat or upright. Flat storage will give the documents overall support and will prevent crumbling edges, slumping, and other mechanical damage to which upright storage might subject them. Flat storage, however, causes documents on the bottom of the box to suffer from the weight of those above. If boxes are stored flat, they should be stacked only two high in order to facilitate their removal from, and replacement onto the shelves.

- Upright storage is acceptable when documents and folders are well-supported to prevent slumping and edge damage. 'Spacer' boards made out of stable materials can be used to fill out boxes that are not quite full.
- Vellum documents and maps, etc., are highly susceptible to fluctuations in temperature and relative humidity and should be placed in an enclosure. Suitable enclosures include encapsulation, folders, mats, and boxes, or a combination of these.

Fascicules

Rare and unique single-sheet items, such as letters, have been traditionally bound into guard books. These are satisfactory if they are kept fairly thin and allow a support sheet for each manuscript page to ensure that the support and not the manuscript is handled. A simpler method is to make up fascicules. A fascicule is a single-section, pamphlet-sewn binding comprising support sheets of bifolia and hooked leaves (acting as compensation guards) with an acid-free stiff paper cover.

Sizes are made to fit commercial boxes. All items are foliated and placed loosely in the fascicules by librarians. The leaves on which the items are to be attached are also foliated. A Japanese paper hinge is pasted onto the edge of the item. The hinges are then pasted and the items attached to the recto of the support sheets.

The fascicules are then boxed. Fascicules have several advantages:

- Each item is kept flat and supported.
- Items can be easily removed and replaced if necessary (*e.g.*, for exhibition).
- Flexing of the object is reduced.
- Abrasion between items is reduced.
- Handling is reduced.
- A variety of materials within a standard format can be accommodated.
- The contents are protected from light and airborne pollutants.

Oversize Single-sheet Material

Oversize material includes architectural drawings, blueprints, maps, large prints, posters, and wallpaper samples. These items are best stored flat in plan chests. They should be placed individually in folders cut to fit the size of the drawer. If several items are placed in one folder, interleaving with acid-free tissue paper is desirable, especially if the items have colours or are of special value. There should be sufficient space between chests to facilitate the safe removal and replacement of oversize material. There should also be an adequate surface on which to place items once they are removed or prior to replacement.

If they are not brittle or fragile, oversize material can be rolled when flat storage is not possible. Some items need to be rolled individually; others can be rolled in groups of four to six similar-sized items, the exact number depending on the size and weight of the paper.

A tube several inches longer than the largest item being rolled and at least four inches in diameter (larger diameters are preferable) should be used. If the tube is not made of low-lignin, pH-neutral materials, it should be wrapped in neutral or buffered paper or polyester film. Alternatively, place the items between two sheets of polyester film or acid-free tissue cut several inches larger in both dimensions than the largest item being rolled. Roll the item or items onto the tube. Wrap the assembly with neutral or buffered paper or polyester film to protect it from abrasions. Using flat linen, cotton, or polyester tape, loosely tie up the wrapped roll. This assembly can be stored inside a larger rectangular box for added protection if desired. Tubes should be stored horizontally.

Handling and Transporting Oversize Single-sheet Material

- Use both hands when handling large items.
- Take care that large pendant seals are supported and turned with the document.
- Consider the route and destination before setting out, even if simply moving items from one room to another.
- Place maps, plans, and large single-sheet material in a portfolio or purposemade folder.
- Use two people for carrying large portfolios.
- Carry portfolios vertically.
- Use waterproof portfolios when moving items outside.

EXHIBITIONS

When exhibiting library material, special attention should be paid to the following:

- Selecting items which are fit for display.
- The security of the exhibit-cases should have locks, shatter-proof glass, be alarmed, and the room should be invigilated at all times.
- Materials used for case construction should be chemically stable and checked for offgassing.
- The climatic factors of temperature, relative humidity, light, UV radiation, and atmospheric pollutants should be tightly controlled and monitored by appropriate equipment.
- Materials used for mounting exhibits should be chemically stable and pose no detrimental threat to the artefact.
- Books should be strapped with polythene to tailor-made card or acrylic cradles which acurately follow the profile of the opened or closed book. Books generally should not be displayed at an angle

greater than 20° from horizontal, nor opened wider than 120°, and should be provided with a text-block support when appropriate.

- Acid-free card with an alkaline reserve should be used for window mats and mounts.
- Exhibits like paintings, not in cases, should be secured to walls or floors and cordoned off for security reasons so that visitors cannot touch them.
- A record of all items exhibited should be kept.

Loans to other institutions for consultation or for exhibition may involve risk or damage. The librarian has a duty to see that such requests, if granted, involve the borrower's making adequate provisions for safekeeping. All items should be protected against wear and damage in transit, and for security reasons the lending library may require such items to be carried both ways by personal courier, preferably a conservator or librarian.

The mounting of the exhibit should also be carried out or supervised by the courier. Loan items must be adequately insured, on an all-risks basis, again at the borrower's cost. The librarian needs to be satisfied that the conditions for exhibiting the item are appropriate on conservation grounds, and also that the security arrangements for the exhibitions are dependable.

Travelling exhibitions pose particular problems for conservation, because the likelihood of damage is multiplied. Lending institutions should make condition reports, including photographic records, of items being sent away for exhibition; they also should consider making a complete microfilm of each loan, for the sake of security.

PHOTOGRAPHIC AND FILM-BASED MEDIA

PHOTOGRAPHIC MEDIA

Since the birth of photography in 1839, photographs have been made employing many different methods. Some of the materials used were extremely self-destructive, others were very sensitive to physical contact, and almost all photographic material is sensitive to the environment – not only temperature, relative humidity, and air pollution but also oxidising substances found from emissions in building materials, wall paints, wooden furnishing, cardboard, wall paints, and even the enclosures used to protect them.

While the conservation of photographic material should be left to specialists, library staff can take certain precautions to safeguard the welfare of photographs within their collections.

Composition of Photographs

A typical photograph consists of three different parts:

- Support – the support layer may be of glass, plastic film, paper, or resin-coated paper.
- Binder – The emulsion or binder layer, most commonly gelatine,

but also albumen or collodion, holds the final image material or image-forming substance to the support.

- Final image material – The final image material, made of silver, colour dyes, or pigment particles, is usually suspended in the emulsion or binder layer.

Many different final image materials and binders have been used over the years. Today, however, almost all black-and-white photographs are composed of silver suspended in gelatine.

Handling

Photographic media are extremely susceptible to damage from careless handling;

Staff and users should therefore:

- Provide copies rather than originals whenever possible
- Wear clean, lint-free cotton gloves when handling photographic media and never touch the emulsion side of any photographic image (*e.g.*, print, negative, transparency, lantern slide, etc.)
- Prepare a clean work surface
- Use two hands to hold a photograph, or support it with a piece of stiff card
- Not use adhesive tapes, staples, pins, paper clips, or rubber bands on photographic material
- Consult a photographic conservator on issues of storage and handling.

Enclosures

All enclosures should pass the Photo Activity Test (PAT) as described in ANSI standard IT. 2 1988. This stringent test evaluates the effect of housing materials on photographic media. Many manufacturers and suppliers of housing materials now conduct this test on their products. If at all possible, purchase products that have passed the PAT, or specify that any housing purchased must pass the PAT. Enclosure materials for photographs fall essentially into two groups: paper/board and plastic.

Paper and board should conform to the following criteria:

- High cellulose content (above 87%)
- Neutral pH (around 6.5–7.5)
- Undetectable reducible sulphur content
- Free of lignin, pH buffers, metal particles, acid, peroxides, formaldehydes, and harmful sizing agents.

Plastic enclosure materials should conform to the following criteria:

- Free of plasticiser
- Surface not glazed, coated, or frosted
- Polyester is recommended for most enclosures so long as the environment is stable. The exceptions are prints and negatives with

delicate surfaces (such as flaking emulsion and hand-colouring), glass-based material, Tintypes, cased photographs, and early film-based material.

Environmental Recommendations for Storage

Photographic media are exceptionally sensitive to environmental factors.

- Generally, storage temperatures should be kept as low as possible and measures should be taken to reduce exposure to light, UV radiation, atmospheric, and particulate pollution.
- Black and white prints and negatives should be kept below 18 °C (65 °F) and 30–40% RH.
- Colour material should be placed in cold storage (below 2 °C or 35 °F) and 30–40% RH if its longevity is to be ensured. Place material in cold storage only after consulting a specialist.
- For mixed photographic collections, 35–40% RH is recommended.
- Fluctuations of temperature and RH should be avoided.

Storage

Photographs

Photographs-it is best for each item to have its own enclosure. This reduces damage to the photograph by giving it protection and physical support. Because paper enclosures are opaque, the photograph must be removed from the enclosure when it is viewed; clear plastic 'L' sleeves (two sheets of polyester placed on top of one another and joined along two adjacent edges), with a piece of board behind the print for added support, have the advantage of allowing researchers to view the image without handling it, thus reducing the possibility of scratching or abrasion.

Special care must be given to the storage of oversize photographic prints mounted on cardboard. This board is often acidic and extremely brittle. Embrittlement of the support can endanger the image itself because the cardboard may break in storage or during handling, damaging the photograph. Such prints must be carefully stored, sometimes in specially made enclosures. They should be handled with great care. Once photographs have been properly housed in folders, sleeves, or envelopes, they may be stored upright or flat in drop-front boxes of archival quality. Horizontal storage of photographs is usually preferable to vertical storage, since it provides overall support and avoids mechanical damage such as bending. Vertical storage, however, may make access to the collection easier and decrease handling. With vertical storage, photographs should be placed in acid-free file folders or envelopes that are themselves housed in hanging file folders or document storage boxes. Overcrowding should be avoided. The use of hanging file folders will prevent photographs from sliding down under each other and will facilitate their handling.

In either case, care should be taken not to pack the photographs too tightly:

- *Prints in Albums*: May be interleaved with a photographic conservation paper if they appear to be suffering damage from adjacent prints or album pages. This should not be done if the binding will be stressed by the extra volume of paper. Modern albums of the type that have adhesive coated pages and plastic cover sheets should not be used.
- *Photographic Albums*: Should be stored flat, preferably in boxes lined with acid-free tissue paper padding.
- *Glass-plate negatives*: Should be kept in individual paper enclosures and stored vertically in suitably padded cabinets or strong boxes with a board separator after every fifth plate.
- *Film Negatives:* Can be stored in paper or polyester sleeves. They can then be placed in boxes or in a hanging file system in a cabinet.
- *Cased photographs*: Such as Daguerreotypes and Ambrotypes should be kept horizontally in their cases and these stored in cabinet drawers and/or boxes.

Boxes containing photographic material should be housed on metal shelves. Where possible, items of similar size should be stored together; the mixing of different sizes can cause abrasion and breakage, and can increase the risk of misplacing smaller items. Regardless of the size of the photograph, all enclosures within a box should be the same size and should be the size of the box. Boxes should not be overfilled.

FILM-BASED MEDIA

There are three main types of film-based photographic materials: cellulose nitrate, cellulose acetate, and polyester. These materials have been used as a support for negatives, positive transparencies, motion pictures, microfilms, and other photographic products. Cellulose nitrate and cellulose acetate are unstable. The by-products of their degradation can severely harm and even destroy photographic collections. In particular, institutions should isolate and properly store cellulose nitrate material because of its extreme flammability, especially when in a deteriorated condition.

Cellulose Nitrate-based Film

- It was manufactured 1889-1951 and in use 1900-1939.
- It is unstable and highly flammable.
- At room temperature and lower, it slowly and continuously deteriorates, emitting gases in the process.
- If these gases cannot escape from the container in which the film is kept, then decomposition accelerates-the base turns yellow, then brown, becomes sticky and then brittle, until it disintegrates into ashy-brown powder, resulting in the complete destruction of the picture/sound records.

- The reaction can lead to spontaneous combustion of the film with disastrous consequences for other adjacent material, people, and buildings.

Cellulose Acetate-based Film

- It was introduced in 1935, and from 1939 onwards almost totally replaced cellulose nitrate.
- It slowly decomposes at room temperature, giving off gases that resemble the smell of vinegar-vwhence the process is known as 'vinegar syndrome'.
- It eventually breaks down altogether.
- Until recently, cellulose triacetate films had been considered suitable for archival records; however, stability problems have become evident with this film as well.

Polyester-based Film

Commonly known as 'safety film'. For the most permanent photographic records, films incorporating a polyester (polyethylene terephthalate) base are currently recommended.

Handling

Film-based media can be damaged easily, even when in good condition. All three film types, and the gelatine binder on them, can be scratched, abraded, and creased. Oils and dirt from hands can also damage the support and binder, as well as the final image material. Once deterioration has begun, film-based media are even more prone to handling damage. Deteriorated media can become quite brittle; in this state, repeated removal from a housing can cause considerable harm.

Furthermore, deteriorated materials may become sticky and adhere to other items. Ideally, film should not be handled at all by non-specialists and should be projected or copied only by a film conservator. Handlers should wear lint-free cotton gloves, handle the edges only, and work in a clean, well-lit, and well-ventilated area with enough room for processing. Eating, drinking, or smoking should not be allowed in the processing/examination area. Prolonged exposure to deteriorated negatives can be a dangerous health hazard, especially when in large collections.

Environmental Recommendations for Storage

Recent work at Rochester's Image Permanence Institute makes explicit the relationship between storage temperature/relative humidity and long-term stability. The results, published in the *IPI Storage Guide for Acetate Film*, predict the life span of fresh and already degraded films under different combinations of relative humidity and temperature. The following chart illustrates the predicted life expectancies for the previously cited storage conditions. The first number of years in each storage condition is for new film and the second is for film that has begun to deteriorate.

Table. Estimated Life Expectancy (in Years) for New and for Deteriorating Acetate Film in Selected Storage Environments

Office, Air Conditioned	21 °C D 70 °F at 50% RH	40–5
Cool Storage	18 °C D 65 °F at 35% RH	90–15
Cool Storage	13 °C D 55 °F at 30% RH	200–40
Cool Storage	04 °C D 40 °F at 30% RH	800–130
Cold Storage	–04 °C D 25 °F at 30% RH	1500–400
Cold Storage	–18 °C D 0 °F at 30% RH	1500–400

The Guide is a very practical tool for a collections manager, since the cost of an improved storage environment can be directly compared to quantitative benefits measured in years of additional preservation. As indicated by the Guide, cold storage is the only viable option to increase stability of material that already shows signs of deterioration and for keeping new material in good condition.

If cold storage is not an option over the short term, the storage facility should be well ventilated to prevent the build up of acidic gases that drive the autocatalytic degradation reactions of cellulosic films. As much as possible, the environment should be stable, cool, and dry. Significant fluctuations of temperature and relative humidity should be avoided.

Segregated Storage

Ideally, each type of film-based material should be stored separately, isolated from other types of film supports. Organising storage in this way protects other photographic media from the harmful degradation products of cellulose nitrate and the cellulose acetates. In particular, the nitric acid formed by the degradation of cellulose nitrate can fade silver images, cause gelatine binders to become soft or even tacky, and corrode metal containers and cabinets. This type of materialbased organisation also makes monitoring the condition of the collection more efficient and effective. While it is important to separate different types of material if possible, it is also important to segregate deteriorating media from those in good condition. Deteriorating materials produce degradation products that can induce deterioration in other photographic media.

General Storage

Sheet film, like negatives and transparencies should be placed in sleeves, the sleeves in a box or drawer, and these boxes or drawers on metal shelves or in a cabinet. Roll film, such as motion picture film and microfilm, should be kept wound on cores, emulsion-side-in and placed in canisters which are free from plasticizers, chlorine, and peroxides. Acceptable materials include polyethylene or polypropylene. Any paper or card inside the can should be removed, as should any outside paper wrappings, and stored separately with appropriate documentation. Both flat and roll material should be stored horizontally on metal racking in cool, dry, dark conditions, with good air circulation.

AUDIOVISUAL CARRIERS

AUDIO DISK RECORDINGS

The most likely form of sound recordings to be found in libraries will be longplaying microgroove disks usually pressed on polyvinyl chloride, or the 78 rpm shellac disks.

Shellac Disks

The first shellac disks date from the 1890s, and this format was used until the 1950s, when it was gradually replaced by vinyl disks. Determining the causes of shellac degradation is difficult because a very wide range of qualities of shellac and 'fillers' have been used by manufacturers. In a proper storage environment, these disks suffer a slow, progressive embrittlement of the shellac. High humidity levels accelerate the embrittlement of shellac disks. This embrittlement causes a fine powder to be shed from the disk after each playback, effectively scraping away groove information. Organic materials in the aggregates are susceptible to fungus attack, while shellac itself is said to be fungus-resistant.

Vinyl Disks

Although vinyl is stable, its life is not indefinite. Vinyl discs are made of polyvinyl chloride (PVC), which degrades chemically when exposed to ultraviolet or to heat. Stabilization is therefore achieved by adding a chemical to the resin during manufacture. This does not prevent the degradation but controls it. Vinyl disks are resistant to fungal growth and are unaffected by high humidity levels.

Handling

- Remove grooved disks from the jacket (with the inner sleeve) by holding it against the body and applying a slight pressure with a hand and bowing the jacket open. Pull the disk out by holding a corner of the inner sleeve. Avoid pressing down onto the disk with the fingers, as any dust caught between the sleeve and the disk will be pressed into the grooves.
- Remove grooved disks from the inner sleeve by bowing the inner sleeve and letting it slip gradually into an open hand so that the edge falls on the inside of the thumb knuckle. The middle finger should reach for the centre label. Never reach into the sleeve.
- To hold a disk, place the thumb on the edge of the disk, and the

rest of the fingers of the same hand on the centre label for balance. Use both hands on the edge to place disk on turntable.

Storage

- Store records in soft polyethylene inner sleeves. Avoid using inner sleeves made of paper, cardboard, or PVC.
- Do not leave recordings near sources of heat or light (especially ultraviolet), as plastics are adversely affected by both.
- Do not place heavy objects on top of recordings. Recordings should never be placed on top of each other.
- Shelve recordings vertically, on edge.
- Do not use shelving units where supports put more pressure on one area of the recording or where supports are more than 10-15 cm (4-6 inches) apart.
- Do not interfile recordings of different sizes, as smaller items may get lost or damaged, while larger items may be subjected to uneven pressure.
- Remove shrink-wrap on long-playing gramophone records (LPs) completely. Shrink-wrap can continue to shrink, thus warping the disk.

Environmental Recommendations for Storage

A proper environment for the storage of sound recordings is essential to retard degradation. Elevated and rapid fluctuations of temperature and humidity can affect certain chemical properties of the plastics that make up recording media, causing distortion of sound quality and warping of the disk itself. 18 °C (64 °F) and 40% RH is recommended. Fungi on disk surfaces can cause pitting, which affects playback quality. Dust, combined with the pressure exerted on the grooves by the stylus, can permanently abrade the walls of the grooves, which affects playback quality; dust can also be embedded permanently into thermoplastic substances.

MAGNETIC MEDIA

Magnetic tapes (audio and video recordings on cassettes, audio and computer reel-to-reel tape, computer diskettes, etc.) are most commonly made of a magnetic layer of chromium or iron oxide bound with an adhesive onto a polyester film base. It is the adhesive binder which is susceptible to deterioration, through hydrolysis and oxidation. As the information is stored on magnetic tape in patterns formed by the magnetized particles, any loss or disarrangement of the magnetic oxide causes loss of information. Since the early 1950s, there have been more than forty video formats that have varied in size, speed, and the manner in which the tape is held. Cassette tapes are much thinner and weaker than reel-to-reel tapes, and their useable life expectancy is very short. Use reel-to-reel tape for long-term retention. Magnetic tape has a much shorter lifespan than is presumed. Magnetic tape that is over 15 years old almost certainly needs careful attention, and most tapes over 20 years old need professional help.

Handling

- Minimize handling.
- Avoid touching the surface of any tape or computer diskette. Oil from skin leaves a residue that can coat the equipment's playing head and attract dust.
- Do not touch the tape surface or the edge of the tape pack unless absolutely necessary, and then wear lint-free gloves.
- Do not use commercial products advertised to clean tapes and diskettes. Contact an experienced professional to clean or repair dirty or damaged tapes.
- Return tapes and diskettes to their individual boxes immediately after use to avoid possible damage and dust.
- Never use paper clips or adhesive tape to attach notes directly to cassettes, reels, or diskettes.
- Handle tape only in clean areas.
- Do not let tape or leader ends trail on the floor.
- Return tapes to their containers when they are not in use.
- Do not drop tapes or subject them to sudden shock.
- Cut off damaged tape or leader/trailer ends from open-reel tapes.
- Do not use general-purpose adhesive tapes to secure the tape end or for splicing. If necessary, use adhesive products designed for the purpose.

Use

- Label all tapes.
- Maintain machines according to manufacturer's specifications to ensure that equipment will not damage tapes.
- Clean the recorder tape path thoroughly at the recommended intervals.
- Discard tapes with scratches or any other surface damage, which causes significant debris to be left in the recorder tape path.
- Use a cleaning cassette after playing a damaged tape.
- Ensure tapes to be reused are thoroughly erased before they are put back into service.
- Fast forward and rewind tapes periodically.
- Do not leave a tape stopped in the middle – always rewind the tape fully.
- Protect the operating equipment and tapes from dust.

Backup and Refreshing

The loss of a single computer diskette can mean the loss of a large quantity of information. For this reason, backup copies are critical to ensuring the preservation of computer-based records. If maintaining an active computer database of records is part of an institutional operation, copy the information recorded on the system's hard drive onto backup diskettes or tapes on a daily basis. As a part of disaster prevention, store backup copies in another secure location. Audio, video, and computer tapes which are to be retained for long periods of time will require periodic copying/refreshing to ensure access to information. Every three to five years, re-copy all master tapes onto high quality, polyesterbased tape in the currently established format for the media. Use this copy master only when making another 'use' copy. Make the copies of masters at different times so they do not age together. Use reel-to-reel audio tape for master audio copies. A written transcript of an audio or video tape can also be used as a 'use copy' or 'backup copy'. A transcript may contain every word on the original tape, or only a general rendering of the discussion.

Migration

Information formats disappear as new technology emerges. Within the last twenty years, 8-track tapes, beta format video, ½-inch videotape, 3-inch, 5¼-inch and 8- inch computer diskettes and countless other formats have become obsolete. Access to information is limited when machines necessary to read these records fail and cannot be replaced. To ensure access to information, copy older formats onto a stable technology while playback machines remain available.

Storage

- Keep tapes and diskettes away from magnetic fields – do not stack tapes on top of electrical equipment.
- Keep storage areas clean and free from dust. Dust attracts and traps moisture and will precipitate hydrolysis, a common and serious cause of long-term magnetic tape degradation. Also, dust may cause permanent damage to the tape: the abrasiveness of the dust, along with the pressure exerted between the tape surface and the tape recorder heads, will scratch the oxide layer and the tape recorder heads.
- Do not leave open reel or cassette tapes exposed to the sun.
- Store open-reel and cassette tapes with the reels or tape packs vertical. Reels should be supported by the hub.
- Use high quality reels or cassettes, boxes/containers, and accessories.
- Use protective collars for open-reel tapes.
- Do not store the tapes in poor quality cardboard sleeves/boxes, which may be acidic, or vinyl boxes containing chlorine.

Environmental Recommendations for Storage

- *Tape storage areas should be cool and dry*: 15 ± 3 °C (59 ±5 °F) and 30–40% RH are safe practical storage conditions. Extreme heat and frost will damage magnetic media.
- RH above 40% accelerates the deterioration of the tape binder.
- Avoid subjecting tapes to rapid temperature changes. If storage and operating area temperatures differ by more than 8 °C (15 °F), allow an acclimatization time within the operating area of four hours for every 10 °C (18 °F) difference.

OPTICAL MEDIA

Laser Disks

Laser disks were launched in 1978 and are usually 12-inch (30 cm) disks of glass or plastic. Millions of pits are etched into the surface which are read by a laser beam directed at the surface. A light beam is reflected, which is then converted into a conventional analogue signal.

CD-ROM

CD-ROM (compact disk – read only memory) originated from the audio compact disk which was available in the mid-1980s, and thus its physical dimensions and characteristics are the same. The main difference between CD-ROM and CDAudio is that CD-Audio contains only audio data, while CD-ROM may contain audio, computer, and video/picture data. The moulded plastic compact disk incorporates a continuous spiral of pits, which contain the data. An aluminium reflective layer allows a laser in the compact disk drive to read the encoded information. Data integrity is protected by a lacquer coating on one side and a plastic substrate on the other side.

Handling

The worst handling stresses for an optical disk are caused by severe flexing or application of a sharp point to the top surface. These actions deform the substrate, wiping out pits and causing areas of the disk to become unreadable. A sharp stylus – a ballpoint pen, for example – can cause compression of the polycarbonate substrate and the metallic reflecting layer in the area under the pen point. Do not leave disks in disk drives. Wear lint-free gloves when handling optical media.

Labelling

Applying labels of any kind may unbalance an optical disk and make it difficult for the player to read. Also, labels may peel in humid conditions. Once a label is on the disk, however, it is especially important not to try and remove it. The act of peeling off a label creates a lever action that concentrates stress in a small area. Such stress can cause delamination, especially in a writable CD. If it is necessary to write on the top side of a disk, a soft felt-tip marker is preferable to other writing instruments, but with some solvent-based markers there may be a danger of the solvents migrating into the protective lacquer.

Cleaning

Avoid using cleaning solvents. Light dust or dirt may be safely brushed off with a non-abrasive lens tissue, but the use of an air gun is preferable. Always be gentle and wipe from the centre hub towards the outside edge of the disk. The motion should be in a radial direction (like the spokes of a wheel), not circumferential.

Storage

The acrylic 'jewel cases' provided by many manufacturers and distributors are good protection against scratches, dust, light, and rapid humidity changes. Protect the individually cased CDs further by placing them in a closed box, drawer, or cabinet. This gives additional protection from light, dust, and climate fluctuations. If the manufacturer provides a spacer card or other material as part of the jewel case package, it should be retained.

Environmental Recommendations for Storage

Optical disks should be stored in a dust-free, cool (below 20 °C or 68 °F), and moderately dry environment (40% RH). Warmer and humid conditions will lead to the oxidation of metallic reflecting layers, dark fading of dyes, and deterioration in polymer substrates and coatings. Do not leave disks in sunlight.

REFORMATTING

WHY REFORMAT

Although libraries can take steps to prevent damage to their collections and the rate at which they deteriorate, few institutions can afford the labour-intensive and costly process of conserving their collections. Preserving the intellectual content, by putting it into another, more durable format (reformatting), is all that is feasible and may be all that is required. Many publications are available which cover in detail the issues that reformatting raises and the methods and techniques involved. This part summarises some of the most common points and is concerned mainly with looking after the reformatting media. It is also a reminder that material which is to be reformatted needs to be handled with all due care.

Library and archive material is reformatted for numerous reasons:

- To preserve its intellectual content.
- To reduce wear and tear to originals.
- To save space-brittle and badly damaged material may be disposed of if it has no artefactual worth and if intellectual content is the only concern.

- To improve access-copies of microfilm and digitised media can be distributed to off-site locations, providing access to more than one user at a time.
- To duplicate certain records for security reasons, in case the originals are damaged, stolen, or destroyed.

Reformatting, if it is to be a truly successful preservation process, depends upon the cooperation of institutions on a national and international scale. Projects like that of the European Register of Microfilm Masters (EROMM), a database of existing microforms in the most important libraries of Europe, must be set up. EROMM records what reformatted texts exist and where, so that institutions avoid duplicating their efforts (two institutions microfilming the same newspaper is a waste of valuable resources, as is one institution's reformatting a run of journals when a 'healthy' set exists in another town nearby). Furthermore, cooperation is necessary between libraries in planning what is to be reformatted and by which institution. Many guides have been published to aid librarians in selecting material for reformatting and in setting up reformatting programmes. Generally, the following questions have to be asked:

- Is the item or collection unique or rare?
- Are there other copies of the item in the library or elsewhere?
- Does the item need to be treated (is the paper already, or is it likely to become, highly acidic and brittle)?
- Is it possible to replace the item?
- Is it, or is it likely to be, heavily used?
- Does it need to be retained in its original form?
- Has it been reformatted somewhere else already?

Reducing Wear and Tear to Originals

When the objective is to reduce wear and tear to originals, great caution has to be exercised in preventing damage occurring during the reprographic process. Reformatting increases the risk to an item because of the number of times it has to be handled in the process.

Selecting a Format

There are three main reformatting processes:

- Photocopying
- Microfilming
- Digitizing

Each has advantages and disadvantages over the others, but they can all serve different purposes, and all are worth having present in a library to some degree.

PHOTOCOPYING

Photocopying as a reformatting process is not a complete preservation tool since usually no master is made from which other copies can be taken.

However, it is particularly useful for replacing missing pages or text:

- Damaged or missing items in hard-copy periodical runs can be copied and bound for storage on open shelves.
- Photocopies may also be used when an embrittled item can no longer be used without risking damage, and a paper copy replacement (rather than film) is desired but is not available from a commercial publisher.

In each case, it is essential that photocopies be of the highest quality and on permanent paper.

Advantages

- There is no reading machine interface required other than the photocopier itself.
- The medium and format of the original can be retained.
- It usually costs less than other processes, particularly if the original is a monochrome document.
- Library patrons prefer paper facsimiles to the use of, say, microfilms, except where bulky documents, such as newspapers, are involved.

Disadvantages

- Photocopies made directly from a master photocopy are usually of poorer quality than paper prints of microfilms.
- The costs of making subsequent photocopies is higher than the cost of printing microfilms.
- There is some loss of information, especially for graphic objects other than line art.
- If the original is kept, more space has to be created.

Photocopy Paper, Toner, and Machines

- *Paper*: Photocopies should be made on paper that meets the American National Standards Institute (ANSI) standard for permanent paper, Z39.48- 1992 or ISO 9706, using a black-and-white copy machine, since colour photocopies are not stable over the long-term.
- *Toner*: Other considerations are toner quality (carbon black is recommended), and the fusion of the toner to the paper. Photocopy machines should be well maintained to ensure that the temperature is right for fusing the toner to the paper. If a freshly-made copy smudges when an attempt is made to erase the image, the machine is not fusing the image to the paper properly and must be adjusted.
- *Machines*: Photocopying bound items on common library photocopiers exerts enormous strain on bindings and inevitably damages them. Photocopiers which allow an item to be photocopied face-up are preferable. Overhead photocopiers which also digitise text and images are now available. They have great potential for

being able to capture good-quality images of volumes which do not open well.

MICROFILMING

Microfilming Process

A wide range of standards covering all aspects of microfilm production and storage have been published.

Preservation microfilming comprises a number of steps:

- *Selection* – making informed decisions on what is to be filmed.
- *Preparation* – checking the item is complete; cleaning and repairing pages; preparing 'targets' that denote details such as title and magnification.
- *Filming* – similar to basic photographic procedures.
- *Processing the film* – after exposure, the film is processed to archival standards and tested to ensure residual processing chemicals are removed.
- *Inspection* – after processing, the film is inspected for blemishes, legibility, and completeness.
- *Record creation* – the creation and mounting of machine readable records (MARC) to promote use of film and prevent duplication of effort.

Commercial Microform Bureaux

Using a commercial microform bureau can be more economical than setting up an in-house operation. It is vitally important to evaluate the qualifications of any microfilm service company.

- Talk to other institutions, particularly archives, and enquire about their experiences with microfilming companies.
- Ask potential firms about their experience in filming records that are bound, fragile, or oversized.
- Ask for at least three references from other institutions.
- Contact the referees to see how the microfilm vendor handled records, met deadlines, and responded to refilming corrections.
- Inspect the microfilmer's operation. Ask questions about standards, procedures, and security.
- Draw up a contract between the institution and the bureau.
- Commission sample film.

Advantages

- A well-proven history – library material has been reproduced in microformats since the 1930s.
- Problems with the technology have largely been ironed out.
- Numerous standards exist for filming, processing, and storage.

- Microfilms can be economically created, duplicated, and distributed.
- Microfilms can be digitized if good-quality film has been used.
- Film is very compact.

Disadvantages

- User resistance – usually microfilm reading machines in libraries are of poor quality, and not designed for human comfort.
- Users must access the film manually by
  - Locating the film
  - Loading it onto a machine
  - Spooling through dozens of images to find the required one.
- If the film is not in the library, it may take weeks to be delivered.
- Film can become scratched when handled.
- Each generation or succeeding copy loses resolution (about ten per cent).
- Printouts may be of poor quality.
- Film creation variables are difficult to control.
- Image quality can be determined only after filming is complete.
- Bad pages must be re-filmed and spliced in.

Types of Microfilm

- *Silver-gelatine* – the only type for archival master negatives, which are to be retained indefinitely off-site in tightly controlled conditions. Master negatives are used solely for generating further copies and never for viewing.
- *Diazo* – an interim printing copy can be made from the master on diazo film, from which other copies are taken.
- *Vesicular* – positive copies can be made on vesicular film for use and circulation.

Storage and Environmental Recommendations

Most of the recommendations for film-based media apply to microfilm material. Many films in existing collections are on acetate-based stock. Such film chemically decomposes, giving off a vinegar smell and ultimately leading to shrinkage and emulsion damage.

Indeed, all cellulosic films are susceptible to deterioration. The rate of deterioration of the film base proceeds gradually until it reaches the autocatalytic point, at which time the rate rapidly increases.

Temperature and humidity have a significant impact on how long it takes the film base to reach the autocatalytic point. It is frequently claimed that properly processed and stored, black-and-white, silver gelatine film has a usable life of about 500 years, far longer than the useful life of many poor-quality originals. However, improper processing and storage conditions will reduce film longevity.

- Master negatives should be stored in fire-proof vaults (not safes, as these can not be kept at the required RH), free of dust and atmospheric pollutants and maintained at a temperature of 18 °C ± 2 °C (64 °F ± 5 °F), with a constant level of RH between 20% and 40% for silver gelatine on a cellulose ester base, and 30% to 40% for silver gelatine on a polyester base.
- Intermediate printing copies on diazo film and viewing copies on vesicular film can be stored in less stringent conditions. However, cool and dry conditions will help to prolong the life of these types of film.
- In all cases, rapid fluctuations of RH and temperature should be avoided.
- Diazo film images will fade, and exposure to light accelerates fading, so diazo film should be stored in darkness and always in its container when not in use.
- Vesicular film is particularly vulnerable to dust and the high temperatures produced by microfilm reading machines, so it is important to keep the machine clean and cool.
- Containers should be free from acidic, oxidising and reducing agents and meet the Photographic Activity Test (PAT), specified by ANSI Standard IT9.2- 1991.

DIGITIZING

What is Digitizing

Digitizing is a way of capturing and storing images using computer technology. A digital camera or a scanning device takes an electronic photograph, which is converted into binary digital code (essentially a string of zeros and ones), and can be viewed on a computer screen or printed out on paper. The data are stored within magnetic and optical media. The information content of digital images is not converted to alphanumeric form at the time of scanning and thus is not textsearchable.

Optical Character Recognition (OCR)

OCR software enables a scanned printed document to be converted into text which can be edited using word processing programmes. Unfortunately, the process is not completely accurate and time has to be spent rectifying misread letters. Moreover, OCR programmes are not capable of saving the original document's typography or page layout.

Advantages

- Digitizing offers quick access to multiple users world-wide.
- Images can be electronically restored and enhanced.

- High-quality user copies can be provided.
- Automated retrieval aids facilitate the finding of information.
- Digitizing provides an image which can be reproduced many times with no loss of quality.
- Digital images do not decay with use.

Disadvantages

- It requires an expensive commitment to supporting technologies used to convert and retrieve records.
- A digital image, displayed or printed, may not yet be acceptable as a legal substitute for the original.
- Standards are lacking in many areas.
- Digital storage is not yet accepted as truly archival – it requires continuous monitoring and eventual or periodic refreshing and transfer.
- The drive systems will become obsolete.
- There are relatively high but rapidly declining storage and production costs.
- The time needed to capture and store high-resolution archival images, and the costs of doing so increase as the quality increases.
- It is expensive to reproduce colour images.

Obsolescence Issues

The technological life span of any optical or electronic medium and its associated hardware and software is a major issue that does not exist when considering microfilming as a reformatting process. Computer hardware and software both change rapidly, with new versions of each coming out on a regular basis.

In addition, technologies come and go. Libraries will probably not be able to use many of the technologies of today in the future. Certainly, parts for the hardware will no longer be manufactured, and old software will eventually not work on new machines.

What this means is that libraries may not be able to retrieve information stored on optical media in 25 years, and this will almost certainly be a problem in 100 years. To deal with hardware obsolescence, archival copies of magnetic and optical computer media will have to be 'migrated' when newer technologies become the standard.

Digitizing and Microfilming Combined

The production of both microfilm masters for preservation, and digital masters for access, seems likely to become the preferred preservation strategy for the next decade. On the whole, a film-first policy is currently favoured. However, the rapid advancement of computer technology, the emergence of sophisticated equipment, which can produce microfilms and high-resolution digital images simultaneously and at low-cost, and the ever-increasing pressures of providing greater access will eventually see digital technology in the ascendancy. Nevertheless, until standards are in place, the use of digitizing for preservation will remain questionable.

DETERIORATION OF PAPER COLLECTIONS

Conservation professionals spend many years studying the properties of collections materials and perfecting their examination and treatment skills. While you will not leave this part with a conservator's expertise, a general familiarity with the mechanisms of deterioration will be a valuable tool for evaluating the overall condition of your collections and focusing your preservation activities.

In order to understand the deterioration mechanisms of specific paper-based formats, you need to be familiar with several basic concepts and processes. This part will address the difference between organic and inorganic materials, the types of chemical reactions that affect paper-based collections, and the process of making paper by hand and by machine. A basic understanding of these subjects will inform the discussions of deterioration mechanisms throughout this part.

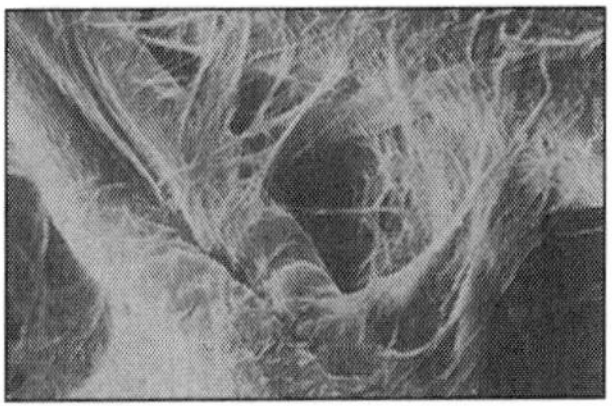

Fig. On the Microscopic Level, Paper Consists of Fibres Bonded Together.

ORGANIC/INORGANIC MATERIALS

All materials are categorized as either organic or inorganic. Organic materials are made from plants or animals. Inorganic materials are made from rocks and minerals.

Organic materials include wood, paper, textiles, and animal parts. They also include some natural materials that are not obviously organic and some synthetic materials. All organic materials deteriorate over time.

Inorganic materials include stone, metal, ceramic, and glass, which are all made from rocks or minerals. Some inorganic materials are found in paper-based formats: photographs contain metallic particles; some pigments and inks contain minerals, metals, or metallic oxides; and metal particles are sometimes found in paper itself. Inorganic materials are generally stable individually, but they can react with other materials to cause deterioration. Some metals react with the cellulose in paper. Like organic materials, inorganic materials can be natural or synthetic.

CHEMICAL DETERIORATION

Chemical reactions are the driving force behind the deterioration of paper-based collections. The most common chemical reactions that you will encounter in this part are described in simplified fashion below. In practice, chemical reactions are very complex. Often one chemical reaction will initiate a series of others, and many reactions are closely related and occur simultaneously.

Hydrolysis

In the simplest terms, this is the chemical reaction of a compound with water to form one or more new compounds. In acid hydrolysis, which is the reaction that plays the largest role in the degradation of paper, acid within the paper reacts with water, causing breaks in the chains of molecules that make up paper and ultimately making it weak and brittle.

Hydrolysis is also a factor in the degradation of other materials, including leather. In leather, sulphur dioxide is absorbed from the atmosphere and converted into sulphuric acid in the presence of an oxidant. The sulphuric acid catalyzes hydrolysis of the collagen in leather, weakening the leather by breaking down the molecular chains within it.

Oxidation

Oxidation is a chemical reaction that involves the loss of electrons from an atom or a molecule. Oxidation requires an oxidizing agent, such as oxygen in the air, ozone, or pollutants such as nitrogen oxide. In some cases, light acts as a catalyst in activating these oxidants; this is referred to as photochemical deterioration. Oxidation causes paper to weaken, and oxidation of lignin plays a role in the darkening of poor quality paper. In addition, metal particles present in paper or inks can be oxidized, producing acids that degrade the paper through hydrolysis. Oxidants play a part in the acid hydrolysis of leather by converting sulphur dioxide into sulphuric acid.

Redox (Oxidation-Reduction)

The complementary reaction to oxidation is reduction, which involves the gain of electrons by an atom or a molecule. Redox reactions typically occur in photographs containing silver image material. In the oxidation-reduction process, the silver in the image is attacked by oxidants in the atmosphere. This forms new colorless silver compounds. During the reduction part of the process, the silver may be turned back into metallic silver but deposited in a different location in a different physical form. Resulting damage can include silver mirroring, loss of detail, and fading of the image.

PAPERMAKING

Paper and board are by far the most common material found in library, archives, and records collections. The invention of paper is credited to the Chinese in AD 105. The technique gradually spread to Japan, central Asia, and Persia over the next 600 years. The first hand papermaking mill was established in Spain in the 12th century, and papermaking spread throughout Europe over the next 300 years.

Hand Paper-making

Fig. In Hand Papermaking, a Screen is Passed Through the Water to form a mat of Fibres, Which is Pressed Between Felts to be Dried.

In this process, a fibrous material is boiled and pounded to reduce it to its constituent fibres, and the fibres are suspended in water. A screen is passed through the water to form a mat of fibres, and the resulting sheet of intertwined fibres is pressed between felts to be dried. The sheet is then sized to make the surface suitable for writing, either by coating the paper by hand or dipping it into a tub of sizing solution.

Machine Papermaking

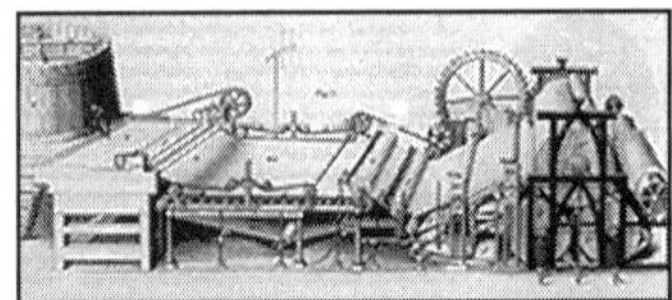

Fig. In Machine Papermaking, Pulp is Poured onto a Continuous Roll of Woven wire Mesh, then run Through a Felt Roller to Dry.

The papermaking machine was invented in France in the late 18th century, and was further developed in England in the early 19th century by the Fourdrinier brothers, by whose name it is still known. The first Fourdrinier papermaking machine was put into operation in 1804. In machine papermaking, the reduced fibres are suspended in water, which is placed in a reservoir; the pulp is poured onto a continuous roll of woven wire mesh, which allows the water to drain through; the wire mesh is moved from side to side to form a mat of fibres; and the sheet then runs through a felt roller to dry it. This method has been refined to make it more efficient over the last 200 years, but the essential process remains the same. Explore The Wisconsin Paper Council's Papermaking

Process Web site for a description of the modern commercial paper-making process. What do you think are some ways in which the materials used and the process itself might contribute to the instability of paper?

INHERENT VICE: MATERIALS

In this part, you will consider the basic materials that make up paper-based collections and the concept of "inherent vice". This refers to deterioration caused by agents present in the materials themselves, as opposed to deterioration caused by external forces. These agents may be inherent in the materials, or they may be added as part of the manufacturing process.

Over the course of time, a variety of materials and methods have been used to produce paper-based collections. Generally the primary goal of using new materials and different manufacturing methods was to make a particular process faster and easier. Unfortunately, many of these "new and improved" methods and materials were not a step forward in terms of the physical longevity of collections.

PAPER

Most papers produced from the mid-19th century to the present become brittle in about 25 to 50 years. Surveys done in the 1980s showed that yellowing and brittleness is present in about 25 to 40 per cent of research library collections.

Materials used to Make Paper

Fig. Newsprint, Made from Groundwood Pulp Paper, Becomes Brittle and Yellowed over Time.

Early paper made from materials such as linen, cotton, and hemp rags was relatively stable and durable. However, there was a chronic shortage of these materials, which became steadily worse as the demand for paper grew. In the early 19th century, the invention of the cotton gin, provided additional relatively good raw material for papermaking. However, by the middle of the 19th century, papermakers began to look elsewhere for raw material.

In the 1840s, a process was developed to use groundwood pulp for paper. Groundwood papers contain more lignin than is found in fibres such as flax or hemp. Lignin is not only acidic, causing the paper to become weak and brittle, but upon exposure to light it oxidizes, causing the paper to darken.

Changes in Manufacturing

The desire to make paper more efficiently, quickly, and cheaply also contributed to the decline in paper quality over the course of several hundred years.

After about 1650, alum was added to the tub of gelatin size to harden it and keep it from spoiling. Alum is extremely acidic and leads to acid hydrolysis of the paper. In about 1680, the Hollander beater was invented, which was a mechanical device for chopping the rags to be made into paper. The Hollander, and later the Jordan resulted in shorter paper fibres and weaker paper, and left residual metal particles in the paper. Chlorine bleaching began in the late 18th century, resulting in the formation of hydrochloric acid within bleached papers.

In the early 19th century, alum rosin sizing was introduced to speed up the papermaking process. The paper was sized in the vat by adding rosin to the vat, followed by alum. Alum rosin sizing creates sulphuric acid as a byproduct of the reaction between the alum and the rosin, and in-the-vat sizing meant that acids were distributed throughout the paper, rather than just on the surface.

Cumulatively, this resulted in more acidic, weaker, and more brittle paper. Alum rosin sizing was widely used by the 1840s, and in the 1870s a cheaper form of the sizing was developed

Permanent/Durable Paper

It is possible to make good quality machine-made papers from wood pulp by using a chemically purified wood pulp but this is a more recent development.

A standard for permanent paper was developed during the 1980s because of demands by interested parties concerned about the brittle book problem. Permanent paper is defined by the National Information Standards Organization in ANSI/NISO Z39.48-1992, Permanence of Paper for Publications and Documents in Libraries and Archives. The standard defines permanent paper as having a 2% minimum alkaline reserve less than 1% lignin, good tear resistance, and a pH of 7.5 to 10.0.

PARCHMENT AND VELLUM

Fig. This Parchment Object Was Stored Poorly and has Become Dirty and Cockled.

The invention of parchment is often credited to King Eumenes of Pergamum, an ancient city in Asia Minor, in the second century BC, but writing on animal skins was common for centuries before that. The term parchment sometimes refers to any skin that has been prepared for writing, and sometimes refers specifically to sheepskin. The term vellum refers to calfskin only. Parchment and vellum were originally used for scrolls and other documents. They were also used as pages in books from the second century AD onward, and as bookbinding material. Until the fourth century AD, skins were treated with salt, flour, and other vegetable products to prepare them for writing; after this, skins were treated with lime water, an alkaline substance. Parchment is generally more alkaline and more stable than leather.

Characteristic Types of Deterioration

Beginning in the early 19th century, chemicals were added to the lime water baths to speed up the process of preparing the skin, but these made the skin weaker. Additional chemicals such as formaldehyde were then added to try to counteract this weakness, but only resulted in stiffer skins with less elasticity. In addition, sulphur compounds remained in the skin after rinsing and were converted into sulphuric acid, which in turn reacted with calcium carbonate to produce gypsum. The presence of gypsum causes parchment to turn a gray colour.

Parchment is also subject to photochemical reactions in which hydrogen peroxide forms, causing the parchment to break down and become brittle and fragile. If gelatinized parchment is brought into contact with water, it will disintegrate into loose flakes.

LEATHER

Fig. Leather Fibres Break Down and Turn to red Powder, Known as Red Rot

Like parchment, leather is made from animal skins. Fundamentally, leather consists of a network of fibres made up of proteins, the most important of which is collagen. There are many different types of leather, and making leather is a complex process, for which different manufacturers have different methods.

Characteristic Types of Deterioration

Perhaps the most well-known leather damage is red rot, the process in which the leather fibres break down and turn into a red powder. In this process, sulphur dioxide is absorbed from the atmosphere and converted into sulphuric acid through oxidation. The sulphuric acid catalyzes acid hydrolysis, breaks down the molecular chains of the collagen, and weakens the leather.

Internal factors related to the leather manufacturing process also contribute to leather decay. Remnants of sulphur compounds used during the manufacturing process remain even after the leather is washed and convert over time into sulphuric acid.

Traces of metals from the rinsing water also remain behind, catalyzing the conversion of sulphur dioxide into sulphuric acid, which leads to acid hydrolysis. In addition, some vegetable tannins used during the tanning process seem to cause leather to decay more quickly. Finally, marbled decorations applied to book bindings in the 17th and 18th centuries can leave black corroded spots on the binding or damage the grain of the leather.

ADHESIVES

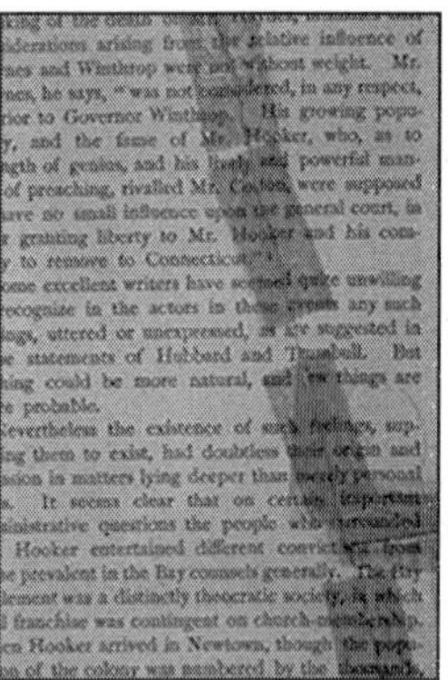

siderations arising from the relative influence of
nes and Winthrop were not without weight. Mr.
nes, he says, "was not considered, in any respect,
rior to Governor Winthrop. His growing popu-
y, and the fame of Mr. Hooker, who, as to
ngth of genius, and his lively and powerful man-
of preaching, rivalled Mr. Cotton, were supposed
ave no small influence upon the general court, in
r granting liberty to Mr. Hooker and his com-
y to remove to Connecticut."[1]
Some excellent writers have seemed quite unwilling
recognize in the actors in these events any such
ings, uttered or unexpressed, as are suggested in
e statements of Hubbard and Trumbull. But
hing could be more natural, and few things are
e probable.
Nevertheless the existence of such feelings, sup-
ng them to exist, had doubtless their origin and
ssion in matters lying deeper than merely personal
s. It seems clear that on certain important
inistrative questions the people who surrounded
Hooker entertained different convictions from
e prevalent in the Bay counsels generally. The [illegible]
lement was a distinctly theocratic society, in which
franchise was contingent on church-membership.
en Hooker arrived in Newtown, though the popu-
n of the colony was numbered by the thousands,

Fig. The Use of Self-adhesive Tape
to Repair Tears Causes Staining.

The term adhesive refers to a compound that bonds one material to another. Adhesives are encountered in various types of paper-based collections, most commonly in book bindings, scrapbooks, documents that have been repaired, and photo albums. Adhesives can be natural or synthetic; starch adhesives share common properties with cellulose, while synthetic adhesives are very similar to plastics. Natural adhesives were first made from plant resins about 6,000 years ago.

Later, animal, fish, and egg white-based adhesives were used. As modernization of adhesives continued during the 18th and 19th centuries, glues were made from various materials, including natural rubber and milk protein. Synthetic adhesives were developed in the early 20th century. Formulas for modern synthetic adhesives vary greatly, are often proprietary, and can change without notice.

Characteristic Types of Deterioration

Animal glues, traditionally used in bookbinding, break down over time, becoming discolored, dark, and brittle. They cause staining or simply crumble and fail. Synthetic adhesives react physically with water to produce swelling and chemically to produce structural weakening and acidic byproducts. In addition, evaporation of components within adhesives can cause them to become brittle.

Many adhesives used in collections in the past have not lasted well. Damage often includes discoloration, staining, and even failure of the adhesive, particularly in the cases of rubber cement and self-adhesive tape. While "archival" pressure-sensitive tapes that appear to be more stable than traditional pressure-sensitive tapes have been introduced, some problems have been observed with these tapes also. Natural adhesives such as wheat or rice starch paste are relatively stable and are often used in book and paper conservation.

COLOURANTS

Colourants of various types are encountered in watercolours, pastels, prints, architectural drawings and reproductions, writing and drawing inks, and colour photography.

General Characteristics

Colourants are divided into two categories—pigments and dyes. Both are colored substances that are dissolved in some type of liquid. A pigment is not soluble in the vehicle, but rather is dispersed or suspended in it. A dye, on the other hand, is soluble in the vehicle and colours an object by being absorbed into it, often with the assistance of another chemical called a mordant.

The science of colourants is quite complex. In some cases, a colorant can be either a pigment or a dye, depending on the vehicle used. Many modern pigments are made from soluble dyes by chemically bonding the dyes with a metallic salt.

Pigments and dyes are customarily classified according to their origins, such as organic or inorganic and natural or synthetic.

History

Natural inorganic pigments made from minerals were the first used by humans about 60,000 years ago. Natural organic pigments have been used since antiquity for many purposes, including cosmetics and textile dying. The first synthetic pigments were inorganic. After 1800, technology had developed sufficiently to produce these pigments on a large scale. In 1856, the first synthetic organic dye was developed from aniline, a chemical extracted from coal tar.

Characteristic Types of Deterioration

The primary form of colorant deterioration is fading, although some historical pigments also deteriorate upon contact with other substances, such as heat, acidic or alkaline materials, and chemicals. Some inorganic pigments of metallic origin may also cause oxidation and acidic deterioration similar to that caused by iron-gall inks.

Fading is a chemical change in which ultraviolet light reacts with the colorant, or triggers a reaction with oxygen or moisture, causing the colorant to change to a colorless compound.

Natural inorganic pigments were very stable and permanent, but due to the difficulty in manufacturing them, they have been replaced in modern times with synthetic inorganic colours. Natural organic pigments were very unstable and subject to light fading. The early synthetic organic colorants, while quite brilliant and intense, were also very unstable. Advances in organic chemistry during the 20th century have resulted in many modern synthetic organic pigments that are much less prone to fading. Lists of historical pigments, as well as modern pigments that are ASTM-approved for artists' use, can be found in The Artist's Handbook of Materials and Techniques. These lists provide rankings for lightfastness in addition to other characteristics. The Watercolors Web site also provides information on the history and characteristics of pigments.

INK AND PENCIL

Ink is essentially a liquid in which one of many possible types of pigments or dyes is suspended. Pencils are made from graphite, a form of carbon. In paper-based collections, ink is encountered not just in documents but also in printed items and artworks. Pencil is generally encountered in handwritten documents and drawings.

History

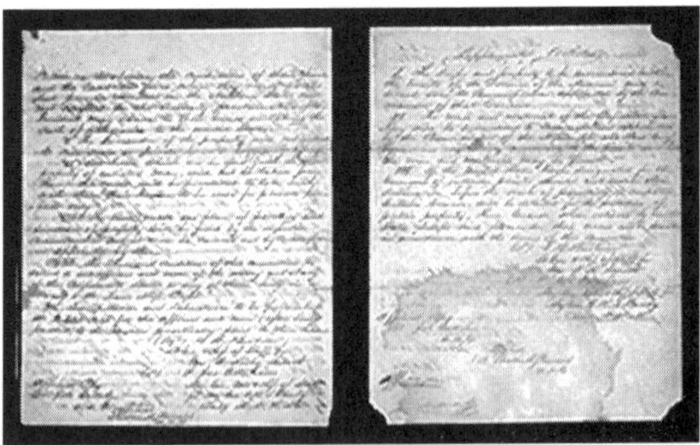

Fig. Some Inks are Water Soluble, Leading to a Loss of Information if Documents Become Wet.

Inks for writing and drawing were probably first made around 2500 BC in Egypt and China. These were made from carbon suspended in water and vegetable gum. Through the centuries, many other inks were developed using berries, plants, and minerals to provide colorants. When synthetic aniline dyes were developed in the mid-19th century, they were soon used in inks. Since that time, a huge variety of ink formulas have been created, most of which are proprietary, and many of which are prone to fading, colour changes, and smearing.

Pencil is a stable medium. The process used to make modern pencils was developed and patented in France in 1795. Henry Petroski's *The Pencil* provides a history of the development of the pencil. Those caring for collections should also be aware of the existence of copying pencils. Markings made with copying pencils can be mistaken for those made with graphite pencils, but in fact the copying pencils contain not just graphite, but also aniline dyes that are water and alcohol soluble.

Deterioration of Ink

Carbon-based Inks

These are the earliest types of writing ink. Good quality early carbon inks do not discolor with age, but can smudge in high humidity. Poor quality carbon inks may turn a brown colour over time.

Iron Gall Ink

This was the predominant type of writing ink for many centuries. It was used as early as the fifth century and was common from the 12th century well into the 20th century. Iron gall ink is made by mixing tannic acid with an iron salt. Both high acidity within the ink and oxidation of excess iron compounds present in the ink make it very damaging to the support. In extreme cases the ink actually "eating through" the support.

Coloured Inks

Coloured inks are made using pigments or soluble dyes. In general, inks made using light-resistant pigments are of better quality. Inks made from soluble dyes are not lightproof and may be water soluble as well.

Traditional Printing Inks

Traditional inks used to make prints such as intaglio prints or lithographs, differ from writing inks in that they are oil-based, allowing them to adhere better to the printing surfaces and to perform well with printing equipment. While many of these inks were quite stable, others used fugitive pigments and were subject to bleeding.

Also, if the ink was poorly manufactured, excess oil sometimes caused staining. Refer to How to Identify Prints for an explanation of printing methods. Refer to Bamber Gascoigne's *How to Identify Prints* for an explanation of printing methods.

Laser and Inkjet Printing

These were introduced on a large scale in the 1980s and have now become ubiquitous. Laser printing uses carbon inks and involves the same process as electrostatic copying. Black and white laser printing is quite stable. Most general-use inkjet printers use dye-based inks that are not very lightfast and are often water-soluble.

Fax Printing

Thermal transfer technology, used for fax printing and other purposes, became common during the 1980s. Printed documents using this technology tend to be very unstable.

INHERENT VICE: STRUCTURES

BOOKBINDINGS

The basic form of the book has not changed fundamentally over the centuries, but changes in the materials and methods used in bookbinding have sometimes compromised the quality of the resulting bound volumes.

Book Structure

The earliest books were in roll form, made from papyrus. As vellum began to be more commonly used, the practice of folding sheets and fastening them together began. Gradually the process of binding that is still used today was developed: individual folded signatures were sewn through the fold, then the signatures were attached to each other by sewing them to cords placed at right angles to the folded signatures. Boards were added to protect the pages, the cords were laced into the boards, and the boards were covered with protective material. Ideally, a binding should be strong and flexible, so that the book opens completely and the pages lay flat.

Decline in Binding Quality

During the latter half of the 19th century and much of the 20th century, poor quality paper was used for book pages. The quality of boards also declined, with wooden boards replaced by various types of boards made from compressed paper pulp that become acidic over time. Many modern bookcloths used as coverings fade easily and are vulnerable to attack by insects or mold. Adhesives used in binding are also often unstable. Sometimes different parts of a book respond differently to changes in the environment, causing distortion.

Changes in binding methods also contributed to a decline in binding quality. Gradually, hand-sewing of books decreased in favour of machine sewing. Books that are machine oversewn rather than sewn through the fold do not open well, and their pages tear easily if they become brittle. Inexpensive case bindings, in which the cover is prepared separately and then attached to the textblock by gluing the endsheet to the case, are less durable than traditional bindings in which the cords were laced in to the cover or slipped into a split in the cover board and adhered. Perfect bindings often fail. Pages or entire parts of the book may fall out.

REPRODUCTION METHODS

Beginning in the late 18th century, various reproduction methods began to replace hand copying of important documents. In the late 19th century, copying options were expanded and copying of original architectural drawings, plans, and maps also became common. Objects produced using some of these copying processes deteriorate more quickly than others, and some have detrimental effects on other collections if they are stored together. Therefore, identifying particular processes is crucial in making storage and other preservation decisions for these materials.

Letter Copying Process

Invented in 1780, this involved writing letters with a copying pencil and then pressing them against water-dampened thin tissue with a screw press. This process became popular in the 1850s and was used into the 1950s.

Hectograph Process

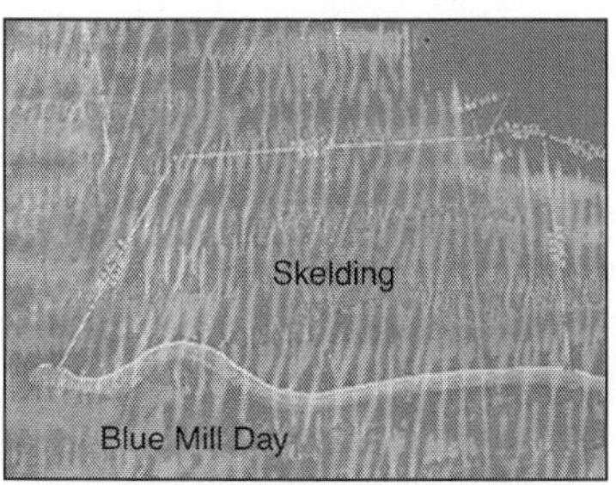

Fig. Blueprints can Fade on Exposure to Light or Alkaline Materials.

This process, which became popular in the late 1800s, used aniline ink and was used both for copying documents and architectural drawings.

Writing was transferred to a gelatin pad from which copies were made. Various other processes for copying documents were invented in the late 19th and early 20th centuries, but many of these were not stable.

Blueprints

Invented in 1871, this process was used primarily to copy architectural drawings, plans, and maps. A translucent original was placed over sensitized paper containing iron salts, and then exposed to light. After exposure, the original was removed and the copy was washed to remove the unexposed compounds under the lines of the original drawing. The result was an image of white lines on a blue background. Blueprints are sensitive to alkaline environments, and light exposure. Similar processes include Vandyke prints, and Ferrogallic prints.

Diazotypes

This process became popular in the 1920s, and by the 1950s it was used to copy office records as well as maps, drawings, and plans. A translucent original was placed on paper coated with diazonium salts; this was exposed to ultraviolet light, which attacked the salts and turned the exposed area off-white. Depending on the specifc type of compound used on the paper, the lines on diazo prints can be various colours. Diazo prints are often processed using ammonia, which causes them to give off alkaline vapors that may harm other materials. The residual chemicals remaining in the print also cause oxidation and discoloration of the print itself, particularly on the edges. Sepia prints, a type of diazo print, can create greasy stains or pink stains on adjacent materials. Diazo prints are light sensitive.

Electrostatic Copying

Also known as xerography, this technology was introduced in the late 1940s and became popular in the 1960s. It makes a copy of the original by forming an image with toner powder using electrostatic charge and fusing the image to paper using a solvent, heat, or light. This is the most common copying process used today. If electrostatic copies are made on good quality paper and well-bonded to the paper, they are very stable. However, electrostatic copies of maps or plans made on matte or transparent Mylar are not permanent because the toner does not bond well to the Mylar.

PHOTOGRAPHIC PRINTS: BLACK AND WHITE

Among the materials collected and organized by cultural institutions, photographs are the most treasured and heavily used. Extensive technical and aesthetic changes have affected photography since 1839, when Louis Daguerre developed a practical method for creating permanent images.

Each photographic process has unique characteristics that affect its deterioration, storage, and handling. In order to care properly for photographic collections, you must understand how photographs are made and learn how to identify their various types. You must also become familiar with problems related to their physical and chemical composition.

The Basic Photographic Process

Photographs are composite objects, consisting of a base, a binder, and an image-forming substance. To produce a photographic image, light-sensitive materials such as silver salts are applied to a support made of paper, cloth, plastic, or metal, and exposed to light. This forms either a direct visible image or a latent image, which can be developed using a chemical developer. The image is "fixed" in order to remove excess light-sensitive material and stop the darkening process. It is then washed to remove residual fixer.

Image-Forming Materials

As photographic techniques developed, a number of different light-sensitive materials were used to form the image. The most important was metallic silver, which was used in most 19th century photographic prints and is still used in modern black and white prints. Differences in appearance in the different types of prints are due to differences in the physical form of the silver particles.

Other types of image-forming materials used during the 19th century included:

- Platinum,
- Iron salts,
- Pigments, and
- Dyes.

Silver images exhibit several characteristic types of deterioration:

- *Sulfiding:* This is the formation of silver sulfide when silver reacts with sources of sulphur. This can result from the presence of sulphur in the atmosphere, but it is most often due to inadequate washing that leaves behind residual processing chemicals in the print. The result is yellowing, staining, and fading of the image, usually beginning with the highlights.
- *Redox*: The visual results of redox reactions vary depending on the type of image, but generally they include loss of highlight detail, fading, and change of image colour to reddish, yellow, or yellow-brown. Silver mirroring is also a result of oxidation-reduction, and is particularly characteristic of silver images suspended in a gelatin binder.

Binders

Various materials have been used as binders for photographic prints. Albumen tends towards chemical reactions that cause it to yellow over time, which is exacerbated by the presence of residual fixative and mounting on poor-quality board. Albumen also becomes brittle and subject to cracking. Collodion is not flexible and becomes brittle, leading to cracks in the emulsion, but otherwise is fairly chemically stable and does not yellow. Gum arabic was used as a binder for gum bichromate prints, which are stable but rare because they were difficult to produce. Gelatin, the most common binder material, is made from animal proteins. It is fairly stable chemically but is quite sensitive to moisture in the air.

Supports

Nineteenth century prints generally had a primary support of high quality stable paper, although the secondary support was often poor quality. In the later 19th century, the primary paper support was often coated with barium sulfate in gelatin; this was known as the baryta layer. This layer was very stable, protected the paper from light damage, and provided some protection against damaging substances from poor-quality secondary supports.

Resin-coated paper was introduced as a support for photographic prints during World War II and became commercially available during the 1970s. This type of paper shortened photographic processing time because it required less washing and it was sturdy, allowing processing to be completely mechanized. Most modern colour prints are printed on resin-coated paper, which consists of a paper base between two layers of polyethylene, with titanium dioxide added to the emulsion-side layer.

Many early prints on resin-coated paper that were framed and exhibited developed cracking of the emulsion layer over time. Some black and white resin-coated prints on exhibit also developed redox, yellowing, and silver mirroring. These problems were due to the titanium dioxide in the emulsion and they occurred most commonly in framed photographs where the oxidizing agent could not dissipate. Stabilizers and antioxidants were added to later resin-coated papers during manufacturing to combat this type of deterioration, but this does not completely eliminate the risk of damage.

Daguerreotypes, Ambrotypes, and Tintypes

Strictly speaking, these photographic images are not paper-based, but they are positive images and are frequently found within collections of photographic prints. Daguerreotypes, positive images on thin copper plate with a silver coating, were popular between 1840 and 1860. They are usually found in small hinged cases and are quite fragile and subject to tarnishing due to exposure to pollutants. Ambrotypes and tintypes are both silver images in a collodion binder, but ambrotypes have a glass support sometimes coated with paint or lacquer, while tintypes have a thin lacquered iron support. Ambrotypes sometimes suffer chips in their original coating material. Tintypes are easily bent, sometimes causing the emulsion to crack.

PHOTOGRAPHIC PRINTS: COLOUR/DIGITAL

The primary difference between black and white and colour prints is in the image-forming material. There are two types of colour photography: chromogenic and nonchromogenic. Modern chromogenic colour photographs are the most common and use organic cyan, magenta, and yellow dyes as the image-forming material. The chromogenic process forms a black and white silver image, which causes the developing chemical to react with dye couplers to form a dye image around the black and white image. The black and white image is then removed with bleaches and the colour image is fixed and washed.

A different type of dye is used in nonchromogenic photography, which was introduced in 1955. This process is known as silver dye bleach and produces photographs with excellent dark stability and better light stability than chromogenic photographs. However, chromogenic materials are cheaper and more versatile, and thus much more common.

Deterioration of Chromogenic Colour Prints

Dye Fading

Fig. Dye Fading is Common in Early Colour Photographs.

Unfortunately, the dyes used in chromogenic processing are inherently unstable. The three dyes do not fade at different rates, so there is often an imbalance of colour in deteriorated colour photographs. It is also very important to note that some dyes that fade faster in the light may be more stable in the dark, and vice versa. In general, early colour photographs were very unstable; many lost 30% of their dyes within 10 to 15 years. Even colour photographs from the 1980s will reach the 30 per cent mark within 20 years. Advances in dye stability were made during the 1980s and 1990s, and contemporary colour materials can be expected to survive 30 to 50 years at room temperature.

Highlight Staining

This appears as a yellowish staining in the highlight areas of the photograph, and is due to residual dye couplers for the magenta dye, which form these stains as they decompose.

Digital Colour Prints

The increase in digital photography in the last decade means that many photographs are now printed on photo printers rather than processed in the traditional way. These prints are created using dyes and inks, some of which are not stable and long lasting. Waterproof pigment-based inks are more stable than dye-based water sensitive inks, but they usually have a smaller range of colour. Many types of paper supports are also used, including laser/copying paper, general purpose inkjet paper, fine art papers, and coated inkjet papers. Ultimately, using the right combination of paper, printer, and ink is most crucial to digital print longevity. Wilhelm Imaging Research has tested many papers, inks, and printers on the market today. In addition to providing guidance on the life expectancies of various digital prints, these tests have shown that using third party inks and paper will not provide the same durability as using ink and paper recommended by the printer manufacturer.

EXTERNAL FACTORS

External factors such as high, low, or fluctuating temperature and humidity; light exposure; the presence of pollutants; and poor storage and handling exacerbate the deterioration of collections. While these external agents affect all paper-based collections to a certain extent, some of them are particularly damaging to specific types of materials, which will be your focus here.

CLIMATE

Temperature

Generally speaking, higher temperatures accelerate the chemical reactions that cause deterioration in paper-based collections. Thus, cooler temperatures are preferred for collections with long-term value.

Temperature plays a particularly crucial role in the fading of chromogenic colour photographs. The higher the temperature, the more movement there is on the molecular level, and the more likely it is that the molecules will be rearranged, resulting in dye fading. For this reason, cold storage is recommended for long-term preservation of colour photographs.

Relative Humidity

Fig. The Parchment Pages of This Volume have Rippled on Exposure to Water.

Humidity provides water to fuel the chemical reactions that cause deterioration. The more moisture there is in the air, the more quickly chemical deterioration proceeds.

High humidity is a primary factor in hydrolysis, which accelerates the deterioration of paper (causing ferrotyping, shiny blotches on the emulsion that result from pressure on the softened binder material; and accelerating), black and white photographs (softening gelatin binders, causing ferrotyping and accelerating the yellowing of albumen binders), and colour photographs (accelerating dye fading). Parchment will ripple in overly humid conditions. Mold and many insects also flourish under hot and humid conditions. Mold causes staining and, in extreme cases, disintegration of paper, while insects can eat holes in paper-based collections.

If humidity is too low, materials such as adhesives and book leathers may become brittle and more susceptible to cracking, particularly during handling. Extended storage at low humidity can cause photographic emulsions to shrink and crack, supports to curl, and mounts to warp. Parchment will split and warp in overly dry conditions. Fluctuating humidity levels also cause damage. Most materials expand and contract with small changes in relative humidity (RH). These changes weaken physical bonds and set up stresses that can shorten the life of most materials

LIGHT

Light energy, in the form of waves, is absorbed by molecules within an object. This absorption of energy activates a variety of chemical reactions that have the potential to damage paper-based collections. This is termed photochemical deterioration. Shorter wavelengths of light such as UV light have more energy than longer wavelengths. They bombard an object with more energy in a shorter time and so cause photochemical deterioration to accelerate. This is why UV light is more damaging than visible light, although all light is damaging.

Fig. Lignin in this poor Quality Paper Caused it to Darken when Exposed to Light During Exhibition.

Practically speaking, light causes paper, bookbindings, and many media (such as inks and dyes) to fade, yellow, or discolor. Light exposure accelerates the oxidation of lignin, which causes paper to darken. Light also contributes to the weakening and embrittlement of paper fibres, textiles, and leather. Some types of light (incandescent lamps and direct natural light) also produce significant heat, accelerating the rate at which materials deteriorate. Materials that are particularly sensitive to light include colour photographic prints, early black and white images (especially salted paper and albumen prints), cyanotypes, blueprints, diazo prints, and hand-colored images.

POLLUTANTS

Fig. The Outside Edges of the Pages in this Book have Darkened Because of Exposure to Pollutants When the Book was Stored Closed on the Shelf.

Airborne contaminants in the form of gases and particulates jeopardize the preservation of collections. For repositories in urban areas, gaseous pollution from sources such as industrial discharge, motor vehicle exhaust, and other combustion products can be a serious concern. Gaseous pollutants can also originate indoors, given off by common substances such as paint, cleaning supplies, untreated wood, photocopiers, and certain kinds of adhesives and plastics. Various types of gaseous pollutants initiate chemical reactions that contribute to the deterioration of paper-based collections. These reactions are usually worsened when high relative humidity is also present.

Particulates come in the form of tiny solids-grit, grime, smoke, dust-which originate largely in industrial processes, vehicle engines, wood-and coal-fired heating systems, smoking, and cooking. They are generally abrasive and acidic and often highly reactive chemically. Photographs in particular are extremely sensitive to atmospheric pollutants. Particulate pollutants may cause abrasion of emulsions and attract mold or insects. Gaseous pollutants such as sulphur dioxide, nitrogen oxides, ozone, and formaldehyde contribute to sulfiding, redox reactions, and dye discoloration.

STORAGE AND HANDLING

Fig. The Sewing in this Volume has Broken Due to Excessive Handling.

Poor storage and handling can also cause physical and chemical damage to collections.

Physical damage due to poor storage and/or handling might include tears, creases, dog-eared corners, scratches or abrasions, or damage to book bindings. In some cases disfiguring marks may be made on items (*e.g.*, vandalism or writing on the back of photographs that either bleeds through or creates indentations). Rusting staples and paper clips can stain and deform paper documents.

Chemical damage due to poor storage and/or handling might include staining due to acid migration from acidic storage enclosures or adjacent materials such as news clippings or bookmarks.

EVALUATING YOUR COLLECTIONS

You have explored how the components of paper-based collections deteriorate; you have considered the complexities of some of the composite objects found in paper-based collections; and you have briefly examined the role of external factors in collection deterioration. Now you will begin to relate this information to your own collections.

IMPORTANT

This examination of your collections is not meant to serve as a formal collection condition survey, but it will assist you in determining which materials need further attention. You may decide that one or more collection condition surveys are required for specific subsets of your collection (*e.g.*, rare books, photographs, scrapbooks). This type of inspection most often takes the form of an item-by-item survey by a conservator with detailed knowledge of that particular type of material

BOUND MATERIALS

Fig. These Books are Held Together by Rubber Bands (which can Themselves Cause Damage) Because their Spines and Covers are Damaged or Detached.

Bound materials in your collection may include printed books (general or rare), handwritten record books, and bound pamphlets of various types (*e.g.*, catalogs, directories, guidelines). Common types of physical damage to printed books and handwritten record books include page damage (*e.g.*, tears, dog-eared corners, missing pages, markings from vandalism, damage from iron gall inks), binding damage (damaged sewing, detached signatures, deteriorating adhesives, broken or loose joints, wholly or partly detached covers, endcap damage), and distortion (caused by climate fluctuations or previous water damage). Older pamphlets are often very deteriorated due to handling and acidity, and may have been placed in acidic pamphlet binders to protect them.

Common types of chemical and biological damage include fading or darkening/discoloration of pages (due to light damage and acidity), acid migration from acidic inserts such as bookmarks, fading of binding materials, red rot of leather bindings, holes from insect damage, and staining caused by mold. Note that darkening of pages due to acidity often shows up first on the edges of the textblock, which are more exposed to pollutants and climate fluctuations.

DOCUMENTS/MANUSCRIPTS/EPHEMERA

Documents and manuscripts found in cultural institutions can range from medieval manuscripts to 18th century letters to modern office files. They may be copies or originals, and they may have been produced using a variety of inks, papers, and copying processes. Ephemeral materials may include cards, postcards, brochures, patterns, papers dolls, etc., some of which may have raised surfaces or three-dimensional decoration, and may include adhesives. Common physical damage to flat paper items includes tears, folds, and creases; dog-eared corners; abrasions; staining from rusted paper clips, deteriorated rubber bands, or pressure-sensitive tape; loss of parts of the paper (usually around the edges); and distortion and staining from previous water damage.

Fig. Foxing (Small Brown Spots Probably caused by Mold or by the Presence of Tiny Metal Particles) Often Occurs When an Item is Stored in a Poor Climate.

Common chemical and biological damage to paper documents includes brittleness and fragility due to acidic deterioration and light exposure; discoloration or darkening due to acidity and light exposure; staining and weakening from mold growth; holes from insect infestation; foxing (small brown spots that appear on paper, probably caused by mold or by the presence of tiny metal particles in the paper, in combination with high humidity and temperature); and acid migration, where better quality papers are stained by poor quality papers stored with them.

NEWSPRINT

Newsprint is generally found in several formats within cultural collections:

- Newspaper clippings within general document files, bound newspapers,
- Loose newspapers,
- Newspaper clipping scrapbooks.

Newsprint is almost uniformly made from poor quality paper and is usually very brittle, fragile, and darkened. Recent news clippings may still be in good condition, but they will ultimately be subject to the same deterioration processes. Clippings in scrapbooks may be further deteriorated due to the use of poor quality adhesives.

OVERSIZED AND FRAMED MATERIALS

Most cultural collections include at least a few maps, plans, and architectural drawings. Perhaps they are maps of the surrounding area or plans of buildings within the institution. Many cultural institutions also hold collections of artwork on paper, which may include posters, watercolors, pastels, and drawings of various kinds.

In general, these materials are subject to the same types of deterioration as paper documents. Many of these materials are oversized and may have been stored rolled for many years, complicating the problems of acidic deterioration. If materials that have been rolled seem too brittle to unroll for examination without causing damage, do not unroll them;consult a conservator for assistance. You may also encounter maps or other items that have been coated with varnish or other coatings, which has darkened and deteriorated.

Various copying processes used for maps and architectural materials have different vulnerabilities, and different processes stored in proximity to each other may damage each other, resulting in discoloration or fading.

Artworks on paper also exhibit a range of deterioration problems, which include fading or alteration of watercolor pigments smearing of pastel, charcoal, or pencil drawings; yellowing, fading, or browning of the paper support due to acidic deterioration; foxing; surface mold growth; cockling due to climate fluctuations; and tide lines or stains due to water damage.

Framed materials (which might include artworks on paper, documents, or photographs) often show characteristic signs of deterioration: browning and yellowing due to acid migration from poor quality backing materials (these might be wood, corrugated board, newsprint, or cardboard); knot patterns or a dark central stripe down the paper due to wooden slats used in backing; mat burn (darkened lines around the margin where the beveled edge of acidic matboard meets the paper); tape stains due to poor quality tape used for repairs; and adhesive stains due to poor quality adhesives used to hinge or mount the item to the backboard.

SCRAPBOOKS

Various types of scrapbooks are found in cultural collections. News clipping scrapbooks are common, as are personal scrapbooks that contain a variety of materials, including documents, photographs, pamphlets, and pressed flowers. Scrapbooks, being composite objects, exhibit various problems common to documents, bound volumes, and photographic materials. Their pages may be brittle and weak, photographs may be faded and stained, news clippings may be yellowed, items may have become detached from thc pages due to adhesive failure, the pages may have been stained by adhesives, and the bindings may be broken or otherwise damaged.

PHOTOGRAPHIC PRINTS

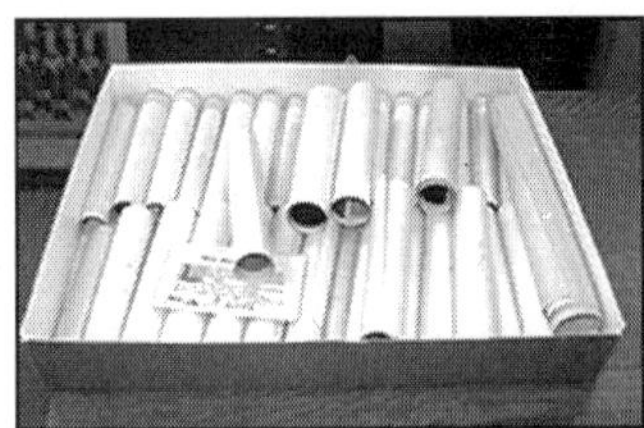

Fig. Older Rolled Photographs Can be Difficult to Unroll Without Damaging them; Always Consult a Conservator if in Doubt.

The most common types of photographic prints found in cultural institutions are cased photographs, albumen prints, silver gelatin prints, and modern colour photographs. These may be stored with documents in files, in boxes or albums, or even loose in drawers. Different types of photographic processes have specific vulnerabilities. However, there are some major categories of damage to photographs that you may observe within your collection. As with paper documents, photographic prints are subject to physical damage such as tears, creases, dog-eared corners, and mold or insect attack. Special concerns for photographs are abrasion and scratching of emulsions (binders), cracking emulsions, emulsions that are peeling away from the support layer, and indentations or staining caused by writing on the back of photographs.

Fig. Damage to this Photograph has Been Caused in Large Part By the Brittle and Acidic Board on Which it was Mounted.

Chemical damage to photographs may manifest itself in black and white images through fading of the image, loss of image detail, yellowing of the image, silver mirroring of shadow areas of the image, and/or staining. For colour prints, colour change and fading are the primary results of deterioration.

Rolled photographs are often found in collections. As with documents, these should not be unrolled if it seems this may cause damage; a conservator should be consulted. Photographs mounted on acidic boards are also common (these are frequently albumen prints, which tend to curl up if not mounted). There is often physical damage to the board and chemical damage to the photograph.

Photograph albums pose additional problems, since the albums themselves may damage the photographs. Many older albums have acidic pages that can accelerate photograph deterioration. Adhesives used to attach photographs often cause staining and sometimes fail, leaving the photograph unattached. Modern "magnetic" albums in fact use adhesive to hold the photograph to the page; this adhesive darkens and stains photographs over time. Modern albums with plastic pages made from polyvinyl chloride (PVC) also accelerate photograph deterioration. Polyester, polypropylene, and polyethylene are the only acceptable plastics for photo album pages.

13

Library Materials Reformatting and Treatment

Preservation reformatting of paper collections encompasses microfilming, photocopying, duplicating, and/or digital imaging. These options may be used alone or in combination, depending on the circumstances. Reformatting of film and electronic media (*e.g.*, motion picture film, negatives, and sound and video recordings) involves duplication onto new media, sometimes in alternate formats. Treatment options for original paper-based items include professional conservation treatment, in-house repair (also known as collections conservation), and library binding.

Reformatting and treatment can be time-consuming and expensive and may not be justified for all deteriorated collections. How do you decide which collections deserve attention? What role should reformatting and treatment play in a systematic preservation programme for paper-based collections?

PRESERVATION MICROFILMING

Despite increasing interest in new technologies, preservation microfilming remains an established and valued strategy for producing copies of deteriorated paper-based collections. Since the late 1980s, a national Brittle Books Programme, funded through the National Endowment for the Humanities (NEH), has been in place, using preservation microfilming to produce master microfilms of deteriorated books.

Overall, microfilm is an important preservation strategy for collections that have greater informational value than artifactual value and for those with such tremendous artifactual value and/or fragility that they should not be routinely handled by researchers. While microfilm is no longer the most user-friendly medium for access, it is the product of a tested technology governed by clear standards and guidelines.

It provides a master copy from which relatively inexpensive duplicates can be easily made. And unlike digital media, which cannot be read without computer access, microfilm can be read by the naked eye with only a light source and magnification.

STANDARDS/GUIDELINES

Microfilming is governed by a variety of standards, but it is important to keep in mind that most of these standards were developed for commercial microfilming applications, where the microfilm being produced only needs to be retained for a limited time. Thus, certain practices may be acceptable in the production of commercial microfilm that are not appropriate in the production of preservation microfilm.

General Microfilming Standards

Preservation microfilming of paper-based collections makes up only a small fraction of the micrographics industry, so addressing preservation filming is not a high priority for standards-making organizations. The American National Standards Institute (ANSI) issues various standards pertaining to imaging materials, including microfilm, and the Association for Information and Image Management (AIIM) also issues standards for micrographics. These standards can be useful in providing general information, but it is up to the individual institution to decide what level of quality is acceptable.

Guidelines for Preservation Microfilming

For specific guidelines for preservation microfilming geared towards libraries, archives, and other institutions that hold paper collections, the Research Libraries Group (RLG) has produced three publications that have come to be considered de facto standards. The *RLG Preservation Microfilming Handbook*, the *RLG Archives Microfilming Manual*, and the *RLG Guidelines for Microfilming to Support Digitization* should be consulted by any cultural institution planning a preservation microfilming project. Another basic resource is the Association of Research Libraries' *Preservation Microfilming: A Guide for Librarians and Archivists*. All of these publications are referenced in Additional Resources.

These guidelines specify materials and procedures that must be used to ensure the permanence of the film that is produced:

- *Film Type*: All preservation microfilm must be produced on a polyester base. Types of film include silver gelatin (the most stable); diazo and vesicular (less expensive, but not as stable); continuous tone microfilm (a silver gelatin film that can be very stable and is used for filming photographs and similar materials), and colour microfilm (Ilfochrome colour film, which likely has a lifetime of several hundred years in dark storage).
- *Film Format*: The RLG guidelines are based on the 35mm roll film format, which provides a larger, better-quality image than microfiche or 16mm film.
- Film generations: Three generations of microfilm must be produced:

the camera negative (*e.g.*, the film used in the camera); a duplicate negative; and one or more positive service copies for researcher use and interlibrary loan.

- *Film quality and processing*: The RLG guidelines specify requirements for reduction ratio (the number of times the original is reduced); orientation of the image on the film; the legibility of the image (background density and resolution); processing of the exposed film; and inspection of the film and correction of mistakes (*e.g.*, number of splices allowed).

THE FILMING PROCESS

For most institutions, contracting out for microfilming services is the most efficient and cost-effective choice, since setting up an in-house lab to produce microfilm that conforms to standards and guidelines for preservation filming is extremely difficult and expensive.

The basic procedures involved in preservation microfilming are as follows:

- *Preparing Collections for Filming*: The materials are examined page-by-page to ensure that they are in the correct order and nothing is missing. Targets are created (informational sheets with bibliographic and condition information that are photographed with the item to assist the user), and reel breaks are determined. During the review process, special instruction for the filmers are noted. The materials are shipped to the vendor.
- *Filming*: A planetary camera (where both the camera and the materials are stationary during filming) is most commonly used. Bound materials may be filmed using a book cradle. Manual exposure is usually necessary for collections with variations in paper colour, texture, and/or ink.
- *Film Processing*: Silver gelatin film processors may be tabletop or deep tank models. They develop, fix, wash, and dry the film. Filmers should use control strips daily to check the performance of the processor.
- *Polysulfide Treatment*: This treatment was developed to combat the formation of redox spots or rings on silver microfilm, which are a result of poor environmental conditions and exposure to pollutants. Polysulfide treatment (which converts the silver to a form that better resists oxidation) can be used during initial processing, it can be provided for the master and duplicate negatives after all quality control inspections have been done, or it can be applied to older film, as long as it is not yet deteriorated.
- *Quality Control*: Before duplication, the master negative is inspected for proper resolution and density; a methylene blue test (for residual thiosulfate from processing) and a polysulfide test are conducted;

and the master negative is inspected frame-by-frame to ensure that each document has been filmed in the correct order and each frame is legible. If necessary, mistakes are corrected using ultrasonic splicing.

- *Duplication*: The choice of film for duplicates will depend on cost and use patterns. Silver film is preferred for duplicate negatives, and should receive a polysulfide treatment. Diazo and vesicular films, which are cheaper and less prone to scratching than silver films, are often used for service copies. Duplicate films are inspected for resolution, density, and completeness as required in ANSI/AIIM and RLG standards and guidelines.
- *Return of Film and Originals to the Institution*: Original materials are generally returned at the same time to facilitate in-house inspection of the film, but master negatives should never be shipped in the same box, or on the same day, with their service copies or duplicate negatives. If possible, master negatives should be shipped by the vendor directly to off-site storage.
- *Post-filming Activities*: You must conduct in-house quality control inspections once the film is returned. These should include a general inspection of the film, packaging, and labeling, as well as a more comprehensive technical inspection that might include testing for density and resolution, as well as scratches, problematic splices, and other problems.
- *Storage*: Once materials have been filmed, house all preservation microfilm in archival enclosures, maintain microfilm readers regularly, and insist that researchers use the microfilm instead of the original materials. Master negatives must be stored off-site, preferably under the proper temperature and humidity conditions.

PAPER REPRODUCTIONS

PRESERVATION PHOTOCOPYING

Photocopying in-house onto permanent durable paper can provide a paper copy of fragile or brittle documents that are not easily usable in microfilm format (*e.g.*, news clipping collections, indexes, finding aids).

In archival collections, preservation photocopies can be used to provide initial access so that researchers can identify which materials they need to see; to reproduce unstable documents (*e.g.*, faxes); to provide copies of valuable documents that should be stored more securely; or to provide surrogate copies for materials that are too fragile to handle.

Traditional preservation photocopying, however, does not provide a master negative from which additional copies can be made, as microfilm does. If the photocopy becomes unusable, the original must be copied again, which can be problematic for fragile or brittle items.

PRESERVATION FACSIMILES

The production of preservation facsimiles is an option for brittle books that are heavily used (*e.g.*, for which a paper copy would meet the users' needs better than a microfilm copy). This type of reproduction is normally contracted out to a vendor. Production of a facsimile is appropriate when reprints are expensive or unavailable, duplicate copies are not available, and other editions cannot provide an adequate substitute. Ideally, the item should be filmed as well, either by your institution or another.

Preservation facsimiles were traditionally done using a photocopier, but now they are produced using digital scanning. Items are normally disbound, then scanned and printed on alkaline paper on a digital laser printer. This produces a digital file that can then be used to print additional paper copies in the future without rescanning the originals. Keep in mind, however, that if the digital file should become inaccessible for any reason and the paper copy wears out, the original must be reproduced again, or the information may be lost.

STANDARDS/GUIDELINES

A high-quality preservation photocopy or preservation facsimile requires the use of permanent paper, as well as equipment and procedures that will ensure a long-lasting copy. Although there are no specific standards for preservation photocopying or for the production of preservation facsimiles, there are related standards and guidelines that cover elements of the process.

Paper used for preservation photocopies or facsimiles must comply with ANSI/NISO Z39.48 1992 Permanence of Paper for Publications and Documents in Libraries and Archives. The standard sets out requirements for pH, tear resistance, alkaline reserve, and amount of lignin permitted. A partial list of papers that meet the ANSI/NISO standard is available online in an excerpt from North American Permanent Papers, 3rd ed. Procedures for ensuring the quality of scanned images in preservation facsimiles should follow guidelines and best practices for digital imaging that are generally accepted within the preservation community. Copiers used for preservation photocopying must be kept in the best condition possible and should not be used for other types of copying. Carbon black toner must be used, and the adhesion of the image to the paper must be tested periodically.

PRODUCING PHOTOCOPIES AND FACSIMILES

It is best to contract out the production of preservation facsimiles, since complex machinery and procedures are involved. Small-scale preservation photocopying can be done in-house, but staff must be well trained in the proper procedures and the equipment must be properly maintained.

The basic procedures involved in producing preservation photocopies and facsimiles are as follows:

- *Preparation*: The materials to be copied are examined page-by-page to ensure that they are in the correct order and nothing is missing. If there are foldouts or other oversize materials in a bound volume, these are measured.

- *Photocopying*: Books are normally disbound for copying. During the photocopying process, a daily peel test (sometimes called a tape pull test) is recommended, to ensure that the image is adhering properly to the paper. When photocopying two-sided pages, care must be taken to ensure that the placement of the text or image on the verso and recto sides of the pages are maintained in relation to each other. Oversize and colour materials may be copied separately as needed.
- *Scanning*:When scanning, items are also normally disbound (unless their value warrants reproducing them without disbinding). The institution must specify how illustrations will be scanned (gray scale, colour), at what size foldouts will be scanned, etc.
- *Inspection*: Once copying or scanning has been done, the finished product is inspected to ensure that there are no pages missing, the copies are legible, the contrast is good, and the general quality is acceptable compared to the original.
- *Binding*:Paper copies are bound according to the NISO standard for library binding. A statement is placed in the copy identifying it as a preservation photocopy; this should be noted in any catalog records as well.
- *Storage*: The copy or copies should be stored according to guidelines for paper-based collections. The original items may be retained after photocopying in case additional copies or another type of reformatting is needed in future. For books that have been disbound, the loose leaves can be foldered and boxed.

DIGITIZATION

Many collections managers, particularly those in small institutions, have been confronted with a member of the board of trustees who asks: "Why don't we just buy a scanner? Then we wouldn't have to worry about preservation." The short answer to this question is that while digitization (the conversion of analog data into machine-readable binary code) is an excellent tool for researcher access, it cannot yet stand on its own as a viable preservation reformatting strategy, particularly for small institutions with limited resources. For the future, the preservation community envisions a gradual partnership between preservation microfilm and the evolving technology of digital imaging. Digital scanners and cameras are ubiquitous, however, and numerous digital initiatives, on varying scales and with varying goals, are occurring in cultural institutions.

Key challenges of digital preservation include:

- Creating digital objects worthy of the effort and expense required to preserve them;

- Creating effective systems for accessing the digitized images; and
- Dealing with the problem of rapid obsolescence of the hardware and software that support those access systems.

STANDARDS/GUIDELINES

Unlike preservation microfilming and photocopying, there are no formal standards that govern the capture, processing, and storage of digital images.

There are, however, a number of projects and publications that have set forth best practices for creating high-quality digital images, access systems, and storage systems. If you choose to undertake a digitization project, you will need to create your own technical guidelines that reflect your institution's needs and your project's goals. Explore Cornell University's Moving Theory into Practice: Digital Imaging Tutorial.

DIGITIZATION PROCEDURES

Despite the possible variations in technical requirements, there are several standard steps in digital imaging. As with other reformatting methods, most institutions will find digitization too complex and expensive to undertake in-house; contracting with a vendor experienced in working with historical paper-based collections is recommended.

The Digitization Process

The basic steps in digital imaging are as follows:

- *Image capture*: The document(s) or other materials are captured in digital form using a scanner or digital camera. Decisions made about the desired image quality during benchmarking (*e.g.*, the type of scan, the resolution of the scan, the bit depth) are implemented.
- *Image processing*: This includes image editing if necessary (*e.g.*, compression of files, sharpening of images) and the creation of metadata (sometimes defined as "data about data"). Metadata indexes and describes the scanned materials. A table explaining the types of metadata can be found within Moving Theory into Practice: Digital Imaging Tutorial.
- *Image delivery*:This is the process of getting the scanned images to the user through computer networks, monitors, and printers. Delivery methods, file formats, file compression, and acceptable image quality will differ depending on various user characteristics. It is crucial to consider image delivery needs during project planning, not after the images have already been created.
- *Quality control*: This involves both initial and ongoing evaluation of whether the technical requirements for image capture, processing, and delivery are being met. At the beginning of the project, it is a good idea to digitize a representative sample of documents to be sure that all quality requirements are being met.

Storage and Maintenance

After digital objects are created and appropriately indexed and described, they must be stored on-line, near-line, and/or off-line. Over time, however, obsolescence of hardware and software (the technology chain used to access digital objects) becomes a far greater concern. If a CD-ROM survives intact for 50 or even 100 years, but no device survives that can retrieve the data, then the data have effectively been lost.

At present, there are significant obstacles to maintaining the integrity and functionality of the technology chain. Upgrading to new hardware and software platforms may prove prohibitively expensive over time. To further complicate matters, a practical and universally reliable way of migrating existing digital data to newer hardware and software platforms has yet to be developed. Even if migration procedures were more standardized, they would necessarily involve a significant commitment of time and resources, making them challenging to implement.

HYBRID OPTIONS

Given the challenges of digital preservation, it makes sense for most institutions to use digital imaging as an access tool while simultaneously relying on more traditional approaches such as microfilming for preservation. Over the past 15 years, several grant-funded projects have explored the possibility of combining microfilming and digital imaging technologies. Yale University's Project Open Book studied the feasibility of converting existing preservation microfilm of 19th- and 20th-century brittle books to digital images (known as the "film-first" method). Cornell University's Digital to Microfilm Conversion Project studied the feasibility of scanning the same type of collections and producing computer output microfilm (known as the "scan-first" method).

These projects proved that both methods could be used successfully. Detailed technical guidelines for filming first and scanning first were devised, and information was gathered about costs and workflow. The project administrators concluded that the choice of where to begin a hybrid project would depend on the condition of the original materials, whether or not preservation microfilm already exists, and whether or not disbinding of bound volumes is permissible, among other issues.

REFORMATTING MEDIA COLLECTIONS

This is partly because, unlike paper-based collections, many audiovisual materials must be played in machines to retrieve their information. Even minimal playback leads to wear and tear, and playback machinery can become obsolete in a relatively short time. Magnetic and optical media may also be subject to catastrophic failure without any warning. In addition, new still and moving images and sound recordings are now frequently being produced in digital form. These are then subject to the difficulties of preserving digital information. Duplication or reformatting onto appropriate media is an important preservation activity for audiovisual collections. Reformatting can provide service copies for deteriorating materials, preservation-quality copies on a more stable medium, and/or preservation masters to replace deteriorating or obsolete formats.

PHOTOGRAPHS AND NEGATIVES

If photographic prints do not have negatives, it is important to produce a negative so that the image will be preserved even if the original is lost or damaged. Conversely, prints should be made from negatives when an original print does not exist.

Duplicate prints of deteriorating historical photographs may be needed if the original is in very poor condition and/or if it is subjected to frequent use. Deteriorating negatives (such as broken glass plate negatives or nitrate- or acetate-based negatives) may also need to be duplicated.

Duplicating Photographs

There are several options for producing use copies of photographs. Duplicate prints can be produced, a microfilm index of photographs can be created, or a database of digital images can be prepared. A very inexpensive (albeit lower-quality) option is to produce photocopies in-house that can be used to identify which photographs are needed by the researcher. You may be able to find a local photographer or camera lab that provides copying services for historical photographs.

It is a good idea to use a service provider that has experience dealing with older materials. If the duplicate photograph is intended to be used as a preservation copy, it should be printed on traditional photographic paper, not on a digital printer, since prints from a digital printer or a colour photocopier will not last as long as traditional processed prints.

Duplicating Negatives

Duplication inherently involves a loss of image quality and detail, so it is crucial that duplicate negatives are printed on stable materials and that the reproduced image is the highest quality possible. As with all reformatting, choose a vendor who is experienced with historical collections.

Methods for duplicating negatives include:

- Producing a print and photographing the print using a large-format camera to produce a copy negative;
- Making a direct duplicate negative using duplicating film;
- Contact-printing the original negative onto film to produce a positive image, called an interpositive. The interpositive is then contact-printed onto film to produce a duplicate negative. This has the advantage of producing a master (the interpositive) and use copies

MOTION PICTURE FILMS

The optimum scenario for motion picture film preservation is to undertake film-to-film duplication, producing a preservation master, a new viewing print, and additional access copies. Film-to-film duplication is very expensive, however, and will be justified only for the most valuable and significant historical films.

Videotape Service Copies

For most small institutions with limited resources, the best option will be to have service copies of films made on videotape and to store the originals in cold storage offsite. Since the two media are very different, the copy will not be a completely accurate reproduction and thus cannot be considered a preservation copy, but it will allow access to films that would be unavailable otherwise.

While videotape copies can be created on VHS videotape (which is well known to users and can be played on equipment already found in many institutions), you should also consider creating the first copy on better-quality tape, which can then be used as a master to make additional copies as needed.

BetaCam SP (a half-inch analog tape) has often been used for this purpose, although in recent years some institutions have begun to use DigiBeta (a half-inch digital tape) because of its increasing presence in the broadcasting industry.

Analog and digital reproductions each have advantages and disadvantages. Analog systems are much simpler than digital systems and reproduce the content more accurately—digital copies by definition sample the original information rather than reproducing it exactly—but digital formats can be easily transmitted over the Internet, copied to other media such as DVD, and recopied many times without data loss.

Digital Preservation

As many other materials are converted to digital format, the question arises of whether to simply convert film to digital for preservation purposes, rather than film to film. For now, the answer is that current digital technology cannot yet capture all of the images and sounds of an original film adequately. In addition, the problems of digital preservation would also apply to digitized films.

AUDIOTAPES AND VIDEOTAPES

For audiotape and videotape that is deteriorating rapidly and/or becoming obsolete, create a preservation master, which will then be used to produce use copies for viewing and listening. The preservation master should be stored in a stable and moderate environment and restricted from use.

Copy Formats

As with motion picture film, preservation masters and service copies can be made either in digital or analog format, each of which has advantages and disadvantages.

It is generally recommended that sound recordings be reformatted via analog recording onto quarter-inch polyester standard-play tape with a ferric oxide coating. The preservation master should reproduce the original as accurately as possible, while the service copy can be altered to improve the sound quality if desired. Videotape can be copied onto VHS videotape, or you can create the first copy on better-quality tape, which can then be used as a master to make additional copies as needed. BetaCam SP (a half-inch analog tape) has often been used for this purpose, although DigiBeta (a half-inch digital tape) can also be used.

LIBRARY BINDING

Although it is primarily a strategy for general collections, library binding can be used for deteriorated historical volumes that have informational rather than artifactual value. Damaged books that have artifactual value, however, should not be library bound, but should instead be treated by a professional conservator.

The long-term preservation and usability of re-bound volumes has increasingly become a primary concern in library binding. While older library binding techniques were strong and economical, they sometimes resulted in books that did not open well and could be damaged by handling and photocopying. Also, the bindings were too strong for the text blocks they were meant to protect. Today's library binders have addressed these issues and provide bindings that are more durable and longer lasting.

STANDARDS/GUIDELINES

The binding industry has adopted formal standards for library binding. The binding industry has adopted formal standards for library binding. At present, ANSI/NISO/LBI Z39.78-2000 Library Binding is the library-binding standard of record..

The goals of modern library binding are:

- To produce a durable and economical binding;
- To alter the text block as little as possible;
- To ensure that the binding itself is as nondamaging as possible; and
- To produce a re-bound volume that will open easily To 180 degrees and stay open as the researcher is working.

Because the *Library Binding* standard is geared primarily towards professional library binders, it became clear that staff of collections-holding institutions would benefit from additional explanation and discussion of the standard so they could make informed binding decisions. In response, the

Library Binding Institute (LBI) sponsored a *Guide to the Library Binding Institute Standard for Library Binding,* originally published in 1990. This publication is in the process of being updated, and a draft version can be reviewed at the LBI Web site.

BINDING OPTIONS

The many options available for library binding of historical items can be confusing to those with little experience in the field. Always remember that if a volume has artifactual value, it should never be library bound; it must be treated by a conservator instead. Any volumes to be library bound must have paper that is not too brittle and is strong enough to withstand the binding process. When making binding decisions, keep the following general guidelines in mind.

Preserve the original signatures and sewing by choosing from the following options:

- *Recasing*: If the original sewing is intact, the volume should receive a new case (*e.g.*, new boards and covering that are attached to the text block by gluing them to the endsheets).
- *Resewing and recasing*: If the sewing is deteriorated, the book should be resewn through the original sewing holes (by hand or machine) if possible, even though this can be an expensive option. The volume should then be recased.
- *Double-fan adhesive binding*:Volumes that cannot be recased should usually be double-fan adhesive bound. In this type of binding, the spine is milled, and a machine applies adhesive to the leaves as they are fanned back and forth.
- *Oversewing*:This technique (machine sewing of single leaves at an angle through prepunched holes) could be needed for very heavy and thick text blocks, but oversewn volumes often do not open well, and the sewing can easily tear the pages if they become brittle in the future. This option should be avoided if at all possible.

When rebinding materials from historical collections, there are some additional issues to consider:

- *No-trim policy*: Specify that the binder should not trim the edges of the text block unless the page edges are damaged or the pages are uncut. Otherwise, any images or text that extend to the edges of the pages will be lost.
- *Paper repairs*: If paper repairs are needed, a paper-based pressure-sensitive tape with acrylic adhesive should be used (document repair tape, available from conservation suppliers). It is important, however, to remember that these repair tapes are only reversible with the use of organic solvents. A conservator would be needed if a volume is later reclassified into special collections. If the book has

value as an artifact and would merit page repairs done with Japanese paper, it should not be library bound.

CONSERVATION TREATMENT

It is important to differentiate between conservation of general collections and conservation of special collections. The former refers to the repair and protective housing of general library collections that are shelved in open stacks, while the latter refers to treatment by a professional conservator of library materials that have been separated from the general collection because of their value as artifacts, as well as archival materials, scrapbooks, photographs, etc.

Collections conservation (also sometimes known as in-house repair when on a smaller scale) can be an important element of a systematic preservation programme for academic and public libraries.

For those institutions that are concerned primarily with special collections materials, however, in-house repair is usually not appropriate. In all cases, it is important to follow proper procedures for repair, since unintended damage can result from improper repairs. Professional conservation treatment, while not appropriate for every deteriorated item, should be considered by any type of institution for deteriorated materials that possess significant artifactual, historic, associational, legal, aesthetic, or financial value as artifacts. A conservator's goal is to chemically stabilize and physically strengthen the item(s) being treated. Conservation treatment by a professional conservator is time-consuming and costly, so it must be limited to those materials that are the most valuable and the most deteriorated.

PRINCIPLES OF TREATMENT

Special Collections Conservation

The primary goal of conservation treatment for special collections is twofold: to stabilize the item in the collection so that it survives over the long term and is available for use, while at the same time changing its physical characteristics as little as possible. All repairs should be obvious to the trained eye (although they should not clash aesthetically with the item). It is important not to mislead the researcher into thinking the item was never damaged.

Conservation treatment must maintain the integrity of the object to the extent possible; thus, conservators follow the principle of minimal intervention.

Specifically:

- *Do no harm*: Use stable materials, and, in the event that the treatment turns out to be damaging over time or improved treatment options become available in the future, use reversible treatments wherever possible. This caution arises in part because some conservation treatments used in the past (*e.g.*, the use of silking, soluble nylon, and lamination to reinforce brittle paper) have caused unforeseen damage to collections.

- *Less is better*: Consider the effect that treatment will have on the aesthetic and physical characteristics of the object. Sometimes limited treatment, or even no treatment, may be the best choice.

Ultimately, it is important to remember that compromise is unavoidable; a conservator must weigh all factors before making a treatment decision and then work with the institution to make the best decision.

General Collections Conservation

While collections conservation shares the goal of stabilizing an item so that it can be accessible in its original format, there is less emphasis on maintaining the integrity of the object and more emphasis on lengthening the useful life of the item (*e.g.*, producing a durable item that will withstand heavy use). The need for relatively quick and low-cost treatments is a factor, as is the need for an organized workflow and the ability to treat materials in batches. Thus, compromises in treatment techniques are sometimes made that would not be acceptable in special collections conservation.

COLLECTIONS CONSERVATION/IN-HOUSE REPAIR

Collections conservation is normally carried out by either a collections conservator (a professional conservator specializing in general library collections) or a conservation technician (someone with more limited training who is knowledgeable about specific techniques). In small institutions, in-house repair is often carried out by a regular staff member who has been sent to one or more workshops; this can be problematic, though, because the training is usually brief and ongoing supervision unavailable.

Collections Conservation

There are a number of procedures that are carried out as part of collections conservation, including preparing new materials for library use (binding pamphlets, attaching book pockets, etc.); preparing books for library binding; constructing protective enclosures; and carrying out basic book repair.

Look at the following sites to explore what is involved in implementing a book repair programme. How do the sites differ?

What activities do you think might be appropriate for your institution?

- University of Illinois at Urbana-Champaign
- Dartmouth College
- University of California, Berkeley
- Cornell University

IN-HOUSE REPAIR OF HISTORICAL COLLECTIONS

In the context of historical collections, "safe" in-house techniques are limited to rehousing objects in appropriate enclosures and simple cleaning of books and some paper using preservation-quality procedures and materials. Instructions for simple page repairs and surface cleaning can be found on the

Northeast Document Conservation Center's (NEDCC) Web site, but these activities should be undertaken only when absolutely necessary and after training and extensive practice on unimportant items. In reality, most institutions will have higher-priority preservation needs than the repair of individual items.

PROFESSIONAL CONSERVATION TREATMENT

There are a number of treatments typically carried out by professional paper, book, and photographs conservators. These might include surface cleaning of paper, removal of damaging backings or mounts, removal of adhesive tape, washing in water, alkalization, mending or backing weakened items, bleaching to reduce stains, retouching areas of loss, re-sewing book pages, re-backing books with damaged covers or spines, and full rebinding of damaged volumes.

MANAGING REFORMATTING

Managing preservation reformatting involves identifying collections in need of reformatting; setting priorities among those collections; choosing the appropriate reformatting method(s); finding funding for the project; and carrying out the project. Because institutions are usually working with a limited budget, and numerous collections may be good candidates for reformatting, selecting the materials to be reformatted and setting priorities are often extremely challenging. In this part, you will identify strategies for effective selection and project management.

SELECTING PAPER COLLECTIONS

Identifying Collections in Need of Reformatting

Reformatting can provide preservation copies of collections that have only informational value, service copies to lessen handling of valuable originals, and/or security copies to guard against loss of information.

To identify collections that are good candidates for reformatting, consider the following:

- Is the collection extremely deteriorated?
- Does the collection have informational or artifactual value?
- How important is the collection to the institutional mission?
- Is the collection frequently used?
- Is the collection important in the context of other local, regional, or national collections? Is it a good candidate for a cooperative reformatting project?
- Have the materials been reformatted elsewhere?
- Is the collection a particularly good candidate for grant funding (perhaps because of its format or subject matter)?
- Does the collection have copyright or donor restrictions?

- Are there a variety of formats within the collection, and how easily can the materials be filmed, scanned, or copied?

Choosing a Reformatting Method

Once you have prioritized a particular collection or collections for reformatting, the next step is to decide which of the various options for preservation reformatting is the most appropriate. Keep in mind your overall goals of ensuring continued access to the information, protecting the original from additional damage, copying originals in poor condition only once, and creating a copy or copies that will last as long as possible.

In general, it is best to start by thinking about the end results of the project. Is microfilm needed for security or preservation purposes? Is a hard copy also needed? Is an exact reproduction needed (*e.g.*, do images need to be colour, or is black and white sufficient)? Is an enhanced version of the material, such as online searchable text, needed? In many cases, a combination of more than one reformatting method will be appropriate, such as preservation photocopying and microfilming, digital imaging and microfilming, or digital imaging and creation of a bound copy on permanent paper.

SELECTING MEDIA COLLECTIONS

Reformatting audiovisual materials is very expensive, and there is rarely enough funding available to reformat large numbers of items at once. While general concerns about level of use and importance to the institution apply to all types of collections, selection issues to be considered for specific types of audiovisual collections include:

Photographs and Negatives

Cellulose nitrate or cellulose acetate negatives that already exhibit signs of deterioration should be a priority, as should colour photographs, slides, and negatives. Deterioration of acetate negatives can be very quick, so frequent monitoring of their condition is essential. Priority for duplication may also be given to valuable negatives and to negatives that are frequently used, whatever their type. If you cannot store nitrate negatives according to the guidelines given by your insurance company and local authorities, their duplication and disposal should be a priority.

Motion Picture Films

For films, cultural significance must be determined, as well as whether or not the institution's copy is the best surviving copy. Completeness of the copy, the number of generations your copy is from the original, and the physical condition of the film must be considered. Films on nitrate or acetate base that already exhibit signs of deterioration should be a high priority. In general, if materials can be placed in cold storage, individual films can be copied as time permits, with the most significant and deteriorated films duplicated first. As is the case with nitrate negatives, if you cannot store nitrate films according to the guidelines given by your insurance company and local authorities, their duplication and disposal should be a priority.

Audiotapes and Videotapes

In addition to determining cultural significance, you must identify damaged tapes, recordings made on obsolete or unusual formats, recordings made early in the life of a format (these may be of inferior quality), older tapes, and unique copies (*e.g.*, the only master). All of these should have priority for copying.

WORKING WITH A VENDOR

For most small institutions, contracting out to an experienced vendor for preservation reformatting will be easier and more cost effective than trying to reformat in-house.

Evaluate the Vendor's Experience and Services

High-volume commercial microfilmers do not have the equipment or expertise to film fragile materials without damaging them. For valuable collections and/or materials that are being filmed because they are too fragile to withstand extensive handling, it is best to use a special service filmer who is experienced in dealing with hard-to-film collections (*e.g.*, tightly bound books, faded documents). For digital imaging, the vendor should have experience working with historical materials, as well as current equipment and the expertise to use it.

For audio and video recordings, an audiovisual or multimedia lab experienced with library and archives collections (as opposed to commercial customers) must be chosen. Professional-quality equipment and properly trained staff are essential to the production of preservation masters and service copies for audio and video recordings. Video recordings are especially vulnerable to data loss during the copying process because of the large amount of data in video signals.

Similarly, a specialized commercial film laboratory is needed for film duplication. Some duplication laboratories have developed particular specialties, such as specific formats or types of film (*e.g.*, 8mm film, colour film, nitrate film, soundtracks). Contact several different vendors to compare costs and services. You will need to estimate the size of the project, which will allow the vendor to provide a cost estimate. Visit the vendor to make sure that housekeeping, environmental control, and security are acceptable for temporary storage of the collections. This is especially important to prevent damage to original materials that will be retained rather than discarded after reformatting.

Draw Up a Contract

Once you have identified the vendor you wish to use, negotiate a contract. Be sure to find out whether your institution has specific procedures that must be followed for bidding and contracts.

You will need to specify standards and guidelines to which the vendor must adhere (*e.g.*, for image quality, quality control measures, etc.) in the contract.

Insurance and shipping requirements must be covered in the contract, as well as any special services (such as the creation of microfilming targets) that the vendor will provide.

MANAGING REFORMATTING PROJECTS

For institutions that contract with an outside vendor for reformatting services, the basic elements of project management are:

- Selecting the collections to be reformatted;
- Determining which reformatting method is most appropriate;
- Creating a project plan (often as part of preparing an application for grant funding);
- Preparing the collections for reformatting;
- Keeping in touch with the vendor during the reformatting process to ensure that all is proceeding as planned; and
- Examining the final result to ensure that all technical specifications provided by the institution were met.

Planning a Reformatting Project

Begin with the following questions: Will you be instituting a systematic ongoing reformatting programme or undertaking one or two special projects? Do you have the expertise in-house to determine the condition of collections and decide which merit reformatting? Will you need a collection survey by a specialist prior to making reformatting decisions?

Who will plan and manage the reformatting project(s)? A professional staff member is usually recommended, but in some cases a paraprofessional may perform this function. Choose someone who can successfully interact with other institutional staff as well as with the outside vendor.

What will be the responsibilities of various staff members within the institution during the project? How will you fund the project(s)? You will need to estimate the size of each specific project and determine how much in-house staffing and time will be needed. If the project is to be grant funded, this will be done as part of your grant application.

Most importantly, what are your goals for the project? This is particularly important for projects that include digitization, where you must begin by deciding what products and results you want from the project, and then determine the technical requirements for producing those results.

MANAGING CONSERVATION TREATMENT

Managing conservation treatment of paper-based collections involves:

- Identifying collections in need of treatment;
- Setting priorities for treatment among those collections;
- Choosing a conservator;
- analysing use and preservation needs, and choosing the appropriate preservation strategy;
- Finding funding for the project(s);
- Interacting with the conservator or technician during the treatment process; and
- Integrating the treated item back into the collection after the project.

For most small institutions, in-house repair and library binding should be used only minimally for historical collections, and professional conservation treatment should be reserved for those materials of greatest value to the institution. For medium to large institutions, a collections conservation programme, a library binding programme, and/or individual special collections treatment projects may be appropriate.

SELECTING COLLECTIONS FOR TREATMENT

General Collections Conservation

Because library collections conservation programmes handle a larger volume of material, and because these programmes focus on general circulating collections, all staff must have a role in identifying collections in need of treatment. Circulation staff, shelvers, and interlibrary loan staff should all be trained to identify damaged volumes (*e.g.*, loose hinges, torn or detached pages, broken spines, damaged corners).

Depending on whether the book is worth keeping (a bibliographer's opinion may be needed), whether the book is needed by patrons, whether there are other copies available, and whether the needed repair is simple or complex, repair may not be the best option. Alternatives include ordering a replacement copy, sending the book for commercial binding, reformatting the book, and/or rehousing the volume.

As books are flagged for repair, damaged items should be sorted into groups by type of repair (*e.g.*, pamphlet binding, hinge tightening, page mending, etc.) for efficiency.

Special Collections Treatment

Deciding which special collections merit treatment by a conservator can be challenging. There may be a variety of reasons for undertaking conservation treatment: if an item is fragile and must be frequently handled; if a reproduction cannot substitute for the original deteriorated item (*e.g.*, when physical characteristics of the item such as the binding or ink may have meaning for researchers); if the item has special characteristics such as colour illustrations or foldouts that preclude reformatting; and/or if it is necessary to repair the effects of past damaging treatments.

Treatment methods for individual items must be decided in consultation with a conservator experienced with paper collections (or books or photographs, as appropriate). The choice of a particular treatment will depend on the value of the object in its original form, the importance of the information it contains, the condition of the object, the potential for treatment to cause additional damage, and—realistically—the funds available for conservation.

For any item, there are usually several possible levels of treatment. When a conservator examines an object, he or she will provide a treatment proposal that sets out these options and their varying costs.

CHOOSING A CONSERVATOR

Since professional conservators usually specialize in a particular type of collection (*e.g.*, photographs, books, art on paper, paintings, furniture), and because qualified conservators may have been trained in various ways, it can sometimes be difficult to find the right conservator for your treatment project. When choosing a conservator, you will want to get information about the conservator's training, experience, and professional involvement.

Education and Experience

Conservators receive their training through graduate-level degree programmes (two to three years of coursework, plus an additional year of hands-on experience) or through lengthy apprenticeships. Apprenticeship is particularly common in book conservation, since formal educational programmes in that field are limited. Whatever the type of training, gaining hands-on experience in treating materials in their chosen specialty is an important part of a conservator's education. When choosing a conservator, be sure to ask about the conservator's practical experience, and obtain client and peer references.

Professional Membership

There are a number of respected professional organizations for conservators, including the American Institute for Conservation (AIC), the International Institute for Conservation (IIC), and various regional organizations. Membership in such organizations can indicate a conservator's interest in keeping up with current developments in the field.

Locating a Conservator

There are several ways to locate a qualified conservator. Getting recommendations from other institutions with similar collections is always a good idea. You should also consult the American Institute for Conservation's online guide to conservation services. This resource does not endorse specific conservators, but will provide you with a list of professional conservators in your area, along with their specialties. There are also a number of regional conservation centers that employ conservators in different specialties to provide conservation services.

If you are located in an isolated area, you may need to get referrals from a broad geographic area. Regional centers and many conservators have experience in packing, shipping, and transporting fragile collections and can provide advice.

MANAGING TREATMENT PROJECTS

Planning a Collections Conservation Programme

Because of the complexities of planning such a programme, management issues can only be touched on here. Issues to address include the following: where in the institutional structure the collections conservation programme will be located; what staff will perform collections conservation activities; how staff will be trained; what space and equipment will be provided; what repair procedures will be performed (simple or complex?); and how damaged collections will be identified. The answers to these questions will depend in large part on the size and financial resources of your institution.

Planning Special Collections Treatment

As with other reformatting and treatment options, organization and funding are crucial. Who will plan and manage treatment projects? A cooperative relationship between the project manager and the conservator will be very important. How will you fund the project(s)? Will you apply for grants? Do you need a collections survey to determine treatment needs?

If you are applying for a grant, items will have to be taken or sent to a conservator for a detailed examination; in some instances, a conservator may be willing to come to your institution. The conservator will produce treatment proposals, perhaps with options, which you will incorporate into your grant application.

Once you have funding, you will sign and return the treatment proposal. As treatment proceeds, unexpected changes in the treatment plan are sometimes needed (for example, if the object does not respond as expected to the proposed treatment). The conservator will consult the project manager if changes are required. When the material is returned, the conservator will provide a treatment report describing what was done to the item(s), which must be retained permanently.

Planning for Library Binding

Binders should be members of the Library Binding Institute (LBI), which is the primary membership organization for library binders. To become a certified member of LBI, binders must undergo a certification process in which their work is inspected to ensure that it meets the *Library Binding* standard. The binder must pledge to adhere to the standard when undertaking work to which the standard applies.

Your institution should have a contract, or at least an informal agreement, with its library binder that specifies the institution's preferences for leaf attachment and the other binding issues noted in the Exploring part of this part. Books returned by the binder must be individually inspected for quality of work and adherence to these specifications.

Index